/EAST·E184·R9G871991/

92

D0569733

From

Lenin

To

Lennon

Also by DAVID GUREVICH

TRAVELS WITH DUBINSKY AND CLIVE *(a novel)*

David Gurevich

From
Lenin
To
Lennon

A Memoir of Russia in the Sixties

Harcourt Brace Jovanovich, Publishers

San Diego   New York   London

OAKTON COMMUNITY COLLEGE
DES PLAINES CAMPUS
1600 EAST GOLF ROAD
DES PLAINES, IL 60016

DISCARD

Copyright © 1991 by David Gurevich

All rights reserved. No part of this
publication may be reproduced or
transmitted in any form or by any
means, electronic or mechanical,
including photocopy, recording, or
any information storage and retrieval
system, without permission in writing
from the publisher.

Requests for permission to make copies
of any part of the work should
be mailed to: Permissions Department,
Harcourt Brace Jovanovich, Publishers,
Orlando, Florida 32887.

Parts of this book appeared in changed
form in the *New York Times Review
of Books, Boston Globe Sunday Magazine*,
and the *Guardian*.

Library of Congress
Cataloging-in-Publication Data
Gurevich, David.
From Lenin to Lennon/David Gurevich.—1st ed.
p.   cm.
ISBN 0-15-149825-3
1. Gurevich, David.   2. Russian Ameri-
cans—Biography.   3. Soviet Union—Biography.
I. Title.
E184.R9G87   1991   90-5218
973'.049171—dc20

Printed in the United States of America
Designed by Camilla Filancia
First edition   A B C D E

Acknowledgment

I wish to thank my successive
HBJ editors—Daphne Merkin,
Bill Goldstein, and Willa Perlman—
and Molly Friedrich, the most
long-suffering agent in the world, for
their useful criticism of the manuscript.
Last but not least, my sincerest
thanks to Erich Eichmann and—
especially—Elizabeth Harper, whose
editorial advice was truly invaluable.

Part One

One

Since 1976, when I arrived in the States from the USSR, I have lived as a full-fledged Russian-American. I have worked, paid my taxes, made car payments, taped *LA Law*, and even rooted for the Seattle Seahawks. At the same time, I open a newspaper straight to reports from Moscow. With my borscht-thick accent, I do not need to advertise my roots. As a result, the same questions about Russia must be answered ten thousand times. It does get tiresome, but you can't blame people for being curious.

Besides, talking about Russia can be fun. The eighties have been a decade of nostalgia for the sixties, and sometimes I have been made to feel like a party crasher at these nostalgiafests: I never went to the Haight-Ashbury or marched on Washington. I point out that Hendrix's music transcends borders, and, as for marches, the Russians expressed defiance by *not* marching. The Big Events—well, yes, the assassinations of Bobby Kennedy and Dr. King, the Tet offensive; but we had Prague . . . who will argue which was more epochal?

Nowadays, thanks to glasnost, my tiny New York apartment is invaded regularly by Moscow friends, and we nostalgize no less ardently. This reinforces my conviction that, whether one grew up in Boston or Kiev, we are all a part of the same generation; we all treasure freedom above everything else—whether we were born to it or had to get it on our own.

———

On my first morning in the West I waited to be interviewed at the offices of the Joint Committee, which processes Russian émigrés in Vienna. Bright lights were hurting my eyes, and hordes of noisy children were running around, giving me a headache. I was not exactly hung over, but my head felt a bit heavy and vague after a night of celebrating my "coming out." Although I was dying for a coffee, I was afraid to go out and lose my place in line. On a morning like this I should be in bed, I thought.

I numbly leafed through the *Newsweek* I had bought on the way. It did not help: all the ads seemed to be for coffee and aspirin. Suddenly my eyes picked out familiar words: "Russia," "Jews," "Vienna." In the picture a bearded man was toting huge suitcases on an airport cart . . . *Hey,* I almost cried out—*that's me!* Twenty-four hours had not passed yet, and I was already a subject of a *Newsweek* piece.

On the other hand, I had come with one meager suitcase and a typewriter. And the more I read, the less the story seemed about me. The émigrés it described were famous computer scientists and dedicated Zionists. The KGB had ransacked their dachas, slashed their tires, and confiscated their Talmuds on a weekly basis. They had been refused exit visas on the flimsiest grounds for six years straight. By the time my name got called, I was in a severe depression. They were the real thing; I was an impostor.

I had to fill out a long form. One of the questions read, "State your reasons for leaving the Soviet Union."

I paused. It looked like a trick question. "Two lines is all I get?" I asked the girl. "It wasn't a simple decision, many factors went into it . . ."

The guys in the *Newsweek* story—they would know what to write. I was Jewish, too; but I had never been in jail, never signed a petition, and could not tell the Talmud from the Torah. How could I sum up my life, all twenty-four years of it, to meet the rigorous standards set by those martyrs? I had not even had coffee yet.

The girl gestured at the room packed with people waiting for their turn to sum up their lives. "Do you think they had an easy time deciding?"

Translation: *Do you think you're special?* I had been asked this before, but, curiously, the sight of others waiting made me feel better. "Fine," I said. "So what's the formula you guys use here?" I felt nostalgic. In Russia I would have known the formula for any form *before* approaching the clerk.

"Just write 'political,' " she said.

" 'Political'?" My jaw fell. It was the other way around: all my life I had tried to stay out of politics. If anything, I would write 'apolitical.' (With coffee, I would have realized that in this context it meant the same thing.)

"Mr. Gurevich," she said patiently. "This is for the State Department, do you understand?"

I pictured a stadium-sized room with desks spread as far as the eye could see and files moving from desk to desk on a conveyor belt. Who was I to throw a wrench into the works?

"You are holding up the line, you know."

That did it. The phrase I knew from shopping for shoes or apples or anything: *Don't hold up the line.* People behind you never give a damn—they grab whatever is offered and tear you apart for interfering with their right not to give a damn.

I signed, unhappily. I was still a cog in the machine, still classified as a member of a collective—this time the "huddled masses yearning to breathe free." I was still being told what to do: pretend that I fit the hagiography specifications set by *Newsweek*.

The girl was not mean, merely practical. She was about my age; before I left, I asked her where she came from.

"Connecticut." She smiled, for the first time. "It's lovely. You come from Moscow—did you grow up there, too?"

"No. I grew up in a place called Syzran." Reminding me of Syzran was like adding insult to injury.

She sensed my mood and beamed at me again. "I'm sorry about the bureaucracy. I don't like it myself, but what can you do?"

"Nothing," I agreed. "Have a nice day."

At the time I thought it was the nicest thing you could say to somebody.

I should have written "freedom" on my application. But I had grown up oppressed by Big Words and had come to distrust them. And it *is* a big, sweeping word that denotes a seemingly accessible concept; perhaps this is why it is so overused and has become too facile a term. Now, with the passage of time, I have come to realize it was foolish of me to try to measure up to the activists from the *Newsweek* piece. They paid for their freedom in full; I got off with a discount. Although I could honestly say that my life until then had been characterized by various degrees of unfreedom—which was why it needed to be changed—on that day in Vienna making so grand a claim would have made me feel uncomfortable. The feeling was vague, inchoate; it felt so precious that I was afraid I would squash it with a Big Word.

Fourteen years later the world is changing at a pace unmatched in history. The House that Lenin and Stalin Built has turned out to be a house of cards. It is a time of catharsis, and as we watch young Berliners guzzling champagne atop the Wall, our mouths open in awe: what a powerful notion freedom is.

Experts will be analyzing for years how this could have happened so fast and so suddenly. They will draw distinctions between hungry Polish workers and relatively well-off Germans; for the sake of balance they will throw in Chinese students and Salvadoran campesinos; they will scrutinize various meanings of the word "freedom," subdividing it the way a greedy developer carves a plot of land into the greatest possible number of units. Drawing geometrically pleasing, pencil-thin lines between "political" and "economical," between "intellectual" and "ethnic," is undoubtedly convenient for bureaucratic and grant-soliciting purposes, but these trees obscure the proverbial forest. To me, "freedom" is one, a monolith of an idea, grounded immovably on the single most important decision of my life: leaving the country I was born in. What could I have been looking for if not freedom?

Two

The passage of time allows me a bird's-eye view of my meandering road to Vienna. Unaided by map or advice, I rambled and stumbled and tripped and went on. In my very first conversation in the West the name of the town where the road had started popped up. Syzran and unfreedom are linked in my mind today just as closely as they were then in Vienna.

Americans love comparing their lives to those led behind the Iron Curtain: an easy, flattering comparison. But they often think of Gulag prisoners behind barbed wire, which is not what I'd call a typical Russian environment. I have met enough ex-inmates not to belittle their ordeal, but the Gulag is at best a *concentrated* form of Soviet life (no pun intended). Syzran is a more placid, a more common, and, if you will, a more nuanced place than a labor camp. It sits on the bank of the Volga River, about seven hundred miles east of Moscow: almost in Asia. It is in towns like this—not in the Gulag, not in metropolises like Moscow or Leningrad, not in Baltic resort towns, not even on sprawling collective farms—where the majority of Russians live.

My friend Irene grew up in Syzran, too. She left Russia about the same time I did and now lives in LA. She treats "being out of Syzran" as a cure for all ills. We were driving on the Pacific Coast Highway one day, and I was venting my frustration with book editors, car mechanics, the IRS: all the hurdles on the way to the American Dream. Irene, who is a quiet and patient person, said, "But David—you're in your own car—"

"You haven't seen the garage bill—"

"—driving on this beautiful road—"

"Can't you hear the ping in the engine?"

"—you could still be in *Syzran*, you know."

Don't rush to label this exchange as "positive versus negative." Irene is not exactly a disciple of Norman Vincent Peale, nor am I a nattering nabob of negativity. The reference to Syzran is a clincher, an effective way of terminating an argument.

We reminisce about our Syzran days sometimes, but we talk mostly about our schoolmates and what might have become of them. We haven't been back since we left Russia in 1975, although my father still lives there, and so does Irene's mother. Syzran remains officially closed to foreigners, which is what we now are, with our dark-blue State Department–issue passports.

I was born not in Syzran but in Kharkov, a large city in the Ukraine, which my family left when I was three. My father was in the Air Force, and for six years we lived on bases in the Volga area. Finally, when I was nine, he settled down as an instructor at a flying school. And so I stayed in Syzran for seven years, till I graduated from high school.

I left Syzran without remorse, and I feel none now. My dominant memory of the place is a ten-foot-tall poster of Lenin, his empty eyes rolled skyward, perhaps to avoid the sight of the drunks lying in the mud below. I am not striving for dramatic effect: with so many likenesses of the Founding Father on the walls, and so many alcoholics, I do not need to stack the deck.

There is a local museum, a small, nondescript building, well hidden at the end of Syzran's main street. I remember going there on a field trip in the third or fourth grade, and I remember the place being enveloped in gloom and dust, but when it comes to the exhibits, my memory grows dim. I vaguely recall a crudely painted pterodactyl fighting some other dinosaur; a grainy black-and-white picture of an exhausted, sooty-faced factory worker from the tsarist days; and large Civil War tableaux of solemn-faced Red Commissars and mean-looking White officers. It is easy to tell the two apart by their mustaches: the Reds' are thick and bushy, while the Whites' are pencil-thin and sometimes curved. Perhaps the painter believed that a thick mustache better conveyed the macho image of the Revolution. More likely, he was creating an allegory of Stalin's victory over Trotsky.

On the other hand, I may be thinking about the local museum in another Syzran-like town, Orsk or Oryol. I visited many Syzrans in my travels around Russia, and all provincial museums were run along the same Ministry of Culture guidelines.

Small Russian towns look much like one another: a Revolution Avenue, a Gorky Park, and a windswept central square, used solely for Revolution Day and May Day parades, with a Lenin statue and a Board of Honor with pictures of the best workers. In that sense Syzran is no better or worse than Orsk or Oryol.

It's the sound of its name. In English it sounds merely exotic, like Gdansk or Harare. But in Russian it sounds a bit like "*sran*," which roughly translates as "shit-like." If you come from New Jersey and feel slighted by New Yorkers, at least you can always invoke the names of Springsteen or Sinatra in your defense. Try living in Moscow and admitting you are from Syzran.

We lived just outside the Air Force base, in a neighborhood around the large turbine plant. The main drag, Gidroturbinnaya Street, was lined with monotonous five-floor concrete buildings, of an indistinct grayish color whose variations were unintentional: the paint started peeling and sprouting graffiti before each new coat could be completed.

The town plans must have been drawn in a drier climate;

even a few inches of rain created huge puddles, spanned by boards that served as makeshift bridges. For six months a year, mud was king. The scarce asphalt paths were badly cracked. In spring the snow melted, and puddles became oceanic.

In places like Moscow or Leningrad they wear galoshes, but such footwear was inadequate for our puddles. We wore boots through spring and fall and carried a change of shoes to school in a bag. Women and children wore plain rubber boots—thin, light, and easy to wash. Military officers, including my father, wore expensive, soft leather boots that were polished to a high gloss. I put in a lot of time shining my father's boots (as well as the brass buttons on his overcoat). As usual, his motivation was pedagogical: I was to learn neatness and discipline. But I was too slow, or too easily distracted, to be a good shoeshine boy, and I resented the futility of it: with mud all over the place, how long would the shine last? And if you still had to watch where you were going, what was the point of wearing such boots?

Workers and soldiers wore boots made of *kirza*, low-grade leather that always looked a shabby gray, polished or not. They were the pedestrian equivalent of a Jeep in the Syzran jungle. They were immune to polish; in fact, they looked better un-polished, and with a healthy smattering of mud they looked positively *bad*. They made heavy, menacing sounds on the floor. Their wearer was not to be messed with: not only did they look heavy enough to knock your liver out with one kick, but they could follow you into the deepest mud to finish you off. My working-class schoolmates' *kirza* made me feel like a mama's boy in my rubber boots. Perhaps I saw *kirza* more as an attribute of manhood than as one of freedom—or am I splitting hairs? Whatever *kirza* boots stood for, admitting to my parents that

I yearned for them was like asking them for money to buy cigarettes: both sounded like lower-class ("hooligan," they would say) ambitions.

Our first Syzran apartment was a studio, and it seemed like paradise to the three of us: no longer did we have to share a bathroom and a kitchen with another family, the way it had been in Kuybyshev and Saratov, Father's previous postings. Then, when I was nine, my sister was born, and my grandma moved in to help out with her; five people in a room felt a bit cramped. When my father was promoted to major, we moved into a one-bedroom apartment.

(Years later, when my mother left Syzran and moved to Kharkov, she sold the rights to the apartment—in New York we call it "key money"—for two thousand rubles, what she would make in a year and a half. In Kharkov, moving into a new building, she parlayed a ten-dollar Colibri lighter, which I had sent from LA, into a better apartment with a terrace. Now the Kharkov apartment is worth twenty thousand rubles—still under the table, naturally.)

The Syzran move, too, involved chicanery and plotting, but a two-room apartment with running water and central heating for just four people (Grandma went back to Kharkov) was the Syzran equivalent of a penthouse. People talked of an astronaut having a three-room apartment in Moscow all to himself, of Georgian orange sellers living in villas on the Black Sea coast— but that was another planet. And how our leaders lived, we could hardly imagine: was it true that Brezhnev really had a live-in maid?

The Soviet haves are reticent about their possessions; *Pravda* does not advertise seven-room penthouses. There was privately owned housing in Syzran: crumbling shacks without heating or indoor plumbing. But most people, plant managers and janitors alike, lived in the same dilapidated breadboxes, known in this country as projects. Inside, some apartments had pianos and rugs; others, just bare boards. But on the outside it was Socialism at its egalitarian best.

Our courtyards may have looked palatial on drafting boards, but in reality they were little more than weedy patches of wasteland. Some bushes were planted, but few survived the hot summers. Women sat on the benches outside, nibbling sunflower seeds and arguing about whose husband drank more. Men, gloomy with hangovers, slammed down dominoes on the rickety table between the sandbox and the volleyball court (two poles with a laundry line between them). In the middle of the yard we set up schoolbags or piles of rocks in lieu of a goal and wildly kicked up clouds of dust with a soccer ball till we could no longer see it in the dark. The only interruption came around six, when the garbage truck arrived and we had to drag out the pails and empty them into its maw.

Your father could be the plant manager, you could have rugs in the bathroom, and you could be eating caviar by the bucketful at home; but if you were lousy in soccer, you played goalkeeper—the position no one else wanted. This seems like a triumph of athletic meritocracy, but, looking back, I think it went further than that.

Some of us, including myself, changed before going out to play; others stepped out in their school clothes, carrying a slice of sugar-sprinkled bread. What is so tasty about *that*?, I used to wonder. And why was it that those kids always seemed to play better? It couldn't be just because they played more, ignoring school; I didn't do much homework, either. But they seemed to be faster, more dogged and tenacious—they wanted to win more than we "nicer" boys did. I would lose the ball in a scramble outside the goal to Kolka, the janitor's son, and I read disdain in his eyes.

Once, as I was passing the ball past Kolka, he gave me a shove that knocked me off my feet. As I lay in the dust, yelling "*Pendal!*" ("Penalty!"), I was aware that it was a gray-area shove, a judgment call; only a referee could say whether Kolka had played "at the ball," which is legal, or "at the player," which is not. The strength of the tackle had nothing to do with the rules.

We pushed and shoved each other for a while, and were about to come to blows, when something held Kolka back. I ducked as his fist went up, but it never came down. I got my free kick, and five minutes later he did it again—this time to my teammate Petka. Petka screamed bloody murder, and this time Kolka took a swing; they rolled in the dust, kicking and punching. I felt uneasily that the strike was really meant for me. Why had he held back the first time?

It was a rare game that passed without a fight, and I don't think I was the toughest on the field, nor the most conciliatory. Yet I recall little injury to myself. Am I suppressing my shiners and bloody noses, trying to mythologize my past? I keep trying to recall things as best as I can, and I come up with an odd memory, a whisper behind my back: "His dad's a colonel." "His mom's a doctor."

Really? Did Kolka really believe that my father would have beaten up his father over my black eye? Or, more likely, lodged a complaint at his place of work—that "he cannot bring up his son properly"? Was Kolka afraid that my father, a man obsessed with fair play, would do *that*? Or that my mother, a pediatrician, would refuse to treat him or his siblings? This is preposterous, I say to myself; neither of my parents would do anything like

that, not unless I was hurt badly enough to land in a hospital—
which would then be a matter for the police. Yet the more I
think about it, the more plausible it seems. Another man in my
father's social shoes might do just that: go to Kolka's janitor
father and demand that he tan his son's hide, or else there'd be
the factory and the school involved. But I cannot imagine Kolka's father coming to mine with a complaint. And if he did, I
cannot imagine my father doing anything about it. He would
have asked me, Did Kolka have a knife? a rock? Was it a one-
on-one? Assured that the fight had taken place in the proper
sporting spirit, he would have given me a pat on the back. True,
I'm projecting from the safe distance of twenty years; in those
days, amid the grabbing and punching and tripping, I never
thought of parental backing and never pulled a punch, no matter
whom I was facing. But that's exactly what Kolka did—and
then took it out on Petka, the plumber's son.

The thought keeps nagging me: what was it like for Kolka
to hold back? To know that "my dad can*not* beat up your
dad"—and it had nothing to do with physical strength? Would
it have been better for Kolka to have his ass belted till he could
not sit down? I don't know; I never held back, and my father
never laid a hand on me.

At twelve I was not analytical and did not spend time wondering whether we were rich or poor. As I said, you were only
as good as your dribbling on the field was. I hardly ever visited
Petka's or Kolka's house. But two floors above us an alcoholic
woman named Kuzina shared a room with her son and her
daughter. The boy was known as Kuzka, after his last name;
no one cared to learn his first name. He was a year or two my
junior, and I doubt that he went to school much. His complexion
was pale and sickly, the expression on his hamster-like face was
always embittered, and he tended to look at you slightly side-

ways. His clothes were a quilt of patches, he always had a runny nose, and his cough was bad enough to spark rumors that he had TB. No mother in the building would encourage her children to play with Kuzka, and we needed no extra warnings to avoid him. Kuzka did not look like he would live through a fight. He was teased mercilessly—he was Tamara's brother.

Tamara, in her twenties, was known as a good-time girl who brought soldiers home on a regular basis. In the evening she would lean against the wall, facing the base gate, and strike up conversations with potential boyfriends. With her high breasts, plump lips, and towering blond beehive, she looked like a poor man's version of Brigitte Bardot. She wore a lot of rouge and powder—to cover the black eyes she got from her lovers, we assumed. To us, she was Sin itself. We whistled and hooted, and sometimes, in an unwittingly Biblical gesture, even cast small pebbles at her. At twelve, sexual excitement takes bizarre forms. She cursed us and made menacing gestures, but what could she do? She could not lay a hand even on Kolka—his father, the plumber, would beat the hell out of her.

Come Monday morning, Kuzka, shivering in his half-torn shirt, would take the empties to the store, while Tamara threw a rough worker jacket over her bare body (I peeked on my way to school), filled the bucket, and got on her knees to scrub the stairs. To pay her, the neighbors kicked in a ruble a month. What's a ruble? Half a liter of cheap red wine cost 1.37 rubles. On the American scale Tamara was a sort of illegal alien—in her own land.

Once I had to take the ruble upstairs myself. Kuzka opened the door just wide enough to peek outside. Ignoring him—*I'm not giving* you *this ruble*—I marched in. The room was bare of furniture; balls of dust rolled along the walls. In one corner was a small table, cluttered with cosmetics, and a cracked, yellowed mirror flanked by postcards of movie actors and a cheap, glossy picture of Jesus. The only sound was the snoring of Kuzka's mother on a straw pallet in another corner. The room stank of alcohol and the odor of an unwashed body. I glanced at Kuzka; he looked away. I realized, with a pang, that he was ashamed—and for a moment I was ashamed, too. I gave him the crumpled ruble note without a word and left.

Back at our apartment, I paused at the door to the living room, seeing it with new eyes: the couch with broken springs, covered with a moth-eaten rug; the piano, badly out of tune; the black-and-white TV with a faded embroidered doily on top; the table, its deep cracks covered by a yellowed lace-trimmed cloth. I knew we were not rich—not by a long shot. In Kharkov I had been to my mother's cousins' apartments: they had stereos and cabinets with imported liquor. I was skeptical about their possessions: to me, bookshelves were the measure of affluence, and we certainly had more books than all our cousins combined. But, then, what we had—those were the *basics*! How could one function below that?

I knew of poverty from books, but Chekhov's illiterate peasants lived in medieval villages, Gorky's bums preserved a certain nobility of spirit, Dickens's colorful paupers were on the verge of winning their long-denied fortunes and lived in nineteenth-century London—light-years away. But this was right here, at my doorstep, and there seemed to be no pride or beauty in it.

After I saw Kuzka's apartment, I began to realize that my teammates never changed out of their school clothes because they *had* no other clothes. And that their bread-and-sugar sandwich was their entire lunch—there was nothing else in the house. This did not make me feel superior, just envious: they still played better, and the idea of poverty had become inextricably linked in my mind to athletic prowess.

I have since been to places where people lived far below Kuzka's level—he, at least, had indoor plumbing and central heating. But I remember my first brush with poverty best, perhaps because I was less affected by the physical shabbiness of the room than by the expression of shame on Kuzka's face. Unlike me, the babe in the woods, he knew his station.

Three

It is hard to say now whether it was the books that interfered with my soccer or the soccer that interfered with my books. On rainy days I had no problem; on sunny ones I was torn apart.

Unlike Americans, Russians still worship the printed word (we'll see what happens when they get cable). No living room is complete without a bookcase holding the collected works of prestigious writers. The largest collection I saw as a kid was at my granduncle Berchik's house in Kharkov. He loved to parade it before visitors. "So many books," he sighed, "so much wisdom." The rows were arranged meticulously by author—Thomas Mann, Zola, Dickens—and volume number. They were Berchik's white-gloved guard of honor, frozen at attention: you passed them with bated breath, slowly and respectfully, keeping time to a march that played in your head, and you saluted his refined taste. Then Berchik would crack up: "Never read any of them!" Giggling, he pointed, one by one: "Never read Maupassant—he wrote smut, right? Never read Stendhal, never read Zola . . ."

I looked away. He was an old man, born in a shtetl; no one expected him to be a bibliophile, but his blatant pride in treating books as property made me squirm.

As a bookstore manager, Berchik could get Zola ahead of the general public. This was his investment, his nest egg. He did not need to read them to know their black-market worth. In the first place, they were translations—"imported" by implication and, as such, superior to Gogol or Pushkin, who never graced his shelves. Second, they were collected works—which look more impressive than individual books, their chief asset being the design on the spine. Berchik's favorite author was James Fenimore Cooper, a six-volume collection of whose work would bring over a hundred rubles on the black market: about ten times its nominal value, or what my mother made in a month. The Cooper spines featured a bright, colorful American-Indian motif. You could spot them from across the room, shining behind the glass, locked securely with the key that Berchik kept in a vase by the door. Cooper was a sterling status symbol: its owner presumably had no problems getting meat, either.

My parents did not have Uncle Berchik's resources, but they, too, felt it was proper to have books in the house, and spent unstintingly. Yet my mother read very little, and my father preferred "serious" thrillers, the Soviet equivalents of le Carré. They were unable to steer me to Plato or Dante, and school did its best to turn me off Gogol and Turgenev. My father could not haul books from the library for me fast enough. Jules Verne, Jack London, assorted Soviet sci-fi and KGB-CIA thrillers—anything set in another time and place; anything not about a small Russian town.

I was used to the notion of books as Great Escape until I discovered the Russian translation of *The Catcher in the Rye*: a modestly bound black book with a fuzzy black-and-white drawing on the cover; a quiet, unobtrusive presence on the library shelf. I had never heard of Radio City Music Hall or the Rockettes, the class distinctions of a Park Avenue apartment or Mark Cross luggage were lost on me, and going to school away from home sounded odd—in Russia boarding schools were for orphans. But Holden's anger at hypocrisy, his spiritual loneliness, could not help striking a chord. I was amazed to discover that someone growing up thousands of miles away could have exactly the same feelings I did. This title had never reached the local store, and I did something I had never done before nor would do after: I did not return the book to the library. Otherwise, I rationalized, I'll never see it again.

Our high-school English reading was made up of Sherlock Holmes stories in "adapted" form: that is, shorn of "difficult" language. When I entered a language school in Moscow, *Catcher* was the first book I read in *real* English. The going was rough (fortunately, it was a Soviet edition, with the slang explained in copious footnotes), but I plodded on, fueled by the joy of rediscovery. When I came home on a winter break, I proudly turned in the library book—two years later.

Among my peers, the only one who might have had more books in the house than I did was Sasha Sharomygin, whose parents taught at a local voc-ed school. His apartment was in a permanent state of chaos—books scattered amid sandwiches and socks—so I could not tell with certainty who had more. I was ashamed of the thought; it made me feel like Uncle Berchik.

Sasha could not tell a basketball from a soccer ball and seemed perpetually distracted. He reacted with "Huh?" to any question and was teased at school, but I knew that in his head he was in ancient Rome or medieval Paris, anywhere but here. Minds that travel in time have no use for combs: no wonder he was permanently disheveled. At his house we put our feet up and, inhaling the dust, spent hours musing on how the world might be different today if only Spartacus or Wat Tyler had had access to automatic weapons. Or, following our hormones, we leafed through the color plates in history books, pondering the relationship between women's fashions and public morals. With long dresses and stays and petticoats, sex could hardly be casual, could it?

Looking back, I understand why I preferred historical adventures to spy thrillers and even sci-fi: musketeers and pirates were after honor, love, money—motivations I was more comfortable with than patriotism or national security. And the attraction of spy novels, I now realize, lay in their settings: the genre dictated that at least part of the action take place in the West, so even if the KGB was thwarting a CIA operation, the CIA agents always held their meetings in a strip joint. The authors crowded their crude descriptions of New York or Munich with booze and loose women, drawing scenes a thousand times more mouth-watering than those from the exemplary family lives of brave KGB agents.

Sci-fi authors did not have much choice in setting, either: any story that took place in the future had to be a peaceful Communist idyll, with Comrade Jones and Comrade Dong working alongside Comrade Ivanov aboard the spaceship. If it took place in the present, the aliens were always threatened by the profit-hungry Americans and bailed out by the altruistic Soviets. (Not that Hollywood has done much better, of course.)

But sci-fi had ideas, telekinesis or time travel, that made us overlook the villains trying to convert the ideas into dollars and the good guys trying to turn them to the good of mankind. My friend Sergei Petukhov and I were briefly involved in the construction of a time machine. It never got off the drafting board, though, due to Sergei's stubbornness (at least, that's what my memory tells me, with servile convenience). As Chief Designer, he thought he had the first shot at testing it; at the same time, although every sci-fi writer swore that you could spend years in the past and come back in the present seconds after you had left, Sergei was skeptical. He was afraid of missing the chemistry test. I offered to go: besides my curiosity about the past, I was secretly hoping that the geographical calculations would be off and I'd return to modern-day New York and the strip lounge filled with dangerous CIA agents—a scene that beats a chemistry test hands down. But Sergei would not give way. Thus one of the great modern inventions never saw the light of day.

Another reason why Sergei was nervous about not coming back from the past at the exact scheduled moment was his mother, who thought nothing of grounding him for being five minutes late for dinner. With Sergei I hung out outside: there was no putting our feet up at his house. It was exemplarily dust-free, and the books were aligned as carefully as Berchik's. Sergei's mother, however, considered them educational tools: keeping them aligned was a pedagogical statement. She loathed borrowing from the library, and if she did, she ironed the pages to kill the germs from the unsanitary people who had borrowed the book before her. She frowned upon Sergei lending me books: God knows what kind of spots I might put on them. She had a fit when I casually left an open book face down. What would that do to the spine!

In a house where the greatest sin was to serve tea in an unmatched cup and saucer, I was a boor who needed to be reminded to wipe his feet or take off his shoes or wash his hands. Only my parents' "respectability" kept her door open for me. She could not believe that, yes, I had done my homework— "Have your parents seen it?" She would not believe that my parents trusted me enough to leave me alone. She suspected that my only reason for dragging Sergei to the movies was to prevent him from catching up with me in grades.

Mrs. Petukhov had no direct bearing on my life, but later I ran into many of her soulmates who did. Excessive gentility and rigid convention are not inherently Soviet traits. But under Socialism, people's conformist inclination never to stick their necks out fits the official dogma that the collective is always superior to the individual. This is not unlike the Oriental mode of thinking; yet, without a work ethic, Soviet Socialism reduces everything to the lowest common denominator: no one should be any better off than the worst off.

In a sense, Sergei's mother was right to suspect me of wanting to get ahead. She must have been utterly unsurprised when she heard of my emigration, and even regretful that I had not done it sooner. I can see her nodding solemnly, each strand of her blond hair frozen in a perfect Socialist-teacher bun: "I could tell where he was headed when he spilled Polish jam on my rug."

At school I was too impatient to go at the snail's pace of the curriculum. I read the textbooks in September and spent the rest of the year in semi-hibernation. Nor was there any reason to listen to the lectures, which never departed from the Ministry of Education's textbooks. I sat in the back of the class, puzzling the teachers, who were used to the best students sitting up front. Safe behind my classmates' backs, I quietly did the next day's homework or read a spy novel. If my teachers knew about it, they never let on. They were concerned with discipline and 100 percent passing grades. All I wanted was to be left to read in peace.

I had no gift for natural sciences, but by the time we started physics and chemistry (fifth grade), I was so used to top grades that I felt forced to develop a way of beating the system. I boned up on the first day, volunteered, and got an A. For the next fourteen classes I could goof off. Then I boned up and volunteered again . . . and so on.

The humanities game was even easier to play. Learning was reduced to memorizing the textbook; the objective was to say the absolute minimum. In history, for example, two things counted: the dates and the political attitude. If I was called, all I needed to know was in what year Pharaoh Ramses or Ivan IV ascended to the throne, and that Ramses/Ivan was a bloodthirsty tyrant whose rule was based upon exploiting the toiling masses.

I was never tempted to argue with the textbook: neither the Tudors nor the Commissars struck me as real. History was just another story, and a poorly written one, at that. It never involved me as much as any given book under my desk did.

Although I could have raised my hand and talked about the history I got from other books, that would have been contrary to the game; I learned early that showing off knowledge gained outside was a waste. Nobody likes an eager beaver when the class is waiting for the bell. Also, if you have A's, you take pains to avoid being seen as a teacher's pet. Sitting in the back of the class with D-students helped, and I never refused to let my homework be copied. I remember Lyuba Stolbunova, a tough, freckled girl from my building, giving me hell for it: "They can do it by themselves! Are you scared they'll beat you up if you say no?"

That was a grave charge, and not an unfounded one. Between that and the fear of being branded a nerd, I did not have much latitude. Either way, you yield to peer pressure, and if that is conformism, then I was not far removed from Sergei's mother. But now, as I recall Lyuba's large, green eyes wide with anger, I realize that it was not fear of either cowardice or nerdiness that made me look away with such nonchalance as my homework was being copied. My homework cost me so little that I felt I could afford to be generous with it. Anyway, their copying was pointless: they made mistakes as they did it. At best, they got inferior grades; at worst, they got caught, unable to account for mistakes. On my part, it was an ego trip, pure and simple.

I could handle the studies, but the political side of school made me cringe. Its task was to prepare us to function in society. At the age of eleven you discovered whether you had an appetite for power and the willingness to take and give orders; or, if you didn't mind being one of the sheep, then you learned to develop the skills necessary for ovine survival. You learned to nod, to raise your hand in a unanimous vote, to weather the endless boredom of meetings. You learned to conform beyond mere peer pressure.

The first three grades were relatively innocent. As little *Oktyabryata* ("Octobrists," after the October Revolution), we recited ditties about Grandpa Lenin and kept our classroom clean because "little Volodya [Lenin] did that, too." The assault on our minds and souls did not start till we joined the Young Pioneers at age ten. The pagan pageantry, the Leninjugend rituals—starched white shirts, ironed black shorts, fiery red ties, arms bent in a precise forty-five-degree salute, the bugle-and-drum cacophony, goose-stepping behind the heavy, arm-numbing banner; the heart beating with excitement, the finger daring not pick the nose; "Comrade Chairman! The Young Pioneers of School Number 19 proudly report exceeding the scrap metal collection target figures by 10 percent!" "Young Pioneers! To the cause of the Party, to the cause of Lenin, be faithful!" "Always faithful!"

At meetings some poor Kolka would be called on the carpet and forced to repent his truancy, his low grades, his foul language, his smoking in the bathroom. He stood in front of the class, red as a beet, his face pained with boredom and incomprehension; nodding, admitting everything, mumbling promises to mend his ways—anything to get out of the spotlight, away from the thirty pairs of eyes drilling him with scorn. It was but a ritual: afterward, if someone asked us what Kolka had been charged with and how his accusers knew that he had actually done such vile things, none of us—Sergei, Lyuba, myself—would have known what to say.

And *they* on the podium, the teachers and their minions, who together formed the leadership—what did they want from him, really? In a year or two he'd graduate from grade school and join his father at the factory; why couldn't they just let him be? Their persistence had nothing to do with Kolka. They had their careers, their agendas, their averages, their responsibility to the Party. They had to file a report, and the minutes of the meeting had to reflect their prosecutorial zeal.

I endured quietly. I detested meetings in any form, on any subject, from Kolka's troubles to end-of-the-year summings-up of student affairs. I had no desire to either recite or debate the slogans at a solidarity rally with the Heroic People of Vietnam; all I wanted was to stay away from the rally, to go play soccer or read a book. I envied Kolka, who could do that: eventually the system gave up on him. Not me: as an A-student, I was conspicuous, expected to be there, urged to participate. I had to make up endless excuses in order not to be elected to the Pioneer leadership (co-opted, as the procedure went), thus disappointing the teachers: "Others need more time to keep up with their studies, but with your good grades, Gurevich, you can afford to be more active!" Luckily, there were plenty of takers, who wanted to sit on the podium at the Revolution Anniversary meetings, to report "Always Faithful!" at citywide rallies, to persecute the poor Kolkas.

Yawning my way through meetings was doubly frustrating because I never felt I had a valid substitute. I daydreamed of getting up and walking out on a Kolka tribunal, or on a meeting on preparations for the Anniversary of the Revolution, where they decided who would decorate Lenin's picture and who would paint the slogans for the podium. If I had left, they would have accused me of setting myself above my classmates, of forsaking the collectivist spirit, of being unworthy of the name of Young Pioneer. And what would you rather do?, they would have asked. That was the rub: I was ashamed to admit that I'd rather play soccer or go to the movies. Well, so would we!, they would have cried out; but don't you understand how important *this* is? Again, I wouldn't have known what to say. A part of me recognized that neither of these pastimes was a serious alternative to a meeting on the Revolution Anniversary. But another part could not admit the importance of decorating the hall, either. This is ideologically immature, they would have said indignantly; do you disagree with our objectives? My reply: I don't really care one way or another; it's just that you are boring the shit out of me! Is boredom an ideological sin?

My friends agreed with me about boredom. But the adults had meetings, too, they pointed out; the format is the same, from Pioneers to Komsomol to the Party, from school to college to workplace. We were Soviet kids, never questioning the meetings' content or the authorities' right to drag us in; we just learned to find ways to stay away.

I am not happy with these recollections. They are too negative, they smack of one-sidedness and a right-wing, cold-war mentality. No matter how straightforwardly I narrate them, they acquire a patina of cynicism—an attitude many Americans I have met associate with East Europeans and hold highly suspect. As a proud naturalized citizen, I do my best to be tolerant and moderately optimistic, but these recollections get in the way. I cannot accept them. I call my friend Yosif and beg him for a scrap, a happy memory associated with the Young Pioneers.

Yosif hesitates, then says, "Well . . . we played soccer, went swimming. Pioneer camp, y'know?"

"That's just summer camp—"

"Yeah, but officially it was a Young Pioneer camp."

I fall silent. I should never have asked. Nominally, he is right, but he has also unwittingly brought back my worst Young Pioneer memories.

The only summer camp I went to was Artek, the showcase Soviet summer camp. My mother had called in a few markers to get me in—and it cost a fortune, too. Artek is a glittering Pioneer-land on the picture-pretty Crimean shore, with steel-and-glass dormitories and modern facilities for every imaginable children's activity under the warm southern sun. Within twenty-four hours I was counting the days before leaving.

No anti-utopian novel can do justice to this expensively appointed paradise, though Zamyatin's *We*, with its smiling, Party-led proletariat, comes close. If I could not stand Pioneer meetings before, at least at home I had the rest of the time to myself. Here the official free time was half an hour before supper; we were to use it to write letters home. We were issued free, prestamped color postcards, but I instinctively chose to write letters, soaking the envelope's seal flap with saliva. I was less concerned about the State reading my mail than about someone in the camp administration seeing what I wrote. I was not even complaining; I realized it would be a waste of time. Syzran was a thousand miles away, and I couldn't just hop on a train and leave. But Artek was such a nonstop pep rally that even a mere "I'm okay" on a card would have looked like a complaint.

Our days were crammed with wonderful and useful activities, none of which could be missed without a note from the nurse. At seven we got up for our morning exercises, stretching our limbs to the sounds of the accordion. The accordionist smiled encouragingly as the coach walked around to make sure each of us was reaching his toes. After breakfast we marched to the beach, where we positioned our bodies at equal intervals on the pebbles. Patriotic Young Pioneer songs blared through the loudspeaker, interrupted every five minutes by the orders to turn over lest we get sunburned (sun lotion was unknown).

Whether going to dinner or to a concert or to meet Gagarin the First Astronaut, we marched in formation, belting out the same happy Young Pioneer songs about being true to Socialism, and wearing our blue uniforms at all times. We went on day trips along the coast: to Sevastopol, a Navy base and a battlefield of the Crimean War; to the Chekhov Museum in Yalta; to the Vorontsov Botanical Gardens, a former nobleman's estate. Expert guides briefed us mercilessly on the history geography flora fauna of the locale, but mostly on how awful things had been under the tsar and how great they were now. In the interim we were exhorted to sing.

Within a week, singing happy songs became a problem for me. In Syzran, at Young Pioneer rallies, I had no problem lip-synching or muttering or just humming (I could never remember all the lyrics)—besides, the rallies were not that frequent. In Artek we had to sing several times a day, with the counselor walking alongside our formation (I had a déjà vu years later, watching boot camp scenes in American movies)—obviously, to make sure that everyone was singing. And the repertory! Back at school I did not mind paying lip service to hymns like "The Party Is Our Helmsman"; it was a mechanical exercise, like a Pioneer salute. The solemn lyrics commanded a solemn facial expression, behind which you could be thinking whatever you liked. But Artek songs were "site-specific," written specially for the camp; they were all about frolicking in the sun and being thankful to the Party for its largesse; they commanded the widest, happiest smile your facial muscles could muster. I could fake a song, and I could fake a smile, but not both at the same time.

I did what draft dodgers have done for ages. But instead of shooting myself in the foot, I sang full blast for an entire day, which drew suspicious looks from my fellow campers. Predictably, my voice grew hoarse; the next morning I presented myself at the infirmary, looking properly dejected. I was given a soda-like powder and told to gargle. The counselor was sympathetic. Due to my "weak" throat, I never had to yell again.

We had dancing lessons, pseudo-folksy dances done in groups (never in twos). They were site-specific, too, I suspect, since I have yet to see them danced outside Artek. The dance music consisted of the same patriotic songs we had to holler the rest of the time. We had movies, all based on Lenin's life and the October Revolution. We had sports, of course. Now I missed courtyard fights; it was better to punch someone and make up after five minutes than to be yelled at—"Go kill 'em!"—by the counselor.

The action was nonstop; when a musical lecture was suddenly canceled, our counselor panicked: "What shall I do with you?" The prospect of unstructured leisure was anathema to him. I tried to adjust, the only way I knew how: I faked headaches and stomachaches, and I conveniently forgot my sweater when we were taken across the camp one night for yet another Young Pioneer festivity.

"But you'll miss the rally!" The counselor was genuinely upset. "It's a full half-hour walk!"

"I don't want to catch a cold," I whined.

He, a bronzed, muscular specimen, gave me a look: *Sissy*. But what could he do? If I indeed caught a cold, he might find himself in trouble for having knowingly endangered my health. And so I got out of yet another bugle-and-drum extravaganza. What I would really have liked was to go to the beach, which was, of course, off-limits after dark.

Back at the dormitory, I ran into another boy, who was walking to the veranda with a book in hand. Both of us were instantly apprehensive: neither was supposed to be there. Muttering excuses, we fled, now hiding not only from the counselor but from each other as well.

My hatred of the place was compounded by feeling guilty about hating it. I could just hear people say, *For children from poor families, this is the only chance to go to the seashore, to get decent food, even to wear the clothes that you are deriding* . . . True: the food was plentiful, and the scenery was gorgeous. I am sure that, to Kuzka from our building, Artek would have looked like Oz. But there were no Kuzkas at Artek.

I realized soon that I was in the midst of *them*—the people on the podium. I learned my lesson on the very first day. At a get-acquainted meeting for our Troop Four, each of us rose, in alphabetical order, to speak about himself, especially how he had so excelled in Pioneer activity as to be sent to Artek for a whole month.

I panicked. I had not realized that this was a *prize*. At home I had worked so hard to avoid doing precisely the things that my fellow campers were now boasting about. Since G is the fourth letter in the Cyrillic alphabet, I did not have much time to make up a story. When my turn came, I fell apart. "I got here," I mumbled, "because . . . because . . ." My face was on fire. "My mother called the Party Secretary—she's a pediatrician—she treats his kids . . ."

The silence was complete. No one looked at me. Then one of the counselors said pleadingly, "Well, at school—do you have good grades? . . . Seee? And you collected scrap metal and wastepaper and helped on the garden plot . . ." I kept nodding like a dummy. "Seee? Well, then—you certainly deserve to be here. You should not be so modest. Next, please."

The rest of the kids went on about trees planted, drives organized, and Lenin mini-museums established . . . I kept my eyes down, thinking, If only my turn had come later, surely I would have come up with something.

Afterward Zhenya Markowitz, a scrawny redhead from Ordzhonikidze, came up to me. "You're really an idiot, aren't you? How do you think anybody gets here, by picking up fucking scrap metal? My mother is a doctor, too."

I'm thankful to Zhenya. You need lessons in social interaction like this—better to learn it at twelve than at thirty-two. Although I am not really sure how well I have learned.

Four

While I was enjoying the Young Pioneer boot camp, my father's mother, Musya, died. Later that summer, I was shipped to Lipetsk, a four-hour train ride south of Moscow, to stay with my grandfather.

My mother's first reaction was to say that Grandfather Semyon "drove her to her grave." My mother could not stand her father-in-law, and objectivity had never been her forte. I have not seen my mother, who lives in Kharkov, since I left Russia. If she gets to read this book, she will note instantly that I brought up Grandma Musya before her own mother. "I knew it all my life," she'll say, knitting her eyebrows and nodding knowingly. "You've always loved *them* more. And what have they ever done for you? When I—"

I don't wait for her to finish, I flee the room, but I'm no longer sure whether I should go on about my grandparents or about my mother. She has a way of winning arguments: emotionally, she's a street fighter, oblivious of the Marquis of Queensberry's rules.

My grandparents lived in a sleepy neighborhood in the old part of town. Their house was a crumbling shack that consisted of a fair-sized room with a hallway, without heat or running water; there was a coal stove and an outside toilet. On my visits I was the water boy, bringing it in pails from a pump on the corner.

The house's prime asset was a tiny garden in the back, with gooseberries and raspberries and an apple tree.

We did not visit Lipetsk often, and I remember little of Grandma Musya: a tiny old woman, her face rolled up in wrinkles and spotted with huge moles. Out of childish superstition, I dreaded kissing her. She spoke softly, calling her husband "Semochka," an affectionate diminutive; she hobbled around the house, trying to make her cane-rapping unheard— "Semochka is asleep."

Grandfather was the head bookkeeper at a movie theater. He had lived in the town for a long time. As we walked around, he often stopped to talk to people. They treated him with respect, but he did not seem to have many friends. He was hardly what you would call an easygoing person.

Grandfather was seventy that summer. He would get up early in the morning and take a half-hour walk to the beach, a sandy strip on the bank of the Voronezh River. Rain or shine, January or July, he would do his exercises, then go for a swim. He was back in time for breakfast; sometimes he would return to the beach afterward. As he calmly trotted along in his swimming trunks, his bald, pear-shaped head looked enormous, bobbing up and down on his body, which was sparsely covered with gray hair. In the Russia of the sixties his exercise fetish was deemed a benign eccentricity. He was ahead of his time. Or out of place: I often think of him when I see retirees jogging along the beach in California.

No force in the world could get me out of bed to join him on his early-morning run—which made me a *slabak*, a wimp. He did not rail endlessly, as my mother would have done; but his sparse, cutting remarks about "his mother's son" and "all that Khaikin blood" (her maiden name) cut worse. Arguing was beneath him. *"Ai,"* he waved: *What's the point?*

I wish I could ask him now: Is this a way to win your grandson's love? But after all these years his ghost is still wearing a stubborn expression, and I know the argument won't get me anywhere. He took love for granted, as an entitlement—with me, with his wife, with his son. He was temperamentally suited to be a patriarch, to rule a clan of a dozen children and their respective families. Amid the brood he would have found the right grandson, an obedient moron whom he could forge into an Olympic champ. In that sense, he was *after* his time.

My mother never tired of talking about my Gurevich stubbornness. "Taking after Grandpa Semyon, may he . . ." Grandpa thought it was a good thing for me to join them on a boating trip; I did not want to go. "He's your *grandfather*," my father, trapped in the middle, would plead. The sadist in me enjoyed watching him fidget and sweat, torn between his liberal inclinations and his filial/paternal duties. "I hope someday you will show me the respect I'm showing him," he would add, looking away. I can't stomach automatic obeisance. I waved and took off; just like Grandpa. Today I can't even recall what was so awful about boating, which normally I enjoy. It was a contest of wills, nothing else. My mother may have had a point after all when she talked about me inheriting my grandfather's stubbornness.

Grandfather won all the battles; things either went his way or did not go at all. I was a bad loser, pouting for days on end. But sometimes I put on an act and accompanied him on his visits to Grandmother's grave. I went every other day; he, every day. According to my father, he kept going every day till he could no longer walk.

Twelve-year-old egotists want to go to the movies, not to a cemetery, especially since part of the route was downwind from a slaughterhouse, whose smells could knock you out on a windy day. We must have talked on those half-hour walks, but mostly we were silent. Whatever opinions I had, I knew that a careless remark could summon enough of his anger to poison things for a day. And the old man's opinions carried no weight with me. We must have been an odd sight.

The cemetery was small, run-down, overgrown with weeds, just like the rest of the area. Outside the church I would fill a jar with fresh water from a pump and take it to the gravesite. The tiny plot was fenced off with metal bars, but these did not stop kids from stealing the glass jars and cashing them in for deposit money at the store. I put flowers in the jar and joined grandfather in pulling weeds out of the flowerbed. Afterward we sat down on the tiny stone bench. There was a chill in the air; the day was fading fast. We sat, each thinking his thoughts.

My mind was occasionally on the movie due to open the next day. As the bookkeeper's grandson, I got in for free—but never by myself, and sometimes I had to wait a *whole day*, truly a tragedy, before he would come with me. Once, to butter him up, I asked about the movie we had seen last, a Revolution thriller. He sneered. "A pack of lies."

I waited.

"It wasn't like that," he said in the pejorative tone that he usually reserved for comments on my behavior. "But those were the days . . ." His expression relaxed; it was almost like a smile.

I waited anxiously. Something was bound to come. The period in question was the spring of 1917, the brief interregnum between the tsar and the Bolsheviks—how could that lead to another putdown for me?

"There were rallies on every corner, and speeches . . . Lenin was a lousy speaker, by the way."

A chill ran down my back. I closed my eyes. The heavens were about to open and strike us with a lightning bolt.

He must have noticed my expression. "Well, he wasn't bad. But not exciting, either. Now, Tsereteli, the Menshevik . . ."

I nodded. An obscure figure, a minor enemy of the Party.

". . . he was an *orator*! You could listen to him for hours . . ."

On our way out I was still numb from shock. With all my resentment of Artek and the Young Pioneer meetings, I was still a good boy. Even so, I was not going to abandon my Grandpa, I would not throw his soul to the wolves—there was still hope for him in Communist Heaven . . . "So, uh, you were still there, in Petrograd, when *it* happened?" I whispered, already afraid of what I might hear. "The storming of the Winter Palace—"

"On October 25th I was in Petrograd, that's right," he said calmly.

"And what . . . did . . . you . . . do?" Please, dear God, let him be there, rushing in a long black coat across the square, scaling the palace gate, firing at the cowardly guards, yelling, "All power to the Soviets!"

"We were at the opera," he said. "We had tickets for Chaliapin in *Faust*."

I was lost. There was no hope. "And then?"

"Then we went to the nightclub. With your grandma." He eyed me skeptically. "That's where you go after the opera."

Horrible visions stormed my head: Grandpa in a silk top hat and Grandma in furs and jewelry—idle bourgeoisie drinking champagne toasts to the death of the toiling masses . . . At least, they were not openly on the counterrevolutionary side. At the same time a part of me perversely wished they had been, that he had been defending the Winter Palace with a gun in his hand—at least, he would have been doing something historically important, rather than listening to *Faust* and drinking champagne! "And after that—"

"It was getting light," he said. "It was beautiful—the winter's first snow . . ."

"I mean, was . . . anything . . . *different*?"

"There were some new posters outside, something about land and peace—in those days, they had new posters every day. No one paid attention. We were tired after all that champagne . . ."

I was right!

". . . and dancing—oh, how we danced in those days, not like your generation. I see those dances in the park . . ." He spat loudly. "We danced the waltz. We knew how to dance. You—you just get drunk and stumble around, like savages, which is what you are." He fell silent.

"Me?" My voice shook as a huge lump blocked my throat. "Why *me*?"

"You're going to be just like them," he said bitterly. "How can you be anything different?"

"You must have been rich," I said, trying to match his bitterness. "You went to nightclubs while the workers—"

"Shut up already," he waved. "I'm sick and tired of this crap they stuff into your heads." He stopped and turned ninety degrees to face me. "You didn't have to be rich to go to a nightclub in those days! We were young! Do you understand? We didn't count money! We were young and in love! Don't start on me with your starving workers! They only wish they could have now what they had then! In those days a working man had dignity! Now he's been reduced to a drunken bum! What do *you* know about workers? You think you know everything! *Ai* . . ." He waved and hobbled on, hitting everything in sight with his cane. I was left in the middle of the street, thinking, Ten days left before I go back to Syzran. I'll kill him or myself.

At the time, I suppressed this outburst. A part of me felt it was unwise to go around telling people that my grandfather had spent the eve of the Revolution in a nightclub. I suppressed it as securely as he must have done in his time. But I was more fortunate—it took me only ten years before I could unlock this box and inspect its contents; he had kept his box locked all his life.

I did not see much of him in the following years: a week here, a week there. Without Grandma he aged fast. After his death bits and pieces came my way, mostly via my father's Moscow aunts. They said my great-grandfather had been an Orthodox rabbi who combined devout faith with physical force. When young Semyon (*né* Solomon, I surmise) declared he was going to marry Musya Vasilyeva, a shiksa, his father threatened to kill him. Something similar took place in my grandmother's household, where her nobleman father would not hear of mixing blue blood with Jew blood. A midnight elopement in a covered carriage ensued, with eternal curses from both sides.

My Moscow aunts were octogenarian ladies, much given to romantic embellishment, I suspect. I am far from buying these stories wholesale, although they sound wonderful and may have some truth to them. I am not in great need of either a pillar of Judaism or a Russian count for a great-grandfather. If Semyon's and Musya's fathers both were humble clerks who merely grumbled about the marriage, that's okay by me, too. I look at my grandparents' picture, an ocher daguerreotype, and I find no surprises: his huge, stern face takes up two-thirds of it, while Grandma Musya's kindly, patient visage is hidden in the corner. She feared him, he ruled her with an iron hand, yet love must have been there. Is it too romantic on my part to believe that fear and despotism by themselves cannot sustain a forty-five-year union? I have spent enough time under the Soviet system to realize that fear of despotism has its limits . . .

Since I never heard the word "God" leave Grandpa's lips, I suspect that converting to marry Musya involved little sacrifice; so much for the rebelliousness vaunted by the aunts. All romance aside, I'm more curious about how he survived the era that had started with attending a performance by Chaliapin and drinking champagne at a nightclub.

However, I realize that I did not stand a chance of getting him to talk. In all probability, his outburst on the way from the cemetery was just that, an outburst. Certainly, he was not going to allow me more than a glimpse into the luggage he had carried for fifty years.

I am sure that in his own peculiar way he loved me, his only grandson. He may have regretted his outburst as a breach of his usual reticence, which was meant not only to secure his own survival through fifty years but to protect me as well—from having doubts about the benevolence of Communism. Best not to confuse the child, he must have reasoned, just as when bringing up my father.

If these were indeed his motives, I am not sure that I appreciate this protectiveness. Later in life I ran into a number of kids my own age, whose parents had been more outspoken about opening their children's eyes to the nature of Communism. I had to stumble toward the truth by myself; perhaps, if I had been offered a little helping hand, I could have spared myself a few cuts and bruises. But both my grandfather and my father belonged to the silent generations forced by fear into lifelong doublethink.

In college I had a friend named Sasha, who was light-years ahead of me in understanding Communism's true nature. His parents were university professors, with acute political instincts, who did much to keep Sasha's eyes open to the system's rottenness. One day they came to visit him in Moscow. As Sasha was leaving the house, he casually stuck an Iris Murdoch paperback in his pocket. They were in shock. They begged him to wrap it in paper, to keep it from view. It did not matter to them that Iris Murdoch was an officially approved author and that a number of her novels had been published in Russia. The book had come from the West—that was enough for them. Both had grown up in the thirties, and by sheer chance both had avoided being arrested; the fear would stay under their skin to their dying day.

Five

When people compliment me on my English, I put their remarks into perspective. I would gladly trade half of this skill for my friend Mike's ability to sign into a computer system and figure out within hours how to lock all other users out of it. Also, a gift needs to be discovered and nurtured. Any knack I may have for languages, I owe wholly to my father.

He took German at school, then English at the Air Force Academy. His progress in both was limited, and I think he hoped I would accomplish something he had never found the ability or time for. He had an enormous curiosity about the world, yet as a member of the military he was barred from leaving the country for nonmilitary purposes. It was no accident that he had encouraged me to collect stamps long before I plunged into languages.

There was something visceral about the way my father rolled English sounds in his mouth: " '*Cock-tail*,' " he would say, and shake his head with wonder. " '*Petushiny khvost*.' Imagine: they mix booze and call it 'a cock's tail.' Or '*cowboy*.' '*Korovy malchik*.' The words they make up!"

"*Korovy malchik*" sounds faintly ridiculous in Russian. The cow is a symbol of docility; boy, of immaturity: one sees a barefoot peasant kid walking in mud and cowshit and urging the cow along with a twig. How can these words, translated one by one into English and wedged together, evoke a romantic image? (Mostly in America: in Western Europe, with Reagan's ascent to power, the word came to mean "trigger-happy.") My father and I, we wondered together. "They are *pastukhi*," he said. "Shepherds. Why do they call 'em *kovboi*?" Some kind of magic had to be involved. To say nothing of *kokteil*—mixing vodka or brandy with cheap red, the only two drinks that we knew, was a recipe for disaster! We could not see the end result clearly: it was an indescribable, luxuriantly colored liquid, served in the finest cut crystal—everything that life in Syzran was not.

Whether the outside world came to us by image, via the tropical flowers on Sharjah stamps, or by sound, via exotic words like "cowboy" or "cocktail," it was a colorful, exciting place, and English was the key to it. My English was my father's pet project. In the end he was unhappy with the way it turned out: political disenchantment and subsequent emigration. But I wonder if a part of him is proud that I took his encouragement and drove it as far as I have.

Starting with the fifth grade, I took English classes twice a week. Our teacher was an elderly lady, kindly and ineffective, with thirty students in her class. My father had me study by myself, using the sixth- and then seventh-grade textbooks, and so on. When I thus "graduated," he asked instructors from his flight school to tutor me. They were unenthusiastic: teaching was something they did for a living, so they hated to let it encroach upon their free time. Books in English were hard to get, and the few available were boring, too: they were "adapted"—written in simplified language, with "See Spot run" narratives that I could only sneer at. (As I mentioned, in high school I would move on to Sherlock Holmes stories—still "adapted.")

Determined to keep me going, my father went so far as to

have me translate textbooks into English with a dictionary. Unmonitored, the exercise had little value: with no one to ask which word from the dictionary should be used, I improvised wildly, with results that, I suspect, had little to do with the original. My interest flagged, and my father got frustrated. Finally, before I entered the eighth grade, he managed to get me into a "special" school, one with heavy emphasis on English in its curriculum. The principal was reluctant, claiming that my father, being in the military, could be transferred any day, and I would be just wasting a space. (It did not occur to me at the time, but, after hearing stories from graduates of other "special" schools, I cannot help thinking that perhaps mine had already too many students with Jewish-sounding names. True, their fathers were socially a cut above: Efros, the chief engineer of a huge chemical factory, and Rivman, the artistic director of the local playhouse. Caste tended to compensate for prejudice.)

I had mixed feelings about the transfer. My friends were in the old school; I was used to the teachers, who gave me every break in the book in exchange for leaving them in peace; and it was a five-minute walk away, compared to the bus ride to the new school. On the other hand, the new school had cachet, and—it was *new* and *different*: two words that have always been crucial to my decisionmaking.

The new school was an odd place. Its walls carried all the standard slogans—STUDYING IS THE MAIN DUTY OF YOUNG COMMUNISM BUILDERS, THE PARTY IS OUR HELMSMAN, LENIN BEATS IN EVERY HEART—except that here they were in English. The portraits of the Politburo members had English captions. Bathroom signs were in English. Vladimir Nikolayevich Golubev, our principal, did not believe in doing things halfway. He never spoke Russian to us, even—or especially—when suspending us for smoking in the men's room. Later, when I came back to visit on vacation from college in Moscow, his English sounded odd to me. He once remarked at a school dance that a certain student was shaking like "a sack of shit" on the floor (my grandfather would have agreed). It was a strange way of putting it, but foreigners who live in blissful ignorance of a language's native-land usage tend to create their own.

Our teachers' English was odd, but there was a lot of it. Our two or three hours of English a day included classes in English lit, English history, and geography (all in English). My favorite class was "The Paper," where we studied political lingo, using the only two papers available in English: *The Morning Star* (the British Communist daily) and *The Moscow News* (a Moscow-published weekly—which, years later, under glasnost, would become the most popular Soviet paper). Both bored me stiff. When it was my turn to present current events, I reported a miners' strike in Peru, guerrilla warfare in Chad, and a student rally in Italy. I made them up, but who could tell the difference? I used all the right words: "Progressive mankind is on the march, and imperialist reactionary forces are routed around the world."

In class I quickly rose to the top with my twice-a-term cram system. My political obligations got heavier: at fourteen I had to join the Komsomol, the youth auxiliary of the Party—more meetings than the Young Pioneers, each one longer than the last (at least, the pageant-like marching was gone). But I was inured to that; also, the school already had a nascent political machine, a small core of ambitious kids happy to climb on the podium and make a speech denouncing this and that. I was mercifully left alone. But the inside of the school was easier to handle than the outside.

Before, when I lived and went to school in the same neighborhood, I knew most of the kids, they knew me, and the only fights I ever had were on the soccer field. If I had to visit other neighborhoods, I was seldom by myself. Knowing nobody in the new school's vicinity made me a natural target.

It could happen anywhere: on a side street, in a park, in a movie theater. A kid half your size would ask you for spare change. Then a couple of others, twice your size, showed up and looked on as the short one went through your pockets. You could run, but they already knew where you were going, and the next time they would remember you.

The shakedowns went on for weeks. I was being reduced to a hunted animal: always on the lookout and searching for the safest route home. I learned to hide my lunch money, my color ballpoints, even my bus pass, in my shoes; they would throw my schoolbag in the mud. Every day I shook in impotent anger and lost myself in *Death Wish*–like daydreams (though it would be another ten years before I saw the movie). Fighting was useless—in Syzran or New York, muggers travel in packs and never face you one on one. All you can do is join them. Or, short of that, make friends.

I got to know one of them in my class: Lyokha Beletsky. He operated in Gorky Park, in the center of town. He would spot a mark, follow him, and suddenly take his arm: "Like this," he showed me once, grabbing my arm firmly. "You gotta show you mean business. I say, 'Step aside, I got business with you.' And Shurik's right there." Shurik was six feet tall, with a comatose expression and piglet eyes on a wino's swollen mug. He looked like he could break your arm without waking up. "Anyone messes with you, tell them you know me and Shurik," Lyokha winked.

Lyokha was a voracious reader, and I kept him supplied with sci-fi and spy novels. In return he once invited me to come along to the park. "Won't take long. Just to buy enough to roll a *kosyak* [a joint], and half a liter."

I passed. I liked Lyokha, but Shurik made me nervous.

Lyokha robbed to buy hash, leaving the rough stuff to Shurik. But others thrived on it. I can see their counterparts now as I walk down Forty-second Street—hanging out with nothing to do, hoping to be let in on a nickel-and-dime deal. Their clothes and their speech are different, but their body language, the way they lean and slouch: these are familiar. In my mind's eye I can see the Syzran hoods, their faces shaded by their hats' visors; their fake gold teeth; their spitting, aimed from between the teeth with firing-range accuracy; their hands-in-the-pockets stance; the cigarettes held between thumb and forefinger. Elsewhere kids imitate movie stars and singers; our hoods' heroes were their older brothers and uncles doing time for burglary or assault.

After dark the town belonged to hoodlums. They dominated parks and skating rinks, where they settled scores. Every dance drew them, be it in a park, in a workers' club, or in a voc-ed school. You didn't leave the Saturday night dance at school by yourself: they milled around outside, stalking their prey. The school was a poor sanctuary, anyway, more like a fortress under siege. Sometimes they hurled rocks through the windows and even tried to break in; it was the physics teacher's begging that kept them at bay. I once cracked a joke about us taking up positions on the perimeter, but no one laughed.

In the old neighborhood we'd also had a gang—sort of. All we did was roam the streets in a pack, looking as mean as we could. The closest we came to fighting was when we went to another project to arrange a soccer game. Any one of us could have easily done it by himself, but we had to show ourselves off as a *gang*. The oldest of us was twelve, and it would never have occurred to us to actually assault someone.

It was different at the new school. One night I was walking

Lyuba home from class. She lived in Moldavka, a neighborhood more vicious than mine, and visually more intimidating: a hive of shacks climbing up a wide ravine; you can see Moldavkas in places like Tijuana. Lyuba was flirting, but my answers were getting mechanical. Looking around, all I could think was: If I piss someone off here, they won't find my body for weeks.

The hoods stood at the bridge—a couple of boards over the stream. There were no more than half a dozen of them, but in the dark they looked like an army. "Hey, you!" one of them yelled. "Come here!"

We walked on in silence. I did not dare take her hand: she would know I was sweating. I was sure she could hear my heartbeat. "They're just a bunch of fools," she said before we parted. "You should ignore them."

"I know," I tossed off lightly, wishing I could ask if she knew of an alternative route back.

They yelled again on my way back. I walked briskly, curbing the urge to break into a run. I was beyond losing face; but when an animal senses your fear, it is more likely to attack you. They were lazy that night, though, and there was a huge puddle between us. "You come back, we break your ass!" one of them yelled by way of farewell.

"You're crazy," Lyokha said when I told him of my Moldavka adventure. "*I* wouldn't go to that place after dark. You should date where you live."

Syzran was awash in violence, but not in the same way as an American inner city. The turf wars were not over drug sales, nor were guns common, although Shurik carried brass knuckles and a switchblade. Fifty-men-strong rumbles would explode from a drunken remark or a pass at a girl: no one ever knew the exact *casus belli*. The line between the gangs and the law-abiding citizens was blurry: soldiers battled factory workers; one voc-ed school fought another with sticks, rocks, and chains. On Saturday nights we stayed away from the Workers' Club, the scene of many a battle; so did the police. Sharing a smoke in the men's room, I heard endless sagas of heroes like Squinty Sashka, who got off on parole and slashed his girlfriend's face for not waiting for him. Who needed stories of pirates and treasure troves? Once someone pointed Sashka out to me on the street, cautioning me not to stare. Compared to him, Shurik looked like a brain surgeon.

Whence such a climate of terror? The standard array of reasons includes broken families, unemployment, drugs, lack of education and cultural facilities, and so on. I recognize these arguments made by the American anthropologists who study inner-city culture (they would feel at home in any Soviet town, from Syzran to Moscow's blue-collar outskirts). Yes, Syzran was a cultural backwater; yes, vodka ravages the fabric of Soviet society as brutally as any other drug; but there is another factor that is seldom mentioned: the effect of the Gulag on the social climate.

In my later travels across the Soviet Union, I could see that Syzran was meaner than an average town its size, but hardly *the* meanest. In Syzran, at least, I could walk down Sovyetskaya, the main street, which I was strongly urged not to do on No-vosibirsk's Red Avenue. In Bratsk, in the heart of Siberia, I saw a rumble with a cast of hundreds. It was Hollywood-unreal, with sirens wailing, police lights flashing, and men lined up against the wall to be frisked. The locals shrugged: camp inmates on weekend passes, I was told.

In a way it seems inevitable: the Soviet economy is domi-nated by large, heavy-industry projects, none of which could have been built without convict labor. Friends of mine who in 1970 went to Togliatti, where Fiat was building a huge car factory, told me later that crime was so rampant that the streets were patrolled by the military in jeeps, rather than by regular police.

While there are fewer camps in Russia now than there were under Stalin, the criminal culture they bred has left its imprint on the society at large. Even as nine-year-olds sitting around our courtyard, we were already singing songs about happy-go-lucky Soviet Bonnies and Clydes, who preferred a heroic death to ratting on a fellow thief. Not until later, when I went to school in Moscow, did I discover, with some embarrassment, that much of the slang I was using had originated in the camps. It is no accident that, while Vladimir Vysotsky, the most beloved Russian songwriter/actor/poet of the sixties and seventies, was from a Moscow intelligentsia family, he was first acclaimed for his prison songs.

Thieves and robbers sound noble in Vysotsky's songs, but after seven years on the streets of Syzran I find it hard to feel what the French call *nostalgie de la boue*, or to romanticize hoodlums. Years later I saw *West Side Story* at the Moscow Film Festival. The dancing and the music thrilled me, but I squirmed: how can you glorify *that*? I realized that my visceral reaction was the opposite of the filmmakers' intention; nor was I so naïve as to mistake this stylized spectacle for a realistic depiction of New York gangs. But I could not help wondering if it would have been the same movie if its authors had met Shurik in the flesh.

I enjoyed getting high with Lyokha: the ritual of burning the sticky black paste, the stuffing of a cigarette, and, most of all, his priestly mien as he went through these motions. But, excepting the sci-fi, we had little in common, and even that had to be set aside whenever Shurik or another "missing link" joined us: Lyokha was not eager to advertise his reading habit among the hoods. A shared high did not make Shurik and me friends: I was still an alien, a target for little barbs that could rip hostility open at any moment. With this strain, smoking was not much fun, and my "addiction" did not last. On the other hand, my "nice" friends would have had a seizure if I had suggested we pitch in for a joint. In retrospect, it was as if the whole town had seen *Reefer Madness*. Hash was the Devil's seed; but booze was another matter.

Russian Jews do drink less than other Russians; yet they might drink at least as much as gentiles in America. Liquor consumption at family gatherings was relatively mild, but at numerous celebrations with my father's fellow officers at least a couple of people would pass out. I was started out on wine at nine or so, on the assumption that I would do it anyway, and better I should do it supervised. Doctors may disagree, but it may have worked: until the eighth grade I felt no compulsion to head for the liquor store with my classmates—many of whom had started drinking as early as the fifth grade.

There seemed to be a dance every Saturday night—if not at our school, then at another. A dance was never just a *dance*: simply letting students have fun would not have been educationally sound. There was always an official occasion: the Revolution Anniversary, Lenin's Birthday, the end of the term, Armed Forces Day. The Party Secretary would climb up to the lectern and deliver a half hour of soporific blather about Achievements and Progressive Mankind. Next came the arts: the same prodigies, year in and year out, played Chopin's Polonaise and performed Russian folk dances. We sat back, savoring the alcoholic buzz, exchanging conspiratorial glances, waiting for the band to come on.

You could not attend a dance sober; the pressure was too great. The nerve to show up at a barely familiar place (if the dance was at another school), to casually slouch against the wall and discuss the girls' physical endowments, to cross the floor and mutter an invitation to dance—all this seemed beyond our reach without the helping hand of booze.

We would split our first bottle before the dance and bring another one with us. We would step out in the backyard, or into the men's room. The bottle would circulate, like the turn in a poker game: you could fold, or you could stay in the game. You were already reeling, but everyone's eyes were on you. Peer pressure at its most naked. You learned to clench your teeth and allow as little vodka in as possible, knowing that the next drop would be one too many. I cannot imagine the school's bathroom on a dance night without the choked sounds of vomiting.

This rite of passage, I am often told, is common to teenagers all over the world. Perhaps; far be it from me to claim that a Soviet childhood is distinct from every other childhood in all respects. But the quantities we consumed—of vodka and port, not beer—and the almost utter lack of a sober face at these dances . . . if this scale of mass inebriation is matched in Ohio or Iowa, then we are all in bigger trouble than we care to admit.

An outlet for frustration, a response to boredom, a rite of passage—why even try to break down the variety of reasons that led us to the bottle? It is easier just to say that everyone around us drank. There were no teetotalers in Syzran.

The drunks milled outside liquor stores, swaying in the wind, holding on to the wall, slobbering and puking all over themselves, or passed out cold. Their ranks swelled on holidays, like

May Day or Revolution Day. Passing out in their own urine, they slept it off in doorways, in the mud, in garbage dumps, in the middle of the street. No one cared: it seemed like everyone was drunk. People stepped over a drunk as if he—or she—were just another puddle. The police picked up the conspicuous ones and moved them out of sight.

In my fourteen years in the West I have not seen as many drunks as I saw in any one year in Syzran. New Yorkers may think of St. Patrick's Day; Müncheners, of Oktoberfest . . . imagine this revelry going on all year long. But "revelry" is the wrong word. There is nothing festive about Russian drinking; it reeks of despair and frustration and is never complete without an overpowering urge to confess and to proclaim oneself to the world. The body language alone speaks volumes: tearing the shirt on one's chest, as if one were choking, as if torn apart by the desire to bare one's soul. "Vvvanya! Fffriend! I—for—you—anything!" Lightning-fast metamorphoses from teary sentimentalist to feral beast and back to sentimentalist, a soap opera played within minutes—there is nothing like it. Foreigners simply don't know what to make of it. If you have not seen a drunken Russian, you'll never comprehend the dark, desperate frenzy so typical of the Russian novel.

Six

While my father's parents tripped the light fantastic in night-clubs ("where you go after the opera"), my mother's parents, Olga and David, still lived in a shtetl. But for the Revolution, their daughter Gisya, my mother, would have tended cows within the pale instead of going to medical school. Without the Revolution, I can easily see Grandpa Semyon as a bank executive living in a respectable St. Petersburg neighborhood. I have no idea where that leaves his son Lev—my father—but the odds of Lev and Gisya ever meeting would have been remote. In that I owe the fact of my birth to the Revolution.

The pictures look flashy and innocent at the same time: a cadet at Kharkov Air Force Academy, fresh from the war, modestly decorated; and a vivacious medical student. Both good-looking, fun-loving, embarking on successful careers . . . when you're in in your twenties, what else do you need?

Knowing my Kharkov family, I am a bit skeptical of this idyll. As in Burma or Peru, the military have always been a good catch in Russia—especially in a hungry year like 1947; especially for a family one step removed from the shtetl. Since neither of my parents is practical-minded, Grandma Olga surely must have used some of her wiles. It was not hard: a young kid, away from home, taken into the family bosom. The grub in the Academy's cafeteria must have tasted twice as awful after Grandma's *kotlety* (meatballs) with onion and garlic. Next, the solemn sounds of Mendelssohn's Wedding March. Or, rather, the theme from

An Officer and a Gentleman: I can see my father marching through the dusty labs in his shiny uniform, sweeping skeletons and anatomical charts out of the way. They never made a sequel: who wants to see Richard Gere and Debra Winger screaming their lungs out, breaking dishes, and using their son in a tug-of-war?

I did not blame my father for leaving. It was not abandonment; rather, it was escape from the mental asylum that was our house. But I can't blame my mother entirely, either.

Nowadays in Kharkov, if a Jew wants to get into medical school, an envelope passed under the table had better contain five to six thousand rubles—four years' salary for a starting doctor. But my mother graduated from high school in 1943, in the middle of Kazakhstan, in Central Asia, where her family had been evacuated to . . . What quotas? what bribes? Among the dirt and squalor the doctor was the one in a white smock; you could not get more respectable than that. Young Gisya became a pediatrician. After twenty years of working in the field she begged her only son—me—to promise her *not* to go to medical school. Anything but. How's that for a Jewish mother?

The American picture of a doctor's life is soothing Muzak in a spotless reception room and a Florida condo with a view of the golf course. In Russia, too, I met successful doctors with matching lifestyles: mostly men, who had the edge in a field where women are actually a majority. But my mother was speaking from her own experience. On an average day she would see thirty to forty patients in three to four hours in a jam-packed clinic where babies screamed in hallways and drafts blew every which way. More infections were contracted in the clinic than outside it. Medicine being free, most parents requested house calls. Shlepping an enormous bag that bulged with instruments, files, and medicine through flooded, muddy, or snowbound streets; climbing five flights to a patient's home, day in and day out—was this any way for a forty-year-old woman to make a living? She was assigned a car, which was usually broken; or the streets were impassable with snow; or the driver took a day off to nurse a hangover (in the country, where a private car was a rarity, women of my mother's generation did not drive). Calling hours stretched to five from the official three. Then she brought home paperwork, filling out case histories and end-of-the-month reports by hand through long winter evenings. Her salary was 125 rubles a month. Whether you convert at the official rate (about $150) or the black-market rate (about $12), she made less than a factory worker.

But there were important benefits. In Syzran nothing was available if you did not know the saleswoman at the store; you could not even leave town unless you knew someone at the railroad station. Yet everybody has children, store managers included, and children need a doctor's attention. Store shelves might be empty, but not our refrigerator: thanks to my mother's patients, we always had chicken, bologna, franks. It never occurred to me to buy anything, from cheese to galoshes, over the counter; that night one hungry winter when we got up to stand in line for bread was an exception. This is not to say that money was completely without value. Buying a decent suit, whether openly or under the counter, would set my mother back a whole month's salary.

Nowadays, as I watch the fast-food TV commercials with moms smiling widely as they haul McNuggets home, it does not seem odd that even as a kid I ate most of my meals out. I did not mind; I was not choosy. Like an adult, I ordered from the menu (there were never more than two soups and three entrees, but you have to start somewhere); like an adult, I paid at the register; like an adult, I sat at my own table—an independent thirteen-year-old among the rough worker crowd. At every table they poured vodka or wine, hiding the bottle under the table or inside their coats and leaving the empties for the cleaning woman, who would keep the deposit in exchange for looking the other way (as a cafeteria, the place did not serve liquor). The air was blue with smoke and acrid with strong tobacco; now and then a brawl broke out. Part of me was fascinated by being amid adult life, but I had to gulp down the tepid food in a rush, dreading that someone would spot me and I would have to explain how my mother was sick or my father was on garrison duty. I tried to take food home, but the cafeteria was across the courtyard from us, and the tin pots that contained food were unmistakably public property. On my way home I always ran into someone I knew and had to mumble standard excuses. They sweetly nodded understanding, but I could imagine the scuttlebutt later: His mother is not bringing him up properly. He is one step away from juvenile delinquency.

Syzran women were used to standing in long lines at the store, dusting furniture, scrubbing floors, and cooking dinner. A husband would stand in line at the liquor section; the wife, everywhere else. If his line went faster, he would come by to help her carry the groceries, always grumbling. Genuine or not, the grumbling was obligatory: his pals would mock him as being *pod kablukom* (pussy-whipped) if they suspected he did not mind carrying a shopping bag. A man was supposed to do certain things around the house—*men's* things, like fixing appliances (with the shoddiness of Soviet consumer goods, it *was* a chore), moving furniture, and beating the dust out of the rugs with a wooden roller from the kitchen. Even this last generated a few barbs from the domino table habitués. I never heard a woman complain that a husband did too few domestic chores: if he did not beat her, if he did not drink away the grocery money, he was good enough. Perhaps these attitudes are not different from those of any backward country, where women are not far removed from being kept in a harem. The crucial difference is that Soviet women have to endure this after eight hours at the factory or office.

As for my father, being an instructor in communications at the helicopter school was not a demanding job. His classes and the required "ideological" work among cadets left him with plenty of time for the gym and hobbies. And for housework. He did much more around the house than other husbands—but in secret, to avoid mockery from his fellow officers. Other wives kept their houses in apple-pie order, which their husbands considered their Army-given right. He must have shared this attitude, halfheartedly, and brought his bruised ego home. I think he would have been content to lick his wounds in peace; but there was no peace.

He wielded the huge vacuum cleaner, loaded the primitive washer. Both broke down constantly and were more of an engineering challenge than a chore to him. For cooking, he experimented with soup mixes, which were a novelty at the time, and he whipped up lemon and chocolate puddings, also from mixes. Even these culinary feats were challenges: the instructions were written in elliptical prose that left plenty of room for interpretation. Late at night we stooped over the pot with the fervor of alchemists, trying to figure out when the concoction reached the point of edibility. In the middle Mother would burst in: "What is this nonsense? The child has to go to school tomorrow!" I remember the look on my father's face: he was about to cry. "Yeah, Mom," I said bitterly, on my way out, "you'll be the first one to gorge on this 'nonsense' tomorrow." "Did you hear what he said?" she hollered. "Did you hear how he treats his mother? He learned it from *you*—you and no one else!" Father only shook his head at me. *Why don't you learn?*, his eyes begged.

Perhaps she was right when she later accused me of having contributed to their breakup. Compared to my father, with his blank expression, I was quicker to blow my top at her nagging and take off.

Together with her patients' medical files, she brought home her frustration from work. The nagging was constant, the charges mounted: Father was accused of everything on earth— in sum, of ruining her life. My Kharkov grandmother came to visit, took one look, and left, with my three-year-old sister in tow. Complaining of every sickness in the book, my mother stayed in bed and rose only to lash out at my father or me in another fit of hysteria. I knew that she worked hard, but I could not bring myself to believe in all her maladies: when we went on vacation, her outbursts grew even more violent. She yelled and bawled till she collapsed back in bed with her sedatives. My father did not know how to cope.

One of her favorite tortures was accusing him of sleeping with every woman on the Volga. It was a self-fulfilling prophecy: finally he started an affair. From that point on, things rolled downhill fast. The more she lashed out, the more he withdrew— until one day the withdrawal was complete.

The Moral Code of the Builder of Communism, the catechism of Soviet propaganda, affirms the superior morality of the Soviet people. They do not abandon their spouses, on whatever grounds, and it is the duty of the "collective" to set its errant member straight. In the absence of shrinks, rabbis, and marriage counselors, it was only natural that my mother headed for the helicopter school's Party Secretary to help her bring my father back.

(My American friend Michael, a fellow Army brat, tells me that in the US military it is common for a wronged wife to complain to the commanding officer. But in Russia it is common for a wife to go complaining to the Party Secretary, whether her husband works at a factory or serves in the Army. When Golubev, our school principal, left his wife for a young teacher, he was censured by his Party superiors, transferred to another school, and demoted to teacher, with a sizable cut in salary. According to my friend Irene—this happened after I left Syzran—the drive for his punishment was initiated not so much by his wife as by his deputy, who had been after the job. By leaving his wife, Golubev provided his rival with powerful ammunition: "amoral behavior," the Party charge read.)

Mother launched a campaign the likes of which the Air Force had never seen. No longer did she stay in bed; the maladies were forgotten. Suddenly she was exploding with energy, acting for herself as both attorney and private eye, as she interrogated everybody to find out everything about the affair (discerning the truth was never her strong suit—the more bizarre the gossip, the better). She plunged tirelessly into letter writing and complaints; collecting signatures, affidavits of character, statements from witnesses; holding meetings with the most obnoxious women, her self-appointed advisors, who knew of "a case exactly like this." They were not hard to come by; a small town is a breeding ground for busybodies, who feed off cases like my parents'. They came to the house to ooh and aah over me and shake their heads: *How could he abandon a son like this?—not a hooligan or anything, and look at all the books he's reading!* I was sure that they were lapping up the juicy bits and retelling them behind her back.

The house, already like a mental asylum, now became a campaign headquarters. Every day she came home to relate who had come out for her and who—the nerve!—had failed to affirm their unconditional support: she would get them, too! Each scene ended with identical screaming: how dare I just sit there and read a book or do homework, instead of working with her to bring my father back? I fled the house. Before, she had been merely high-strung; now she was demonic. She scared me.

The case moved up through the Party hierarchy, and successive Party Secretaries wrung their hands impotently. She was out of their jurisdiction; they had no means of stemming this avalanche of complaints. Yes, Soviet military honor had been tainted by these acts of vile debauchery; but there was nothing they could do. They summoned my father to meeting after meeting and demanded that he reconcile—or else.

As I search my memory, I cannot come up with much factual data; I made a conscious effort to keep myself out of the picture. I tried to ignore my mother's accounts of her visits to my father's superiors: the slightest show of interest would have been interpreted as support, as a cause to redouble her efforts to engage me in the battle full-time. Also, I knew her too well to believe her accounts. I was ashamed of her; I felt that the moment I turned my back on an acquaintance, he would tap his head with a finger—*Cuckoo*—in reference to her.

As for my father, he undoubtedly tried to spare me the ugliness of the situation and kept me in the dark about his side of the story. I did not pry. To myself I pictured a Party meeting, as an adult version of a Young Pioneer meeting, with my father as Kolka: red as a beet, his face pained with despair and frustration; nodding, admitting everything, promising to mend his ways—anything to get out of the spotlight, away from the eyes drilling him with scorn. When I met his fellow officers, I read in their faces: *What kind of a man is your father, to allow his wife to wash dirty linen in public like that?* To them, it must have been a logical result of too much helping around the house.

The combined pressure of the Air Force and my mother brought him back. But peace did not last. My mother was a gloating winner, picking up the slightest provocation to rub it in, reminding him of his defeat and threatening more warfare.

It was a November morning (the 9th, I think; right after the two-day Revolution holiday), and the scene was pitiful: at thirteen I experienced my first major hangover. The night before, I had puked all over somebody's apartment and then made a long, sinuous trek home, passing out on the way. In the morning my will to live was about equivalent to my ability to move.

My father did not need explanations. He did not moralize. "Two things," he said. "One, always eat when you drink— heavy food. Two, don't mix." No more *kokteil* jokes.

In the dark, somber room we avoided each other's eyes. The fall morning was gray, overcast. I lay in the corner like a whipped puppy and watched him pack his shirts and underwear in a cardboard suitcase. It was obvious to me that his level tone was the result of an effort: by now he was a humiliated, broken man on his last legs. There had been leavings before, but this one was final.

The very same night I drank myself blind. But I ate a lot, and I stuck to vodka. Although I felt the consequences the next morning, they vanished in the shower. At least, my father's parting advice was sound.

In response to my father's new push toward divorce, my mother revived the campaign. She stopped short of appealing to the Defense Minister himself, but this time my father stood firm.

I doubt that his superiors gave much credence to my mother's allegations of sexual debauchery, but the aspersions had been cast, the meetings conducted, and some sort of action needed to be taken. Besides, they must have drawn their own conclusions: a man who could not control his own wife could probably not control his subordinates, either—definitely a drawback for an officer.

Later my father would be transferred and denied a promotion, retiring as lieutenant colonel, rather than as full colonel. It was a Pyrrhic victory for my mother, who thus ended up getting less alimony. But that's what she had wanted, to inflict as much harm as she could.

I did not take seriously my father's affair with "Aunt Natasha," as I was to call her. I had met her a few times and detested her from the start. She treated me with an obsequiousness that made me cringe—and then tried to milk me for information on my mother's next move. She was as much of a plotter, sans hysteria. Natasha was a few years older than my father, unattractive, poorly educated. I was convinced that this would blow over, that he deserved better than this. Wasn't *my* father intelligent enough to see her flaws? And what was the rush, anyway? Why couldn't he take a rest from domestic strife for a while? No one knows more about relationships between men and women than a fifteen-year-old who has read too many bad novels.

In any event, he could not move in with her: she was married, too. Nor, with the shortage of living space, could he count on finding a room or getting an apartment quickly, and there were no motels, either; the officers' dorm was the only lodging available.

We lived close to the base, and I visited it often: the gym, the basketball courts, the movies at the officers' club. For me, these attractions hardly turned the base—or the school inside it—into Oz: they were a dump inside the dump that was Syzran. The on-base apartment buildings were the same drab breadboxes as the ones off base, and the school's grounds teemed with slogans and crude posters about constant vigilance and determination to crush the Yankee aggressor.

Years later I would teach Russian at a school on an Air Force base in Texas. By then I had spent enough time in America to accept calmly the relative luxury of a US Air Force base: the PX, the pool, the tennis courts, the bowling lanes, and the low, subsidized prices at the officers' club. I was amused by the ease of access and struck by the unusual—for the US—proliferation of patriotic posters. But not until I stopped by the cadets' living quarters—they were no different from any college dorm—did memories of the officers' dorm at the Syzran helicopter school come surging back.

Off base we lived among doctors and welders, but we socialized mostly with my father's colleagues. Without giving it much thought, I assumed that I would be a pilot. It bothered me a little that my father taught at a *helicopter* school: compared to the sleek beauty of MiG fighter planes that swooshed down from the clouds, leaving a sonic boom in their wake, the choppers (MI-6's, I think) looked like ugly contraptions to me. Naturally, I accepted Father's invitation to move with him to the dorm as the first step toward joining the club of The Flying Men: sort of an Air Force prep school.

Father was not a typical military man. Once a month, as the officer on duty, he had to carry a gun for twenty-four hours. Despite my begging, it remained holstered: "It's not a toy." He seemed relieved to turn it in. In the war he had been a mechanic, part of the ground crew, and he never talked about it. Afterward he stayed on active duty: the military offered the security that civilian life did not. He was a radio buff, a tinkerer, whose happiest moments came when the lights in the house went out, giving him a chance to bring out his shining tools, religiously oiled and kept in their pockets. Yet, despite his penchant for order, he was as miserable with the Army's insistence on going by the book as with having to carry a weapon.

The gym was the only place where he was different. I was reminded of this side of him when I saw Robert Duvall in *The Great Santini*—well, almost; he never drove me to tears. But the push for athletic excellence was always on. So many evenings I would rather have been reading Maupassant (hidden under Jules Verne) than facing humiliation on the pommel horse. So many mornings I would rather have stayed in bed than put on the skis and do laps around the park; it was no more than a couple of miles, but after a night spent reading instead of sleeping, it seemed like ten. These years filled me with such hatred of sports, other than soccer, that it took me ten years before I got up on skis in Calgary, Alberta, and felt an odd sense of déjà vu.

Yet this was the only area where I resented his pressure. Otherwise I thought that the two of us would get along great. I followed him cheerfully: there were bound to be problems, but it was better than enduring my mother's constant nagging to force him to come back.

On the face of it, she responded to my departure in her usual way: with violent hysterics. But by then I had learned to distinguish among grades of hysteria and knew she was capable of a reaction far more violent. It seemed that a part of her was hoping that, as long as I was with him, not all was lost, and that I would prevail on him to come back . . .

When I walked in, I saw the grim ward, its walls painted an institutional green; the six rough metal cots; and, most tellingly, the tiny lockers next to the beds. Where do they keep books?, I wondered. My enthusiasm began to wane. Something was not right. The dorm inhabitants were not kids; not cadets; nor were we in a state of war. So why were these officers—adults—pilots—confined in jail-like conditions? I had only one explanation, which I accepted reluctantly: their sin was being single. As bachelors, they had no priority in housing. My father had an apartment, but he had left it behind. Perhaps this was what single life was really about.

He could not help noticing my expression, and put his hand on my shoulder. "Remember, it's temporary." He did not know it would be another eight years before he got an apartment for himself.

I felt ashamed. After all, Julius Caesar had inured himself to sleeping on the ground—during his campaigns, to be sure, but still . . .

My dream of being treated as one of the guys came true instantly. On the first night the pilots, all Father's ex-students, threw a welcoming party: a Russian party, heavy on vodka and light on protocol, with wet kisses and assurances of eternal love and friendship. My father could not slow the steady pour of vodka into my glass: "He's fifteen—a man!" Smashed to the gills, I sat quietly, afraid to blabber out my preference for MiGs and thus blow my chances of going on the helicopter ride everyone promised. I was also a bit concerned how I was going to make it to school the next morning.

On the second day I started my homework at the large table in the middle of the room, but I never got around to the prosperity of Soviet farming under Stalin—a poker game was getting under way beside me. I was promptly initiated. They were using a joker, and that was the first and the last time in my life I ever held a hand of five aces. One of the officers went to the liquor store. The party went on.

Two days later, grim-faced, my father deposited me back at the apartment. A few weeks after that he was transferred to another town. The Air Force had finally found a way to resolve his marital problems.

Thus my short life with Father came to an end. He was forty-three, I was fifteen, and neither of us knew much about life. It still felt a bit like a game; it was not until his last visit home to pack, on the morning of my first hangover, that the truth weighed on me.

Seven

After twenty years I still find it hard to sort out the amalgam of feelings that enveloped me after my father left. My immediate reaction was relief. Peace on Earth. The screaming had gone on for so long that the furniture seemed saturated with it; the glasses in the cupboard had absorbed the vibrations, and tinkled. I knew that the peace was temporary, the appearance deceptive: echoes of screams were hiding in the corners and soon would be back in force. Hate was still in the air; my mother's bitterness and frustration would soon be seeking an outlet, and I would be the target. But I savored the respite.

I had reasons to feel relieved. The stay at the officers' dorm, my premature initiation at the flyboys' club, had made me realize how much I valued *privacy*. (There is no Russian word for this concept; it came to me from English, with a flash of recognition: *Aha, that's what I've always liked . . .*)

Between me and my mother, we now had two rooms—a luxury by Soviet standards. I was free from my father's fitness mania: no more morning exercises, no more skiing, no more gym. I was free, period. I was confident that my mother would have no control over my comings and goings. I tried to look mournful—divorce was considered a terrible, terrible thing— and at the same time was forcing myself to bow to convention. Yet in retrospect I realize that I am a lousy actor; I could exaggerate misery but could not create it out of thin air.

At the bottom of it was my pride. I liked to think I was

putting on the act that convention prescribed: I could not admit to myself that, with my father gone, I was in for a rough ride. I welcomed freedom, but I worried about its downside. Like a newly freed prisoner who may now and then long for the security of a hot meal back at the mess hall, I was seized with the fear of having no one to talk to whenever I had a problem, with math or anything else; no one to appreciate a clever solution of my own devising. While I had rarely sought advice and appreciation, now I had the gnawing suspicion that they formed the safety net that had made it possible for me to crack problems, cosines or otherwise. Now he was gone, and I had to fend for myself. I would be finding myself in this situation over and over again.

In a sense, I fended for myself well in the year and a half between my father's departure and my graduation from high school. I hung out till late, drinking—it may not sound outrageous, but it was a lot more than what my classmates could do. My mother tried to impose discipline, but her heart was not in it. What did she have to worry about?, I reasoned—I still had my A's, I did not start my day with a shot of vodka, and the cops did not call her to come pick me up at the precinct. Her hysterics were aimed at having me write my father a strident letter, an ultimatum demanding his return in categorical terms. "He'll see the light, he'll leave that whore—or else you tell him he's no longer your father!"

An old hand at dealing with hysterics, I ignored the outbursts. But if sometimes I showed up after midnight, reeking of booze and/or perfume, it never occurred to me that a forty-year-old woman left by her husband might have reasons beyond my disobedience to get unhinged.

Freedom is like wealth: if there is nothing to spend it on,

nobody to share it with, it loses meaning. I was free to hang out with Lyokha and his hoodlum friends, but I seldom did, because, as I noted earlier, we had no common interests. And my "nice" friends lived under much stricter rules than I did. Besides, Syzran had no nightlife; as far as I was concerned, it did not even have a *day*life.

We hung out at the dances and on park benches (hoodlums rarely attack groups), smoking and drinking and talking about girls. Morals were rigid, there were no easy conquests, even if the desire was mutual—no backseats of cars, no drive-ins, no motels. All we had were bushes in summer and dark hallways in winter. I had the apartment to myself in the afternoon; but afternoon sex does not become attractive to women before a certain age. The girls we pined after were aghast at such proposals; and, even if one agreed, we would not have known what to do. So we kept on drinking and smoking and talking and dreaming.

The dreams sprang from the movies—but in a town of 200,000 we had five movie theaters that played mostly Soviet movies, predictably patriotic. Imports were few and far between, mostly from Eastern Europe. In the US, only movie buffs know a Polish movie called *Ashes and Diamonds*; to us, it was *the* movie. The last American picture I saw in Syzran was *The Apartment*. In one scene Jack Lemmon's character sits down in front of the TV in his lonely bedroom, with a TV dinner, and, chicken leg in hand, starts playing with the remote control: thriller, Western, another thriller, another Western; bored, he turns it off. "Nooo!" roared the Syzran audience.

Movies were our only peek into the world outside. Not that we believed anything about them; any American movie was like science fiction. Although *The Apartment* was based on a problem we understood well—finding a place for a love tryst—to us, that was its only realistic element; everything else, including TV dinners and remote control, came straight from Mars.

America was another planet, but Moscow was closer than the moon. I had gone there for a few weeks two summers in a row. I strolled along the broad avenues and tree-lined boulevards, I gaped at the stately nineteenth-century mansions and Stalin-era high rises, and I was one with the endless stream of people on its streets, people of all colors and shades, dressed in styles most diverse . . .

(In Syzran, as soon as a shipment of Polish coats arrived in the stores, the whole town was parading their new coats, exchanging meaningful glances: *Nice coat isn't it and so warm— Yes very warm damn Polacks know how to make coats don't they.* And gloating at the poor shmo who had gotten to the store too late.)

. . . women sipping drinks in sidewalk cafés on Pushkin Square and Kalinin Avenue; very likely, making sophisticated conversation about abstract art, Bulgakov, de Sica, things I had only read about in magazines; and, without any doubt—look at their long hair, their expert makeup, their tight miniskirts and high heels—expert in other things as well . . .

(In Syzran women wore either tons of makeup or none at all; due to the ubiquitous mud, high heels were solely for the dance floor; a miniskirt, I could not imagine—its wearer would get raped or else arrested for solicitation.)

. . . there were theaters, and concerts, and movie houses— 120 of them. I managed to get tickets to the Moscow Film Festival. It was hog heaven: movies from all over the world, and I just had to see every single one of them. Clutching the crumpled schedules in my sweaty hand, I shuttled from the Rossiya Theater to the Palace of Sports to the Kosmos Theater, devising the quickest routes and catching up to six movies a day. I was starstruck: outside the Moskva Hotel I chatted with Bourvil, the famous French comedian, and got his autograph; and there were bevies of other actors and actresses whom I had only seen theretofore on the screen. It was pure magic. For me, Moscow was the festival, and the world.

When I came back to Syzran, my friends glanced at the movie magazines I had brought with me, but most of my stories fell on deaf ears. The Bourvil story required a lengthy preamble ("Remember him from . . . ? No? C'mon, the guy with the big nose—no?"); the names of John Wayne and Kirk Douglas (I had seen *The War Wagon*) drew a blank; eventually I just shut up. Syzran, I thought bitterly.

My two weeks at the dorm torpedoed my ambition to pilot MiGs. I had little desire to live in a place where you did not have enough room to put your books, and got smashed nightly, whether you were in the mood or not. I decided I wanted to be a journalist.

Two years earlier, in Artek the supercamp, our Troop Four had been in charge of putting out the camp newspaper. It soon turned out that no one was terribly interested in doing it. On the other hand, having to make a bed in a military manner, with every inch of sheet firmly tucked in place and not a ripple along the covers, has always been my nightmare. Soon I was writing the entire paper under a dozen different names; in exchange, these others made my bed and pulled KP for me. None of it made me love Artek, but I discovered that writing skills could bring rewards. I had never thought of it as a career. I was old-fashioned; a career meant hard work, and writing—it was so easy.

About that time a Soviet movie called *The Journalist* came out. Its hero travels from a small town not unlike Syzran to an assignment at the UN. I remember that his editor asked him to do an "essay," a word that impressed me deeply, but I can't for the life of me remember the point of his travels or what story he was supposed to cover. Yet the small-town boredom and crudeness rang true enough to render the UN segment believable, too: sitting in a bar and discussing the world's future with the glamorous Annie Girardot. From twenty years' distance, this seems utterly inane: maybe you had to live in Syzran to be impressed by it.

The movie's atmosphere was not unlike that of the countless trash thrillers I had always devoured. Now I was laying my hands on every reporter memoir available. Journalism was taking shape as a serious possibility. It seemed like a perfect occupation—like never having to decide what you really want to do.

I saw myself catching planes (I had never been in one) from space launch to film festival, from taiga to jungle, from war to Olympics. Armed with a press pass, I would be hanging out in modern bars (like the one in the movie, or the one roped off for reporters at the film festival). Sipping a multicolored *kokteil* through a straw, I'd interview Sophia Loren about her new movie, query a Nobel Prize winner on the meaning of life, ask an important public figure an irreverent question. I would be feverishly banging out stories on a typewriter, dropping cigarette ashes on the pages. A job at a newspaper would entitle me to an apartment with my own telephone (I knew only one person in Syzran who had one) and, if I got to be really good, a *car*. My experiences would make me glamorously burnt-out (perhaps a scar to go with it), a condition that would attract a caliber of women who had never heard of Syzran. The writing itself worried me not at all; the ease with which I banged out newspaper stories in Artek or at school led me to believe that this was something I would be able to do.

I am a little embarrassed to recall this fantasy. The notion of news media as a means of getting at the truth, and thus as an instrument of social justice, was alien to me; words like "cover-up" did not exist in our vocabulary. In the Soviet Union a reporter's material always toed the Party line.

To qualify for entrance exams at any school of journalism, I needed two years' experience. I went to seek free-lance employment with the local daily, *Red October*. The paper was not much. Its four pages were filled with Party directives (reproduced in their gospel entirety), reports on the output of pig iron and wheat, TASS-provided items on new plants in Romania and lynchings in the US; and frivolous items like pieces on the arts, tucked next to the movie schedule—all five theaters. The office was a hole-in-the-wall downtown. On my first visit, predictably, I got lost and strayed into the print shop in the basement. The labels on the equipment were dated 1903. They must have made sturdy machinery under the tsar.

The space allotted to the local news was such that one person could do it without help from ambitious ninth-graders like myself. The arts editor was an elderly lady, her hair in the standard, no-nonsense bun. As she listened to me blurt out my movie-reviewing plans, the horror on her face mounted.

"How old did you say you were?"

"Fifteen."

"Then you are not a Party member."

That was obvious. You can't join the Party till you're twenty-one.

"Then how do you know what to write?"

Finally, I was pitied by an editor in the industrial section, a middle-aged Jew. He agreed to give me an assignment or two so that I would have something to show on my university application. I was not euphoric: first, it felt like alms; second, I can't tell a rotor from a stator. He assigned me to interview a Heroic Worker who had fulfilled the quota by 110 percent or some such thing; and off I went.

On a freezing Monday morning I showed up at the railroad depot where the HW was employed as a mechanic. I was sent to one tool shack, then to another; no one seemed to be in charge. Nor did anyone seem to be working; I was the only one outside, shuffling through the snow from one freight car to another in search of my HW.

At last I found a foreman. He looked me over and shook his head. "You should be at school."

"I need it for the university," I whined. "They want experience."

"In this cold you don't get experience," he said. "You get your ass frozen off. Why don't you hop over to the liquor store and bring us something back. I'll tell you about that s.o.b.," he chuckled. "Who do you think fills out his worksheets?"

Two other workmen, who were warming their hands next to the stove, chuckled, too. I squeezed out an apologetic smile. I felt awful. I do not think of myself as a paragon of integrity, but it did feel like starting off on the wrong foot. And I did not even have the three rubles for the vodka.

"They won't sell me vodka," I lied. "The saleswoman knows my mom."

It worked, and after more chuckling and jokes they pointed at the shack at the very end of the tracks.

The HW was a large man in his forties. He was wearing a padded worker jacket that looked steeped in oil, which made me afraid to light a cigarette. (I had smoked only on occasion, but a cigarette seemed like the perfect prop to project the image of an experienced reporter.) The jacket was pushed up to cover his face. He was lying next to the stove, fast asleep.

I sniffed his breath; he had already had the hair of the dog. I cleared a space to sit amid the rusty, oil-covered parts (whose names I'll never know, I thought sadly) and reviewed my options. On the one hand, I could not sit there all day and wait for him to wake up. On the other hand, if I woke him up, he was not likely to cooperate. I counted my money. With two rubles I could buy a quarter-liter and go back to the foreman. But then I'd be so ashamed and even afraid of being found out that I'd never accept another assignment.

The shack was hot and smelly. In the dim light of a low-watt bulb, with junk strewn all over the place, this could not have been a worse start for my career. The glitter of film festivals' press centers seemed light-years away.

The HW woke up and eyed me warily. His face was grained with soot; it seemed as if no amount of soap could get it out. I explained that I was from the paper. He said I should really talk to the foreman, then turned back to the wall.

"I thought I would make you famous," I said sadly.

"Fuck your fame," he said, without turning. "I already got paid my bonus—what else is there? Everybody takes turns over-fulfilling the quota; it's my turn this month."

I was silent. This did not sound like an HW profile that *Red October* would be interested in. And the best-written, most revealing article would not be appreciated by Admissions unless it was in the form of a newspaper clipping.

"I just want to know what kind of work you do," I said.

"Cables," he said. "I go up there and fix the overhead rail for the electric locomotives."

"Maybe you could show me," I muttered, looking down.

"You think I'm stupid enough to go out in this cold?"

"Maybe I could get you some fuel." I rose. "To warm up."

"Maybe I'll wait." He winked.

Ten minutes later I was back with a quarter-liter. We drank it out of foul-smelling tin mugs; he made a show of rinsing them in a soot-covered sink and wiping them with an oily rag. After we finished the vodka, I no longer felt the need to go outside, after all; the HW played out the cable-fixing scene inside the shack as I meticulously wrote down the names of the ladders and tools he used. Remembering the editor's admonishment, I said, "You dedicated your heroic labor to the coming Party Congress, right?"

He shrugged. "You're the educated one. I dropped out of the fifth grade."

I wrote the piece. "The cables sang and moaned in the freezing January wind as Mechanic —————— climbed his cherry picker, in a stubborn triumph of Man over the Forces of Nature . . ." And so on. It was a perfect imitation of the Heroic Worker style common to Soviet papers.

The editor read it and nodded. "We'll use it." He regarded me skeptically, unsmilingly. "That's what you want, right?" He knows, I thought.

I wrote a few similar pieces, but I never bothered to go "into the field" again. HWs are created by Party Secretaries and are their responsibility. My job was to dress them up.

When I came to Moscow on my last summer before graduation, I stopped by the University's School of Journalism. But it was entrance exam time, and I could not even get to the door.

The driveway was filled with official black Volga sedans. Army generals and gray-haired men in three-piece suits paced the reception lobby, waiting to see the Dean. None of this boded well for a boy from Syzran.

Outside, I got talking to a few people, and the picture began taking shape. My timing was off; journalism was a "hot" career now, and I was not the only one who had seen *The Journalist*. Parents like an Air Force officer and a country doctor could not provide the pull needed to get in, and profiles of Heroic Workers had nothing to do with it whatsoever.

I asked one of the applicants to tell me more, and later that evening we met at the University dormitory on Lenin Hills. Unlike me, he had spent two years working for a paper *full-time*, hoping this would give him an edge against well-heeled high-school graduates. He was quite talkative and spun nonstop yarns of his reportorial exploits. As I listened, I felt worse and worse: all his stories were variations on my HW experience. The purpose of every assignment was to do as little and pad your expense account as much as possible. I left despondent, not knowing what to do.

A new draft law lowered the conscription age to eighteen. This meant that, since I would graduate at seventeen, I would have to get into college immediately—or be drafted. I had spent enough time around the military to see the soldier's life, which was only slightly better than that of an indentured servant. At best, I was doomed to follow my father into the Air Force. I panicked.

At school we had an English lit teacher named Vyacheslav Vladimirovich, nicknamed "Comma" for the way he enunciated this punctuation mark when dictating his notes to us (this was how we learned English lit). His favorite book was *Vanity Fair*; his choked description of Becky Sharp's infidelities made Thackeray sound so titillating as to send me instantly to the source, with ensuing disappointment. The apogee of Comma's life was a two-week tourist trip to France, which he had wangled heroically through many Party officials. The mementos of the trip, a dried-up marker pen and a packet of Air France mustard that he had saved intact, still brought tears to his eyes. After yet another lecture on French civilization and culture that left me with a Voltairean skepticism for all things Gallic, he suggested I try for the Translation Department of the Moscow Institute of Foreign Languages. There is another school that deals exclusively in foreign languages, in Gorky, he added—perhaps I'd like to be closer to home?

I thanked him politely. Gorky simply would not do, I said.

Later I met a number of working Soviet journalists, and nothing about them made me regret having gone into languages instead. In both fields you mouth someone else's words, but at least as an interpreter you do not have to pretend they are your own.

Part Two

One

There it was, in black-and-white: my name on the admissions list. The emotional roller coaster of the entrance exams was over: I was a student of the Maurice Thorez First Moscow Pedagogical Institute of Foreign Languages, Translation Department, English Division. But seeing it was not enough; I needed something tangible. I asked for an official *spravka* that I had indeed been admitted.

The English equivalents of "*spravka*" range from "certificate" to "reference," neither of which carries the import of the Russian word. As a symbol of a society dominated by bureaucracy, the *spravka* has no equal in America. The woman at the office asked me what I needed it for. I shrugged. "Just in case." She nodded; she seemed to know exactly what I meant, and wrote, "To Whom It May Concern: . . ." I folded it carefully, stuffed it in my pocket, and took a deep breath. She added that I was to report three days before school started, for "socially useful work." I didn't mind; nothing could rain on my parade that day.

Smarter—or more confident—students never asked for a *spravka*: they just showed up on the first day of classes. Thus, when I arrived at the construction site and was given a pair of rough mitts and a shovel to clear away debris, I had only my own insecurity to blame.

Ten years later I was flattered to see an item in *Newsweek* that referred to my alma mater as "Soviet Ivy League." I was making a minimum wage in LA then, and it felt good to know that I was an alumnus of the glorious *Institut Inostrannykh Yazykov* (Institute of Foreign Languages), or InYaz, as the school was known informally.

It was named after Maurice Thorez, whose relation to foreign languages, besides his most-preferred-foreigner status as the French Communist leader, is obscure. This is part of a Soviet tradition, whereby the construction of a car plant causes the sleepy Volga town of Stavropol to be renamed Togliatti, for an Italian Communist leader; another small town, Liski, was renamed Gheorghiu-Dezh, after a Romanian Communist leader; and so on. (It is unlikely, however, that Gus Hall, the leader of the American Communist Party, will get anything much named for him after his death: things have changed under glasnost.)

InYaz was exclusive: like the Institute of International Relations (the popular choice for Politburo scions) and the Military School of Foreign Languages (the future élite of the Army-KGB-GRU), it was not even listed in college handbooks. A recommendation from a local Komsomol Committee, which I had obtained with some difficulty ("You were not *active!*"), was required with the application.

If you entered InYaz with such namby-pamby motivations as a yen for learning, a curiosity about other cultures, or the notion that nations need to understand each other better if we are to share the same planet—you were in the wrong place. From day one we were taught that foreign languages are tools for dealing with the hostile capitalist camp, that they are powerful weapons on the ideological battlefield and can be handled only by a responsible individual—someone the Party can trust.

InYaz's handsomely classical, columned nineteenth-century

edifice had once housed the Commercial School, the pre-Revolutionary equivalent of a business school (sometimes I wondered whether the capitalist spirit had been completely exorcised from the building). In front was a small, well-trimmed park with Lenin's bust and a monument to the defenders of Moscow in the Great Patriotic War (World War II to the rest of the world). Inside, a staircase on the left led to a dark, somber hall with a large bust of Comrade Thorez. This route ended in the corner of the hall with the office of the head of the Institute—the *Rector*; it was for official visitors, and thus the only area of the interior that looked presentable. The rest of the inside looked drab and worn, with peeling paint, broken chairs, and knife-carved desks.

But the bleak hallways were dotted with glimmers of bright lights, fuzzy contours of curled neon signs from faraway places . . . students in button-down shirts and rolled-up Levi's and blazers with obscure coats of arms on the breast pocket, whose aura of success transcended the squalor. They had already been *there*, whether it was Senegal or Norway; or else their parents went there regularly, which guaranteed they would, too.

They crowded the hallways in their confident, imported splendor, with their slim attaché cases standing like watchdogs at their feet; they offered one another (never outsiders) Marlboros out of shiny packs, languidly they flicked their Ronson lighters, casually they dropped magical names like Dakar and Oslo in conversation. The heating was poor (in winter we often had to wear our overcoats), the air conditioning nonexistent; ubiquitous drafts failed to move the clouds of smoke that enveloped the smoking areas. But we were not health-conscious. The air reeked exotically of Virginia tobacco, expensive cured leather, and French cologne.

There I am, a seventeen-year-old Syzran hick, standing in line in the cafeteria, hearing someone behind me say, "It really sucks there are no nonstop flights to Kuala Lumpur." What a fantastic sound this is; how fortunate is he who is able not merely to say this without a trace of awe but even to *complain* about having to stop over (where might *that* be—Ankara? Bombay?); who is able to talk about going to Kuala Lumpur the way other people talk about going to Kiev. Is he the rule or an exception? In five years will I be where he is now, will I be on my way to Kuala Lumpur? The line is long, and, as I sidle past the glass case with mayonnaise-covered, greenish hard-boiled eggs in it, I keep practicing, mouthing silently, "It really sucks there are no nonstop flights to Kuala Lumpur," twisting my face into a sneer as I talk to a freshman five years from now . . . "Next!" hollers Aunt Valya the counterwoman, and I humbly order a hot dog and a salad. Twenty years later I have not been to Kuala Lumpur, and the idea of going there is still tantalizing.

There are no electives in Russian schools; all courses are mandatory. Years later, as a student at Columbia, I panicked as I leafed through the slick volume with hundreds of available courses. Part of me felt nostalgic for the time when you showed up on September 1 and faced the schedule: "8:00—Grammar— Room 33." I had not been trained to choose.

In the beginning came phonetics. We were stripped of whatever bizarre accents we had acquired at our high schools and taught snooty Oxonian inflections instead. When I meet people who studied English in Russia, I can tell what kind of students they were. Ones with British accents, like my friend Irene, put in hours at the lab; others, like myself, picked up our accents from records and movies.

Most of our courses were standard for any language school:

grammar, linguistics, Latin. But at InYaz you soon learned that correct pronunciation counted for little; grammar, for even less. To say nothing of your ability to read Tacitus or your knowledge of the theories of Saussure. You could flunk those and take them again and again.

All courses were mandatory, but two were more mandatory than others: Marxism-Leninism and military training. Your knowledge of the intricacies of English could be on a par with Edwin Newman's, you could hold your own in a debate with Noam Chomsky, but if you neglected these two subjects, you did not have a prayer.

Grigoryan, the professor in history of the Communist Party, was the scourge of freshmen. He was an Armenian in his sixties, with a football-shaped bald head, and thin lips frozen in contempt; his piglet eyes scanned the room as he sneered at the motley assortment of sweaters and jeans—a stark contrast to his own crisp-white shirt and rigorously pressed suit. From the moment he walked in, fear ruled the classroom.

I don't know of an American equivalent to those seminars. They had nothing to do with learning or inquiry; there was but one truth, wrought in black-and-white, without shades of gray. It was to be found in Lenin's works and the Party Congresses' resolutions. "Study the sources, comrades," Grigoryan would say. And he wanted to see proof—our notes on Lenin's "What Is To Be Done" and "The April Theses." We were to absorb every word of the Founder's wisdom and arrive at the official dogma. Marxism is a fundamentalist faith: there are no two ways of interpreting Lenin's "One Step Forward, Two Steps Back."

It is hard work to be a Leninist in Russia: one must be blind to the gap between theory and practice. Now, as I read essays by critics who valiantly fought their way through the jungle of

Lenin's prose, I can see that the official reading of his work was superficial and his intentions were never that benevolent, even on paper. Had Lenin been a better writer, I might have realized it earlier, but his convoluted, dense prose bored rather than repelled me. The theoretical basis he concocted for his instructions was derivative and reactive, born of polemical arguments with people I had never heard of. His works were either tracts or extended memos to his underlings on how to combat his rivals, at whom he endlessly directed petty, sarcastic barbs. The Founder was not only a tyrant but also a rather unpleasant person.

In lieu of "sources," we took shortcuts to Truth; we boned up on various textbooks, Soviet versions of Cliffs Notes, whose authors endowed the Party's twisting policies with an appearance of logic. It was suicidal to come to a Grigoryan seminar unable to rattle off Bukharin's crimes or the resolutions adopted at the Third Party Congress. If you did not know the essence of the Party line and, by extension, admit its omniscience, what kind of a Socialist student were you? If you were not guided by Party principles, what kind of a language expert were you going to make? Capitalists, we were taught, would be constantly provoking us into arguments, trying to shatter our faith; and what kind of an ideological fighter would you be if you could not successfully repudiate your foe in an argument? Grigoryan would remind us that, since the Party was giving us a free education, it was our task to study hard. He would rage and sputter, his Armenian accent growing incomprehensible. We had a soft life, he went on; it was mere history to us; if only we had been there, in the heat of the battle, when Trotskyites had stormed the Party Committees, trying to bluff their way to power . . . His voice broke down, he reached for his dazzling-white handkerchief and patted his forehead.

The silence was absolute. Not a breath was heard, not a whimper; we were even afraid to glance at our watches. And that sour taste at the prospect of the oral exam . . .

He means every word, I thought; he's not a fake, he believes it. Like everyone I knew, I was used to politics as something confined to meetings, where the Party line was read from the podium in a monotonous, soporific voice. I was aghast: it was one thing to mouth the Party line—at InYaz it put you on a straight road to Kuala Lumpur or the UN. I already knew that; actual belief, I could not comprehend. One should reserve one's passion for women, wine, movies, rock & roll—but getting worked up on account of *politics*?

Prodded by fear, I did well in Marxism. As at grade school, I used my wits, rather than my brains. It was a tactical exercise that had nothing to do with knowledge or intellectual prowess. Grigoryan even seemed to like me, and once praised me in class, which made me uncomfortable: in order to be treated so well by this monster, I reasoned, I had to have some profound flaws.

If Grigoryan is still alive, it might be tempting to picture his misery as he endures the humiliation that the Soviet media pile daily on his idols. I do not gloat: I would not wish it upon anybody to be told, at the age of eighty, that everything he had fought for was in vain, that his foes had triumphed. His threats were more bark than bite: I never heard of him actually contributing to anyone's expulsion. In his mind he must have wished us well: like many teachers, all he wanted was to cast us in his own image—good Party men.

But I don't believe he is miserable. Fifty years of doublethink does not vanish overnight. In private, among his closest friends, he may grumble at heretical innovations, at the media's disrespect for authority, at the crowds standing around talking what in his time amounted to high treason. And he must cherish hopes that everything will go back to "normal." But I am also sure that he has found a new and wonderful way to accommodate the changes—because the Party is always right, and to speak otherwise would be bringing back the ghost of factionalism. A true Party man does not wash his dirty linen in public.

I'll always remember with rancor the time lost studying Leninism; but the true torment was military training, where I did not stand a chance. Years of living around Air Force bases were no help; I could tell a MiG from a B-52 in a photograph, but what good was that in basic training?

We could consider ourselves lucky: at least, we had *officer* training. If I had chosen to study English at the University, I would have had only two years of "special" training, but upon graduation I could be drafted as a private. After InYaz I was made a lieutenant in the Army Reserve—a military interpreter, to be precise. We were on the Russian equivalent of an ROTC scholarship.

My memories of first-year special training come back to me like snapshots: falling in before each class . . . roll call ("Present!" "Can't hear you." "PRESent!" "Can't hear you." "PRESENT!" "That's better.") . . . marching in the courtyard behind the building . . . shooting a machine gun at the firing range, and its sudden, painful recoil . . . futilely trying to assemble the same machine gun in class. Those who went through boot camp can snicker all they want, but even these brushes with its spirit made me shudder. I can't laugh at Woody Allen fumbling with his bayonet in *Love and War*. I doubt he would still laugh had he gone through the actual humiliation: the sneer on the lieutenant's face, the chuckles among the class. For the vets among us, it was child's play—and a way to bolster their egos. Most of them had gotten into school on the strength of their Party membership and were lagging behind academically. This was their chance to get back. There was an easy camaraderie between them and the lieutenant; there were jokes and hints that only they could decipher and enjoy, and at which we, the seventeen-year-olds, could only idiotically grin.

As future military interpreters, we were expected to be part of Army Intelligence. In the second year of our cadetship we had to read military maps and know all there was to know about our opponents, from the number of Chaparral rocket launchers in a US infantry division to the combat load of an F-15 fighter plane. None of this knowledge, essential for preventing NATO tanks from rolling into Kiev, ever registered in my brain.

The CIA's constant spying was apparently a problem. How else could one account for secrecy? The course itself was euphemistically dubbed "special training" in the curriculum. There were no textbooks: we had to copy down every chart in special notebooks, individually assigned, with all the pages numbered. Each study group's notebooks were kept separately in a somber-colored cardboard suitcase, the kind that costs about twenty rubles in any luggage store. In order to prepare for class, you came to the office and the secretary hauled your group suitcase out of what resembled a train station luggage room. The metal tag on the suitcase indicated that the material was to be given top priority in case of evacuation. Under the secretary's watchful eye you signed for the suitcase and found the notebook with your name on it. Needless to say, at no time could the notebook leave the office. After you returned the suitcase, she checked the notebook to see if all the pages were intact. Then she counted the notebooks in the suitcase. Throughout the procedure she maintained the solemn air of a keeper of nuclear secrets. You didn't joke about special training at school any more than you joke about hijacking at an airport. It was hard to believe that the CIA was not maintaining round-the-clock surveillance.

The aura of secrecy was pervasive. I am sure that, had someone asked us outside school what exactly we studied in our military classes (no one ever did: nothing like virtue untested), we would have clammed up. At the same time, I found hard to believe the usefulness of the wisdom cached in our suitcases. Why would Americans attack? After Napoleon and Hitler, no one in his right mind would attack Russia. Judging by movies and magazines, they were already way ahead of us technologically and economically—what of ours could they possibly want? I was less sure of our own leaders' benevolence. After all, the maps we studied were of West Germany, not of the Ukraine. It made me queasy to think that I might have to accompany Soviet tank troups through Bavaria and, perhaps, all the way to the Atlantic shore. What for? To turn Amsterdam into another Syzran? On the other hand, we would have to be foolish, too, to attack such superior military might—just look at the pictures of these tanks! (We had no inkling of the Soviet Army's strength—now, *that* was the real inside dope that you could not find in a suitcase. Everything about the Army, even its numerical size, was a State secret. My father, too, when I asked him about the size of the military, just grinned: "That's classified." In retrospect, is it possible that he didn't know it himself?)

Even more important than this reasoning—I suspected it had flaws—I felt instinctively there was something inane about the suitcase procedure and, by extension, the course. I wanted to scream as I stared at my fellow students poring over their notebooks. From time to time one would look up with a yearning expression, seeking empathy, proof that he was not going through the torment alone. More often than not, the sufferers' looks would cross, they would shake their heads in despair, and one would say, "Let's go outside for a smoke."

Ours was not to wonder why, naturally; the course was just something else to be endured. With a worthy goal in mind: the Ministry of Defense looked like an appealing employer. After graduation a two-year stint in Somalia, for example, could yield enough money for a car. Few would question the proclaimed purpose of the course, Defending the Motherland: the Soviet masses never felt shy about their superpower military muscle. The Afghanistan adventure changed the national mood, but the group of people who showed up on Red Square to protest the invasion of Czechoslovakia was tiny; the shame that now everyone is so eager to confess hardly spread beyond the intelligentsia. Plain folks—well, they just rooted for our glorious tank forces the same way they rooted for our ice hockey team. I remember Yura Mironov, my ninth-grade classmate, staring at the map of Europe and wondering why we could not annex Czechoslovakia: "We could put Czechoslovak players on our national ice hockey team! No one could beat us then!"

I tried hard not to follow my classmates out for a smoke: after taking a break, I knew I would not be able to go back to work. Mutely I stared at the long, unpronounceable names of German towns, wondering about my imaginary American counterpart, a Joe Smith. What kind of suitcase do they use in military courses in American schools? Is he staring at a map of Poland at this very moment? Is he as bored as I am? More important, is he as convinced of the futility of this exercise as I am? What if he isn't? What if all my logical constructs have just *one* tragic flaw to them—what if the vaunted American technological superiority rests on just one tiny thing? A mineral, for example, that they use in their bullets and that is so secret that our authorities could not even include it in the periodic table. The US just might want to go to war over this mineral—and Joe knows it . . . The thought did not cross my mind often, but when it did, it made me nervous. Not that it evoked images of nuclear mushrooms; rather, it validated the entire suitcase ritual—and *that* was hard for me to accept.

I gave up. I did not want to know how many rifle platoons were in a motorized division. On the maps I confused artillery batteries with tank brigades, infantry platoons with field hospitals. At the orals I stared at the map for an eternity or two and then, emboldened by despair, confessed that my image of the battlefield was purely audiovisual—explosions whistles flashes bursts screams booms burning tanks acrobatically flying bodies charred flesh. No threat of court-martial could make me reduce it to multicolored squares and triangles. It was a calculated confession: the colonel, a quiet, gray-haired man of infinite patience, was rumored never to flunk anybody and could not possibly be looking forward to seeing me again. I knew I was facing the first C of my life, but I was past caring; I wanted to be out of the room, away from the posters like the one that showed maniacally screaming US Marines storming a beachhead for their imperialist masters. The colonel signed and sent me away. In case of war, my poor map-reading skills and my inability to tell an Honest John missile from a Minuteman would make me the Achilles heel of the Soviet Army.

Two

It did not take me long to realize that my classmates' motivations had little to do with either idealism (language as a means of communication) or the Party line (language as a means of class struggle). Just like our better-heeled competitors from the Institute of International Relations across the street, InYaz students had a certain image in Moscow. I could read it in the eyes of the girls I met: *You're from InYaz? Uh-oh*. To some, it was a sign of distinction: you were going places. To others, you were a ruthless go-getter who would sell his mother for a job at the UN. To a large degree, our reputation was well deserved.

One of our most intimidating professors was a woman who taught the history of English. How *"brod"* turned into "bread"—that sort of thing. In academic terms, her course was probably the toughest in our entire five-year curriculum. Her face, framed in dyed red hair, was thin and unsmiling, and she was legendary for the grilling she gave at orals. "What do you care about the Great Vowel Shift?" she said at a lecture once. "You just want to pass—so you can run me over with the brand-new car you'll bring from Egypt." The quip sent shivers down many students' spines: they sensed that with her attitude the exam in the history of English might become a stumbling block to their careers.

At InYaz the goal was to get into the Komsomol Bureau: to rub shoulders with the Party bosses and be noticed as someone who gets things done. Then a future UN bureaucrat could approach the professor: "Uh, I'm late with my paper, I was busy with Bureau affairs, you know what I mean?" Most professors understood; those who did not would get a call from the Party Committee: "Comrade X has been assigned to go abroad—do you want to delay him with a flunking grade in, uh, Latin?"

In the hallway we freshmen would mob a "traveler"—one back from a tour of duty—in a blazer and Levi's. Flattered that he would deign to talk to us, we hung on his every word: What is the screening procedure to go abroad for the Army? for the Red Cross Committee? for the Agriculture Ministry? What country can the Agriculture Ministry send you to? How does one get to Kuala Lumpur? Or the UN, that shining castle on the East River?

No one queried the seniors as avidly as Kafirov. The sight of him made me uneasy: with a ravenous look on his hamster-like face, he seemed the hungriest of us all. He lived with his old, sick mother, and his pants were shiny from wear. But he always wore a suit and a tie, and the yellowing collar of his starched shirt looked harder than steel. Other "hallway analysts" mocked him behind his back, especially when he took to smoking a pipe to emulate his idol Chernov, the Department Party Chief. He leaped at a chance to carry Chernov's papers and was even rumored to have sold Chernov his stamp collection at a bargain price.

I stood around, too, gripped by uncertainty. I was absorbing the information, ticking off the options—Exportthis Importthat Berlin Geneva Komsomol references slot on the Department Bureau . . . Hey, these were important, *adult* things they were talking about—you needed to know this stuff. But an invisible dike rose in my ears, resisting the flood. At seventeen it was hard to fake interest in the Agriculture Ministry's procedure for screening candidates for a job in Mali. I understood my classmates lapping it up, but my heart was not in it—perhaps because I read so much yearning in their expressions, such frenzied readiness to sacrifice anything for a slot on the Komsomol Committee or for a recommendation to the UN.

My mind was somewhere else altogether. I did not utter a word, I nodded along gravely; but once, as the group was dispersing, I could not hold back; I asked a "traveler" who, after a year in Africa, had had a one-day stopover in Paris, "Did you—did you get a chance to go to Jeu de Paume?" Under the others' incredulous looks, I was disintegrating quickly and could only mutter, "It's like a museum, you know . . ."

"Man," he chuckled, "you've got one day, you hit the stores. See this?" He flashed his watch. "Swiss. Sixteen jewels. *One hundred fifty* francs." A chorus of polite "wow"s. "You've got to know the right place," he said importantly.

"You're right, you're absolutely right," I murmured.

Red-faced, I edged toward the exit. I felt destroyed. I was a frivolous type, and now everybody knew it. In one moment the distance between me and Kuala Lumpur had doubled. I needed to remake myself, to redraw my priorities; I needed to grow up, damn it.

By graduation we were supposed to have fully mastered two foreign languages (something like major and minor in the US). The second language started in the middle of the sophomore year. Each group was assigned a different language, though in theory one could apply for a transfer (whether it would be approved was another matter). Nothing else was debated in the hallways.

Most agreed that English alone would not secure you a desk at the Foreign Ministry, or at the State Committee for This &

That with travel abroad. It was understood that jobs involving contacts with (and travel to) Britain and the US were reserved for the highborn, for the children of you-know-who. Command of English could get you a two-year assignment in India or Egypt—you'd save enough for a co-op and/or a car, but counting on that as a career? Don't sell yourself short, sneered the hallway Machiavellis. Of course, if this is what you want, take French or Spanish for your second language. There, you got the Third World in your hand, ha ha; might as well take the bull by the horns—take Arabic.

(The name of InYaz was somewhat misleading. With the odd exception of Arabic, only Western languages were taught there; Third World languages and Japanese were studied at the Oriental Languages Institute, a prestigious school in its own right; Polish or Czech, not even considered foreign, were taught at the University, and reference to them made our hallway tacticians smirk. Whoever picked Polish for a career, it was agreed, did not have "what it takes." Poles study Russian, not the other way around.)

Forget German, the hallway wisdom went: it's been taught for years, all the good jobs are taken. Italian? Not bad: the trade is expanding. But nothing, repeat nothing, beats a Scandinavian language. A long, ponderous pause. Swedish—that's good. How many Swedish translators are there around? I know this guy, someone would always say; he started out at Intourist (the State tourist agency), now works for Filmexport, travels to Stockholm every year; he's got it made.

Sweden might be a swell country, I reasoned; Bergman's *Wild Strawberries* (the only film of his that played in Russia) left me cold, but I had read enough critical essays to know that he was a Grand Master; and the "experts" could not be wrong about the jobs—but I doubted that I would ever bring myself to like the sound of Swedish. My group was assigned Italian, and I saw no reason to rock the boat. When it came to image, Italy had no peer. *Dolce far niente*, "sweet doing-nothing": what a perfect combination of sound and content. Should I beg for a transfer to the Swedish group for the sole reason that everyone said it was *the* thing to do? just to fit in with convention, in order to earn back the respect I had lost after my Jeu de Paume and other frivolous remarks? Fuck 'em.

And then a bomb went off. It was announced that, for the first time in the history of InYaz, Dutch would be taught. The "experts" were in turmoil. What was that? Wasn't it like German? Within twenty-four hours they reached consensus: Dutch is the one to shoot for.

I was restless that night. The lure of Swedish had been easy to resist. But Dutch—that sounded intriguing. I was sure that later I'd learn other languages, too; but Dutch was like a rare book to a collector; how many people speak it? Holland; a tiny South American country called Suriname . . . Afrikaans was pretty close to Dutch, but, in the light of Soviet foreign policy, this was a most unserious consideration.

I got up and trekked down to the dorm kitchen for a glass of water. The idea grew weirdly appealing to me. "What do you study at your school?" "Dutch." "Huh? Whassat?" "Dutch, you moron."

In an odd twist, the second-language transfer approval rested with the English Department. The next day I went to see Comrade Shchekina, the English instructor for the group assigned Dutch, to tell her I wanted to be in her group. I had no intention of begging—with Shchekina, it got you nowhere. And Italian was a fine fallback position.

Shchekina, who was also the Party Secretary of the English Division, was no more than five feet tall, slightly built, and wore her gray hair in a bun. At InYaz you were defined by your attire the way Southern Californians are defined by their cars: if you did not wear imported, you were a stick-in-the-mud. Shchekina wore the simplest, cheapest clothes imaginable: a studio executive in a Chevy. She was a chain-smoker, but where other teachers, stylish young women in leather skirts and high heels, puffed Kents, Shchekina smoked *papirosy*—strong Russian cigarettes with long, hollow filters. Socially, this placed her one cut above a truck driver.

Now she glanced at my application. "I remember you from the first-year's English orals last June."

I remembered it well, too. Her reputation as an examiner was as intimidating as Grigoryan's. There was no getting around her, it was agreed, and there was no bluffing. She saw right through you. But the subject was not military training or Party history—it was English.

At the exam I had not been scared one bit. I stretched in the chair, crossed my legs, and grinned. "Hi."

She shook her head but could not help smiling back. Perhaps my chutzpa was refreshing after the agony of fear from other students. We went through the translation part, the grammar exercises; I was not to be trapped on sequence of tenses or the subjunctive mood. We moved into the conversation part; she asked me what was the last movie I had seen. The rest of the group had claimed to adore this or that patriotic movie. I said, "*The Maltese Falcon.*"

(They showed the thirties oldies at the Illusion, a revival theater. Each movie played one day only. For me, it was a constant conflict: should I go to class or try to catch a Humphrey Bogart or a James Cagney?)

She nodded, ever so slightly. "Humphrey Bogart. A great, great actor." She took a drag on her *papirosa*—highly irregular at an exam, but Comrade Shchekina made her own rules. I noticed that she was holding her *papirosa* between thumb and forefinger: just like you-know-who.

Now, six months later, she said, "I should not have given you an A at the oral. Not that you did not deserve it—but it was a wrong pedagogical decision. You walked into that room with some chip on your shoulder. How could you sit like that in front of a woman old enough to be your mother? And say 'Hi' to a person you'd never met before?"

I was taken aback. In American movies the characters crossed their legs and said "Hi" all the time at introductions. Unwittingly I must have picked up the characters' body language along with the idiom. "Sorry," I said. "I guess language is not all there is to it, Valentina Ivanovna."

"Exactly. You must do something about that attitude of yours." She okayed my application with a big, ugly-looking fountain pen.

When I watched *Casablanca* in Moscow, the knowledge of lines like "Round up the usual suspects" became part of an arcane code that I used like a secret handshake with a few friends. Coming to America, I learned it was a part of standard movie lore—moreover, a cliché, and I felt robbed: the code had been taken away from me.

A friend of mine recently visited from Moscow. Eyeing me expectantly, he said, "Looking good, Lewis! Feeling good, Billy Ray!" I was at a loss. "But this is from *Trading Places*!" he exploded. "Didn't you see it?" I did, I said; I just—well, this stuff no longer registers with me.

As I cut classes (mostly English: for me, they were the easiest to catch up on later) to see James Cagney or Humphrey Bogart,

I was, in fact, creating my own curriculum; I learned more English from *Casablanca* than from Galsworthy. Ultimately, I might have been better off if I had acquired the Forsyte mannerisms from the book.

I don't know whether the movies created my "attitude" or only contributed to it; my friend Irene maintains I had it as early as Syzran. Surely, one could enjoy *The Roaring Twenties* (it played in Russia under the socially ponderous title *The Fate of a Soldier in America*), then walk out of the theater and slip back into the straitjacket of a model Soviet citizen. It was a dream, after all—a powerful dream not meant to be acted out except on the screen. Mine could be a simple case of unwillingness to separate dream from reality. But it also seems that, for me, the movies (and my having to play hooky to see them) contained seeds that fell on fertile soil—whether I got the attitude before or after seeing them.

In any event, Comrade Shchekina had a point. After twenty years her observation still holds. My "attitude" has caused me problems time and again, both in Russia and in the US.

Shchekina had visited England once but did not go on much about it. Only once did she blow up on the subject: "Oh, sure! You go to one of their stores, you see all this junk from here—" she indicated the entire room "—to here! All that pantyhose, underwear, and what-have-you! But what's the point, I ask you? I look at it, and I say to myself, Is this the only thing they are interested in, producing more and more junk?"

"Can you imagine Shchekina's underwear?" someone asked between classes.

I felt that Shchekina was as sincere as Grigoryan in her ascetic Communist idealism. I wonder if she had to exercise self-control when she was in England. In the West, Soviet exchange groups are received in the atmosphere of a lovefest, and hers was invited by a red-brick university, to boot. As the epitome of a Party intellectual, she must have been a heroine to British Marxists; as a woman in a position of power, she was a boon to their feminists. Yet she must have been introduced to a lord or two, or some other class enemy; I am sure she conducted herself with perfect poise, but I would give a lot to know what went through her mind then. Wasn't there one split second when she saw herself for what she was: a relic of another epoch, one that demanded an iron will and strict orthodoxy from *every-one*—not just from a bunch of overambitious, career-obsessed language students?

I would see her march down the hall, puffing like a steamboat on her *papirosa*, and suddenly explode at some nincompoop begging her for a chance to take the test again; I could swear that her hand mechanically reached for her hip—where a gun would be. She was a born Red Cavalrywoman. Why did she have to teach English, of all things? Why not Party history, or algebra, with its immutable truths? She loved John Galsworthy, she told us once; he depicted the disintegration of capitalism better than any other writer.

Along with A. J. Cronin's *The Citadel* and Mitchell Wilson's *Live with Lightning*, John Galsworthy's *The Forsyte Saga* (the first volume, *A Man of Property*) was the staple of our English course. Why these titles, so out of fashion? Why not Hemingway or Fitzgerald? Not only did they have a thing or two to say about capitalism, none of it nice, but they did so in thoroughly modern language. My guess is that our English syllabus, like that in other subjects, had been compiled decades ago, before Hemingway was officially recognized by the Soviets, and never reviewed since.

We struggled through the turn-of-the-century soap opera on a weekly basis, following Soames and Irene Forsyte from dinner party to reception to country house, memorizing the assigned vocabulary and doing exercises based on the novel's situations. In class I could barely keep my eyes open—especially after I had spent the night devouring a loaned-for-a-day copy of *The Godfather*. Now, as I play with the TV remote control, I often find the BBC-made *Forsyte Saga* miniseries: one or another public-TV station always seems to be rerunning it (recently the Soviets showed it, too, to much public delight). When I see a leg-o'-mutton dress sleeve, I remember the time in class when we tried to figure out what the *hell* that was: not only had we never seen this type of dress, we had no idea what a mutton leg looked like.

I don't think Shchekina herself knew much about leg-o'-mutton sleeves. And, although Soames is a convenient peg for exposing bourgeois mores, I find it hard to swallow that Shchekina's love of Galsworthy was based on his depiction of "the disintegration of capitalism." I think she rather liked Galsworthy's world, where money and class knew their place. (Love interfered, to give the author his due, but in a manner so proper.) She liked a good story told in a leisurely, old-fashioned way, with a clear-cut, discernible moral. Aesthetically, she was rather bourgeois—or, perhaps, just black-and-white simple-minded; ideologically, she must have still seen capitalism through Galsworthy's eyes. I would not be surprised if, like many Soviet officials, she actually enjoyed meeting British gentry more than she did her left-wing hosts.

Shchekina may have splurged on a VCR by now (though they still cost a pretty penny in Russia, and her pension cannot be that much). But openly obtaining a tape of the miniseries may still be a problem there, and I'd love to buy one in a legal capitalist store and send it to her. That way she would not have to resort to the black market and compromise her Communist morality. Perhaps then she could retire into Galsworthy's world from the reality of glasnost, which must be bruising to her not only politically but aesthetically as well. (What did she make of *Intergirl*, the saga of a Moscow hooker, the Soviet movie hit of 1989?)

Perhaps age has mellowed Shchekina enough to accept my tape graciously and not to spit in my traitor-émigré face. With her legendary X-ray vision, how much did she see through me then? Quite a bit, possibly concluding that on top of my "attitude" I was as phony as the rest, giving her ideals no more than lip service—just in better English. I doubt that she would have approved my application had she known I would eventually leave for America. (Then again, I did not know it at the time, either.)

My transfer to the Dutch group caused a minor stir among the hallway tacticians. "A quiet one—well, well . . . Shchekina must really love you."

"That's what she said." I beamed at Kafirov. I gloated a little, but I felt sorry for him, so painful was his expression on that day. He took it as a personal affront. But he tried harder, and in the end, five years of brown-nosing paid off: he was the only member of the Komsomol Bureau to be recommended for Party membership. And then for the UN.

I ceased to feel sorry for him, yet, unlike others, I could not bring myself to envy his coup. I lay on my cot at night, worrying: how does one cultivate envy? Somehow I sensed that this was the root of my problem. At InYaz the pressure was to succeed, which requires ambition; and if your ambition flags, you must have envy to prop it up. In learning envy, I mused, it would be helpful to have someone envy *me*, but no one ever did—except for one brief moment when I got into the Dutch group.

Three

Like most out-of-town students, I lived at the dormitory. To this day its hallways haunt me—long and gloomy, lit day and night by ten-watt bulbs, half of which were missing at any given time. Its walls featured the standard visual misery of patriotic posters, which served both to provide the required ideologically sound look and to camouflage the cracks in the wall. Each wing held a kitchenette and a bathroom—one for approximately sixty students. The showers, used by men and women on alternate days, were in the basement, reached—from our seventh floor—through a long series of flights in the back. Many stairwell windows were broken, and in winter you had to bundle up for the trip back to your room and race like hell before a film of ice formed on your hair (hair dryers were not common in that day).

It was a dreary place, but I was not used to luxury: I dumped my cardboard suitcase (the kind we used for storing our top-secret notebooks) under the bunk and happily stretched out on a thin mattress atop screeching metal springs. A corner of my own, with a tiny locker next to the bed, a rusty table lamp on top of it, and some space in the armoire, whose creaky door never shut tight.

My first roommate's name was Hao. In the beginning it felt quite exotic. If they—in Syzran—could see me now! I have a roommate who comes from *Hai*-fuckin'-*phong*! How about that?

(My LA friend Irene works full-time and has a Guatemalan woman to babysit her daughter. When she wrote her mother in Syzran about it, Irene became the talk of the town. "A nanny from Guatemala! Your daughter has really made it!")

We had a third roommate, but he did not stay long. On his second day he made me an offer. "You go to this warehouse, tell them I sent you, give 'em a hundred, bring me the stuff, in twenty-four hours I'll get you five hundred."

"What stuff?"

"French turtlenecks, twenty rubles apiece."

"Why so cheap?"

"Because they're made in Georgia. All French stuff is made in Georgia."

"Where does the hundred come from?"

"Your investment, dummy. You want something for nothing?"

A hundred, I thought; that's more than my entire monthly budget. "Thanks but no thanks." He looked at me and shrugged but did not persist.

He slept late and talked for hours on the hallway phone about shipments and deliveries. I suspect his main reason for being at InYaz—he must have paid straight cash—was to obtain the temporary Moscow residence permit provided by the school. He seemed shocked that some appearances had to be maintained—attendance, for example (he should have been more patient: later, requirements slackened). He must have tried to bribe someone on the faculty to look the other way, but it didn't pan out: either it was not enough, or he picked the wrong person. Perhaps he found another school where those things could be done more cost-effectively.

About Hao, the trader said, "This slit-eye is pathetic, studying all the goddamn time. He thinks it will make him as good as *us*?" I did not inquire what "us" meant; I had no desire to be lectured on white supremacy.

After the trader vanished, Hao said, "He was not a good Socialist." I did not inquire what precisely that meant; I had no desire to be lectured on Socialist morality.

Hao did study day and night. His endurance was phenomenal. To relax, he scrubbed the floors and dusted the furniture. I did not shirk my duty, but the quality of my cleaning never met his standards. In that sense, he came to be a very desirable roommate.

At twenty-two he looked fifteen. When he asked me to look at the composition he had written for his Russian class, I thought that it could not have been written by anyone older than fifteen.

A typical story by Hao (I read more later) featured a heroic Vietnamese lad who left his family, his beloved, and his pet goat, and sneaked into the South to scout the enemy troop positions. He would get caught (Hao was aware of dramatic convention) and endure inhuman torture at the hands of a Yank named John Rockefeller and his South Vietnamese lackeys—without uttering a word. At the scene of execution he inflamed the crowd with patriotic speeches till they assaulted Rockefeller and his lackeys and started a full-scale uprising. In the course of a bloody battle the hero died, with the names of Lenin and Ho Chi Minh on his lips.

Hao's greatest fear was that his stories did not adequately reflect the heroism of the Vietnamese people and their loyalty to Marxism-Leninism, and each one had a standard ending: half a dozen repetitions of "Long Live Lenin [Ho, the Party, etc.]," each on a separate, carefully indented line.

When I finished reading, I did not know what to say. I had seen this kind of prose on posters but never handwritten in a notebook. I stared at Hao, searching for a clue, but all I saw was eager expectation. I looked past him. The wall space over his cot was taken up by pictures of Marx, Lenin, and Ho Chi Minh; in between were Vietnamese postcards with flowers. Suddenly Hao seemed more exotic than before.

Beaming, he asked me if I liked it.

"It's really vivid," I said.

Actually, the torture scenes were the best written. At first I thought that something had gotten twisted in Hao's transition to writing in Russian. Or perhaps it worked the other way: the foreign language gave him a freedom of graphic detail that he did not have in Vietnamese, where he had to face the double constraint of rigid morality and ideology. If, on an outside chance, Hao defected to the US, he might now be writing blood-and-guts scripts in LA. In any event, even his poster-like writing was superior to that of his idol Ho Chi Minh, whose book of poetry I came across in the dorm. It was rather whimsical but hopelessly bland—at least, in Russian translation.

"There are mistakes?" Hao asked, expecting the worst.

"Not many," I lied. On every line.

"I try very much," he said. "But Russian is difficult."

"Hey," I said, "check out my Vietnamese." Then, after a brief silence: "Hao, I don't mind going over this in detail, but, you know, I've got my own homework."

"Of course." He nodded solemnly.

"Also"—I coughed—"it's my turn to clean. Which—let's be honest, now—I am not very good at, right?"

For a moment he looked confused, but then he understood and nodded enthusiastically. I was moved: I have corrected many papers and edited many manuscripts since, for free and for meals and for cash; but never has the gratitude been so ardent, so effusive.

Eventually I moved out of Hao's peaceful enclave. I could not stay with a roommate to whom loud rock was anathema, booze was decadence, and cleanliness was next to Socialism.

Later we would run into each other in the hallway, smile, and assure each other that we were doing fine. But Hao stuck with his Vietnamese friends, and when I saw him on those rare occasions, he acted distant. I filed it away for future reference, and later on it came together.

The Vietnamese composed the largest Third World contingent in the dorm, but there were many others: Nigerians, Yemenites, Cubans, East Germans, and even an occasional graduate student from Vienna or Utrecht. Everybody got along, more or less; the Vietnamese were the only group resented throughout the dorm.

They were resented for their cooking. In the evening the odors of fried herring wafted through the halls, driving other students into their rooms. They were resented for their foreign-student scholarships. Africans were considered sons of tribal chiefs—some of them were—with money to burn. But the Vietnamese were supposed to be poor, and their scholarships irked the Russian students who had to take jobs to survive. Most of all, though, they were resented because they never had qualms about using their special status with the authorities. Rather than argue about Led Zeppelin, I changed rooms after the first year. I could tell, from other cases, that negotiating was hopeless.

My second-year roommate made me uneasy at first. He sat on his bed, back against the wall, an almost-empty half-litre of vodka at his side. In the first ten minutes that I spent in the room he did not move a muscle nor utter a word. Finally I gave up and stared at him openly. He kept ignoring me. I cleared my throat. "I'm Gunga," he said. "From Mongolia." He finished the vodka in one long gulp, picked up a guitar, and hit the chords. He sang—keened, rather—a few lines. "You know the song?"

The Mongolian national anthem? I wondered. "Sounds familiar," I said.

" 'As Tears Go By,' " he announced proudly. "The Rolling Stones."

I nodded. "Got it."

We came to regard Gunga as the epitome of hip. He had spent most of his eighteen years in Belgrade, where his father was a trade attaché. He walked straight as a ramrod, legs slightly apart, making Clint Eastwood look like a wimp. He unabashedly used his Oriental inscrutability in playing poker: nothing could tell us whether he was bluffing with two deuces or holding a full house. His ability to consume booze was legendary. After a liter he'd go out and play with his Mongolian band at the University. This was before David Lee Roth's stage antics; in the sixties it was perfectly all right to just *stand there*. That Gunga did, looking more impassive than Charlie Watts and more cool than James Dean, in his Levi's so torn that by merely holding together they defied the laws of physics.

Everything was fine so long as the band played at the University. But once they came to play at a dance in the dormitory. Gunga stood there, tougher than ever, while their 250-pound sumo wrestler of a lead singer cavorted across the stage à la Chuck Berry until he fell and twisted his ankle. Fun was had by all. The thunder struck in the morning.

The Vietnamese filed a complaint. Performing songs ("Satisfaction") in the language of the aggressor (English), it said, was an affront to the heroic Vietnamese people. But Gunga was not some easily browbeaten Mongolian shepherd. His father was a diplomat, and his grandfather had put away many a jug of fermented camel milk with various Comintern leaders. Therefore, Gunga was merely advised, in the gentlest of terms, not to perform any more songs in English. Perhaps the Dean thought there was enough Mongolian rock for him to pick a repertory from.

Gunga reacted in his usual manner: he got formidably drunk and traded words with the Vietnamese that same night. The next day they filed another complaint, accusing him of drunkenness, hooliganism, and behavior incompatible with the status of a Socialist citizen and an InYaz student.

When Gunga heard of the second complaint, he did not back off. Heated by a half-liter, he marched through the hallways. Russian dorm dwellers dared not cheer openly—*their* parents were not big shots to bail them out of trouble—but he certainly had their hearts and minds. There were smiles and quiet encouragement on the way: "*Pokazhi im*" ("Give 'em hell").

Gunga descended upon his foes with the same fury that his ancestors had unleashed upon the world seven centuries before. Those who had expected fancy kung-fu and taekwondo pirouettes were disappointed. The scene was straight Hollywood: Gunga punched out his first Vietnamese in the kitchen, bloodied another's nose in the hall—his fists were flying. A few students quietly left for their rooms to keep out of trouble, but others stayed to watch; not one would raise a finger in defense of our supposed comrades. Gunga's opponents did not fight back; they just fled as he chased them down the hall, punching and kicking, till they all crowded into one room and locked the door. He went down to the basement to get an ax but passed out on the way.

To be objective, Gunga's prospects at school were not that bright. He cut classes shamelessly, and the only things I ever saw him read were Simenon novels in Serbian. But the Great Asian War, as we called it, brought things to a head.

Two days later Gunga was expelled and, the day after that, put on a plane bound for Ulan Bator, Mongolia's capital and his hometown. At the gloomy sendoff, after a few glasses he started banging his fist on the table. It was all his fault, he yelled—he should've called the US embassy, they would've sent down a platoon of Marines, or at least one guy with a flame-thrower, that's all he needed, he would've shown those little fuckers how to rat on him!

We exchanged doubtful looks. Instinctively we knew that American foreign policy's devotion to high ideals was not without limits. I went outside, tore a poster off the wall, and handed it to Gunga. "Souvenir." On the poster a fearless-looking Vietnamese girl pointed a rocket launcher at an ant-sized GI. "You can use it for target practice. Your dad has a gun, right?" But Gunga was already snoring, dreaming sweet dreams of torching a roomful of Vietnamese.

The Vietnam War was a mystery to us. If Gunga had routed the entire Vietnamese community single-handed, why couldn't the most powerful armed force in the world obliterate all of North Vietnam in twenty-four hours? What were the marchers in the West protesting about? How could John Lennon and *Pravda* be on the same side? But our personal experience out-weighed any doubts: the Vietnamese, whoever they were fighting, could not have had a just cause.

Once in a while a man would come down from their embassy, and the Vietnamese vanished from their rooms for the meeting, held at the study room on the seventh floor. Their attitude toward attending meetings was markedly different from ours.

One day, walking by, I peeked inside. The students sat in rigid poses at the desks. No one in the back was reading a book, doing homework, or playing "naval battle." The official who faced them was intoning something out of the newspaper. Not one student stirred. Once in a while—perhaps at the end of a paragraph—the official paused, raised his hand, and repeated the last phrase. The students raised their hands in a single motion and chanted after him.

I felt uneasy. I had seen newsclips of Nazi Germany and Mao's China. But this was live, feet away from me. I caught sight of Hao in the middle aisle. The face that I had seen smiling, concerned, upset—now it contained nothing but blank obedience as he spewed out the chant. I wished I could understand Vietnamese. But it may have been that the words were a perfectly mundane Party resolution on the Yankee aggressors or on over-fulfilling the rice production quotas—that content was nothing, form was everything.

Much later, after I moved out of the dorm, I heard of a Vietnamese student who had jumped to his death from a sixth-floor window. He had flunked his end-of-the-year exams, I was told, and, as a punishment, was not allowed to go home on vacation—third summer in a row. Like many other stories, it was hard to confirm, but it jibed with what I had seen in the study room. The product of a similar system, I could imagine what they had told him: *You failed the trust of your Party, your people* . . . No wonder the poor saps studied so hard, I thought.

My study room spying had a bright side: things did not look so bad for a while afterward. Just as Irene keeps telling me that I could be in Syzran, I keep telling people that Russia is not too bad: just try Vietnam.

A few years later, in LA, I was looking in vain for New Year's Eve postcards in a Hallmark store. I was apprehensive about sending Christmas cards to Russia. The funny ones might not be understood, and the straight ones had angels and crosses on them—the KGB morons who open the mail might interpret it as religious propaganda. I shared my problem with the manager, a middle-aged Asian woman. "See, I'm sending them to Russia . . ."

"Oh, oh." She nodded eagerly. "Christmas religious holiday, yes? For Communists, no good?"

I nodded back and asked cautiously (by then I was sick and tired of people asking me this question), "Are you from . . . ?"

"I come from North Vietnam," she said. "Many years."

We chatted for an hour, trading stories about the problems in corresponding with relatives; about what goods are best for sending over—which were likely to pass through customs and which were sure to get stolen; and, most of all, how difficult it was to communicate our problems to Americans.

I did not mention the dormitory Vietnamese to her. I'm sure she would have understood and not taken umbrage. But by then I had already met Americans who did not hesitate to lump me together with Brezhnev, the KGB, and other Soviet aberrations. I was not about to say anything that might be construed as a hint that this charming, gentle lady had something in common with the long-suffering, obedient, sometimes vicious robots from the dormitory.

Most Christmas cards reached my relatives safely. The ones that got "lost" featured glossy color pictures of flowers and/or wintry landscapes. They must be popular with Soviet postal workers.

The malodorous memories of my Vietnamese comrades' cuisine have long since faded. In both the US and Paris I've eaten at many Vietnamese restaurants, and never left dissatisfied. Also, a lot of the time, Vietnamese food was the only kind I could afford.

Four

The Vietnamese students were poor indeed. They did not waste money on booze or cigarettes but saved it to buy the Soviet-made electronic gear that we scorned for its shoddy quality. They looked poor, too, in their identical, government-provided cheap suits that seemed to be made of cardboard and that few Russian students would wear. But other foreigners, Arabs and Africans, were warm in their sheepskin coats, they wore blazers and jeans, they drank Cutty Sark and smoked Winstons. Unlike the Vietnamese, they seemed to be loaded.

As a good Soviet citizen, I was resentful. Every day *Pravda* reported loans extended to Ghana and plants built in India— all out of fraternal duty. Why did this money go to Joe Blow from Accra—so he could spend it on Levi's and Winstons? And do you think Joe showed his gratitude? He strutted around the dorm, decked out in shmattes to die for. And you should have seen the long-legged blondes who came to Joe's parties—lured by the perfume and pantyhose, what else? The very sight of them was a daily blow to my white-male pride.

One night, as I was reading a book in my room, a knock came at the door. A black man stood outside. I knew he lived across the hall, but I didn't know his name. He asked, smiling— and what a smile it was, a hundred-watt bulb in my room's dark and gloom!—if he could borrow some glasses; he had company. It was a common request: the Party had not yet found time to invent Dixie cups. I muttered that, yes, sure, he was welcome to help himself—except for they, er, might not be clean, I added, embarrassed. No problem, he said; okay if he returned them tomorrow morning? Uh, fine, I said.

He came back minutes later; would I like to come by for a drink? I was mute for a moment, and then, indicating my track pants, asked, Just like that? I knew that the Africans always dressed up for parties, no matter how informal. He shrugged: *Sure*. Whenever you like, he added; when you're done with your homework. I thanked him; within seconds I was off the bed, changing my shirt. At the time, no book in the world could keep me away from a party.

The room was dark, save for a few candles; powerful speakers were blasting out Otis Redding's "Sittin' on the Dock of the Bay," and shadows of dancing couples were swaying on the wall. The air was smoke, perfume, sweat—all my favorites. Two Scotches went down smoothly—nothing like the throat-searing vodka I was used to. Sam, the host, slapped me on the back and asked if everything was all right. Wonderful, I nodded, dragging on a Winston.

"Should take water with your Scotch," another African said. "You Russians; we have to teach you everything." "Wait a minute," I said, but Sam interrupted: "C'mon, we're all friends here. William's girlfriend didn't show up." He winked. "Now the man's taking it out—"

"I-am-not-taking-it-out-on-anybody," William said firmly. "But everybody lies to you in this country, from day one. They promised to send me to Georgia or Armenia, with a nice climate. How can you stand this goddamn weather? I should've never come here. My goddamn older brother's in London, and I'm here like a goddamn fool with you people."

"London's climate's supposed to be . . ." I started uncertainly.

"Ah, but London!" Sam laughed.

"What does he know?" William spat out. "He hasn't been to a nightclub in his life."

The Scotch stopped in my throat and went through my nose. *Nightclubs.* In Russia we had restaurants, where Russian-style jazz bands (never without an accordion) would play sugary Soviet pop; where by closing time—midnight—everyone was roaring drunk, falling on the dance floor or snoozing face-down in an ice cream bowl (and no one knows who ordered that ice cream). But *nightclubs*—in Soviet thrillers those were the places that CIA agents used for recruiting morally unstable characters . . .

I stopped abruptly. Were these guys agents, too, recruited in a London nightclub? Why not?—the cover was perfect. *So what?*, a small voice said. *What do you know about but those stupid maps in suitcases, anyway . . . ?*

"You guys don't seem to be doing too badly without night-clubs," I murmured, as I wiped—or, rather, smeared—Scotch on my face, which was on fire. "Look at yourselves . . . your clothes alone—"

They both howled. *Clothes—!*

My head was reeling—from Scotch, from smoke, from the nascent, gnawing sense of inferiority. Out of the corner of my eye I saw the dancing stop and the couples—two Africans, each with a Russian girl—sit down on beds and chairs around us.

"In London this stuff doesn't cost much," Sam said in a pitying voice. He priced his shirt, his pants, his tie—but pence and pounds meant nothing to me. All I knew was that I was being humiliated, and I didn't know whom to blame for it. Sam and William sounded convincing, I had to admit; but I hated to believe them completely. I wanted to get them off their high horse, but I didn't know how. I knew about the Magna Carta and John Osborne and the Profumo Affair, but I had no idea how many man-hours it takes to buy a pair of Levi's in London. Now, if they were spies, then, of course: surely, the KGB dresses our spies just as nattily. But how could I bring this up? Civilized people do not accuse each other of spying—and I wanted so badly to be civilized.

I swallowed hard at my impotence. "I understand," I said stubbornly. "I understand you're a bunch of show-offs. Especially in front of the girls."

William poured me another Scotch. "Cheers, my friend. May you find out one day how ignorant you are."

I realized that foreigners avoided taking shopping requests from the Soviets: that would have been like opening a floodgate. On the other hand, the *sub rosa* trade flourished, quietly: sweaters shirts watches briefcases—and jeans, of course. Sam and I grew friendly, yet I could not bring myself to ask him for anything. If it hadn't been for goddamn William, I thought. I was not merely afraid of rejection: I was afraid of rejection with *laughter*.

But one day, as Sam and I were standing next to each other washing our socks, I told him, without any provocation, that my girlfriend would not sleep with me because I did not have Levi's. I am not a compulsive liar, but I have my episodes. Sam took it very much to heart: perhaps, in a way, he could relate to the problem. I must have instinctively realized it; otherwise, I would have told him that I needed Levi's to bribe a teacher. He told me he would keep his eyes open.

Time went by. We ran into each other in the hall, and he never failed to mention that, yes, he was keeping his eyes open. "Thanks," I muttered; Christ, did he have to bring it up? Did I remind him? Either he was extra-considerate, or it was just a particularly complicated way of keeping me off his back. I started regretting I had ever asked.

Until one day he stopped me in the hall. "Do you remember William?" I reluctantly admitted that I did. "I think you're about the same size. He'll sell you a pair."

That night I could not go to sleep. For the first time in my life I was going to commit a crime graver than jaywalking (somehow, sharing hashish with my Syzran classmate Lyonka had never felt criminal). I was about to enter into a commercial transaction with a foreign national. Whether or not my suspicions of spying were true, it still felt like taking pictures of special-training maps and delivering them to the American embassy; it felt like treason.

I kept tossing and turning. The itch to own Levi's was slowly overcoming the fears. Another consideration was loss of face. I did not doubt that Sam would see through whatever feeble excuses I'd offer for not showing up; that he would know the real reason. And not only he—the hateful, arrogant William would know, too, and snicker contemptuously, "You Russians." By morning I managed to rationalize what had started as an act of treason into an expression of ethnic pride.

Strictly speaking, buying jeans from a foreigner was not a violation of the law unless I resold them at a profit. But an InYaz student had higher moral standards to uphold: I would be expelled summarily, with the subsequent "antisocial" reference. My fears may have been vastly exaggerated, but they were not entirely fantasy.

I arrived early at the subway station where we had agreed to meet. Playing back in my head every thriller I had ever seen, I strolled along the tracks, hopped another train, rode to the next station, then back. No one seemed to have followed me.

Sam arrived, grinning his customary grin, and I had no

choice but to return it, hoping he would not detect the tremor in my handshake. As we walked to William's apartment, Sam chatted about Armenia, which he had just visited; I was cursing his blackness. We were not washing socks or drinking Scotch in the cozy nest of the dorm—where both of us lived, after all. We were *outside*—and I was walking next to someone so obviously a foreigner! By now I was convinced that Sam was no agent; otherwise, surely, he would have realized that this made me a sitting, uh, walking duck for every KGB agent in town. Berating my paranoia, I forced myself to imagine that we were in South Africa and that Sam was risking his life walking next to me. The effort consumed me completely: by the time we arrived, I was falling apart.

As I had suspected, William lived in a foreigners' compound: several cars with diplomatic license plates were parked outside. The guard was not there, but invisible surveillance cameras were clicking right and left in my head: someone had to be watching! Yet there was no turning back—no alibi was any good now.

My knees grew weak as I climbed the stairs. Sam said something encouraging, but I could only moan; my mouth was too dry to talk. Sure enough, William was not alone—there was a young Russian girl in the room. Foreigners, including journalists, who have spent some time in Russia and socialized with natives understand that it is imprudent to introduce two Russians in the company of another foreigner. Even at Sam's party at the dorm, the girls and I made a point of not introducing ourselves. William, my verkokte benefactor, simply refused to care; might even find it another amusing peculiarity of our life— was that the meaning of the sparkle in his eye? What was the girl doing there? Was she just a party girl? A *Party* party girl? I had met a few of them. And she must have had the same fears about me.

Finally, armed with the jeans, I stepped inside the bathroom to try them on. Threw cold water on my face. Pulled off my shirt and dried myself with a towel. Despite my fears, I took notice of a multicolored array of toiletries, recognizing a tooth-paste tube and a bottle of cologne. The rest were a mystery: what was "deodorant"? "aftershave"? But I dared not linger. What would they think I was doing? And what about the KGB cameras, reputedly standard equipment at foreigners' com-pounds? Worse than the fears of expulsion for trading with foreigners, I imagined the smirks on the faces of KGB agents as they watched the film of me, a hayseed, agape at foreign puffery: where was my Soviet citizen's pride? (I felt no such shame about Levi's: they were a symbol, they were hip; deodorant was just petty.)

I took a closer look at the jeans, and I wanted to scream. The whole trip—changing trains, shedding the CIA paranoia, making up South Africa stories—it was all for nothing! These were nothing like the Levi's that we worshiped. These were soft, and wide at the bottom—what kind of bronco were you sup-posed to bust wearing them? And where was the leather patch with the horses on it? The tiny red tag on the pocket was not enough. I sat on the john and hid my face in my hands, des-perately wishing someone would tell me what to do. I came all the way for this?

I inserted my leg into the soft denim with all the euphoria of a death-sentenced convict putting his head in the guillotine. But the fit was perfect. And the price was right. It equaled my mother's weekly salary, it meant days of eating nothing but split-pea soup made from powdered concentrate; for this money you could buy dinner for two in Moscow's ritziest restaurant, but it was still below the black-market rate. Most of all, I could not believe for one minute that Levi Strauss & Co. would do a number on me. In Russia we knew what brand loyalty meant.

I came out, grinning weakly. Yes, a fine fit, thank you very much. For an extra five rubles William even threw in a belt. I hated his guts, anyway: partly because, even in the winter dusk of the room, behind the drawn curtains, I could see that the girl was so good-looking; partly because the smirk on his face was so obvious. I sipped the offered Martini Rosso. "This will take care of your girlfriend," Sam said, smiling widely—a smile that his chipped tooth rendered irresistible. "Huh?" I gasped, then remembered: Oh, yeah. The girlfriend. How could I admit my doubts? He was so happy he could fix my sex life for me.

For weeks I dared not wear the Levi's. I was only a sophomore, my parents lived in Syzran—where could my brand-new Levi's have come from? When I finally overcame my fears, the jeans were met with quizzical looks. Not until *Abbey Road* reached the dormitory (several months after it came out in the West in 1969), with its cover showing our idols in soft-looking bell-bottoms, did I realize how far ahead of fashion I had been. Too far: by then the jeans, worn daily, barely held together.

My arrival in the West coincided with the arrival of designer jeans on the scene. And, of course, people have always worn Lee and Wrangler, too. But somehow I stuck to Levi's. On my first visit to The Gap I spent an eternity shlepping pair after pair to the fitting room. But none felt right: if the waist fit, the length did not, and vice versa. Rather than look at other brands, I left empty-handed.

It is foolish, sentimental—other brands may be just as good, and designer jeans may fit better. But no ad slogan has managed to lure me away. It is practical, too: life in the West is already chock-full of decisions, without having to choose what brand of jeans to buy. Had I started trying on other brands, I might have spent a whole day at that store and still left empty-handed. Instead, I stopped by another store—and it had the right size.

Five

In 1986 I drove for two hours from Seattle to Tacoma, Washington, for a Bob Dylan concert. It was the first time that I saw the idol of my youth live, and I was torn by conflicting emotions. On the one hand, the sight of his black-leathered, bird-like figure on stage, playing and stubbornly refusing to surrender to the march of time, brought a lump to my throat; I clenched a fist, my arm shot up in the air. On the other hand, he insisted on singing every song in a different key, even a different tempo, from the classic album version; some of the songs I recognized only by the lyrics. He has a right to do with his songs as he pleases, but I felt disturbed and a little bitter, as if he were telling me to disregard my past and treat these songs as new. I told this to my friend Alison, who came with me to the concert.

Alison, ten years younger than I, was there more for Tom Petty (who was also playing) than for Dylan. She thought I was overreacting. "These are just songs, David."

"They are not just *songs*. He can't do this to me. After so many years they're mine as much as his."

Rock & roll is one thing that continually gets between me and my American friends. For example, if I wrote, "No other socio-cultural phenomenon defines my formative years more comprehensively than rock & roll," their mouths would fall open: *In Russia?* Call this attitude ethnocentric, possessive, even parochial. The truth is, when I hear an advertising jingle set to a Beatles tune in order to sell cars or tampons—yes, I feel a tug at my heart. And I still feel a little condescending toward people who don't remember Blind Faith. No matter what friend or episode I recall in this book, in one way or another it will have something to do with rock. Gunga and the Vietnamese clashed over the Stones. My first Levi's were not authenticated until *Abbey Road* came out. I met my friend Micky as we listened to . . . When I met my future wife, she gave me a record of . . . And so on. It is like a free-association test.

Rock & roll was the battering ram that the West drove into our collective psyche. Then everything else rushed in: art, fashion, books, and, sometimes, politics. The authorities automatically banned any Western music, from Canned Heat to James Brown. To Soviet ideological pundits, the Beatles were every bit as subversive as a miniskirt or Nabokov. You needed to be somewhat politically inclined (and nothing breeds political apathy the way Communism does), as well as have some command of English and the proper connections, to get hold of and read *1984*. You needed friends in high places to see *Midnight Cowboy*. But rock was readily available from the numerous radio stations like Radio Luxembourg or the BBC (the unjammed, English-language edition), and we lapped it up with a gusto unimaginable in the West. For Westerners, it was music to dance or drop acid to; for us, when you multiplied the Beatles' youthful vitality by the forbidden-fruit factor, it was more than a breath of fresh air—it was a hurricane, a release, the true voice of freedom. We paraphrased Mayakovsky's line "I'd learn Russian just because it was spoken by Lenin" to read: "I'd learn English just because it was spoken by Lennon."

I was hooked while still in Syzran, after one Beatles song— a bootleg recording of "Can't Buy Me Love" on an X-ray plate (the material was similar to vinyl). We even had our own rock star: Kostya (Konstantin) Velichko, who led his own band. In his bottle-green suit and preknotted tie, he looked more like a Third World businessman, and his gear was nowhere near a Stratocaster or a Gibson. But, as he strummed his crude guitar with John Lennon's picture Scotch-Taped to it, he had both playfulness and intensity, the same cool, amused expression, the same glint in his eye that I have seen since in the face of Eddie Van Halen and many other rock stars.

At first Kostya and his band wanted to call themselves The Rolling Stones. The name was all they'd heard. They'd never heard of Mick Jagger nor seen his pictures, they'd never heard "Satisfaction," they didn't even know exactly what the name meant—but, hey, did it sound good! It was bouncy, it was bold; it was *in English*. It had that rowdy, rolling *r* and the bang of a rock shattering a windowpane. It made you want to say it over and over again; it made you proud to be a Stone.

Our high-school principal, with all his open-mindedness, informed Kostya that, while they were certainly free to take any name they wanted, as The Rolling Stones they might as well forget about playing the high-school dances. Where else would they play? (I don't remember what name was eventually foisted on them; to me, they were always The Stones.) Kostya did his best to imitate the Liverpool sound in his rendition of "Can't Buy Me Love," but one night, as they were playing, the deputy principal leaned over and pulled the plug. Nobody took up arms: we were simply not like that in 1966. It was understood that the song, with its idealistic lyrics (successfully mangled by Kostya), was too fast, too racy, too free-sounding, too . . . rock & roll? Kostya, with the sour sarcasm typical of our generation, could only nod and go back to an officially approved pop tune about lovelorn geologists in the Siberian taiga (a favorite image in State-made romantic lore: love must spring from being useful to the State). Kostya's face, with his narrow Tatar eyes, was impassive, save for one wink: *Hey, we got halfway through tonight, didn't we—all the way to "Say you don't need a diamond ring."*

When I returned to Syzran on my first winter break, I brought with me a Hendrix tape. At the first chords of "Purple Haze" Kostya took off in search of a second tape recorder. He could not find the right kind of cable, and so the tape had to be copied via microphone. He shared a two-room apartment with his mother and sister, who had to be bribed, cajoled, and bullied into leaving so that the place could be turned into a recording studio. It was far from soundproof: the recording was enlivened by the noises of the garbage truck and the squabbling downstairs about a place in the line for milk. The tape recorder was an old, rattling job; the tape itself must have been used twenty times before, because it tore now and then and had to be spliced back together. But Kostya grinned blissfully and played it and rewound it and played it again.

When Americans hear East European or Third World sob stories of shortages, they are prone to remark of themselves, "We don't appreciate what we've got here." Conservatives refer to the good life—two-car garages; liberals, to the freedom to investigate anyone in government. Me, I see kids swaying to Walkmans or teenagers numbly staring at MTV in their rooms with sports pennants on the walls and Mickey Mouse phones, and I can't help thinking of Kostya splicing that tape (true, it was *Hendrix*, not Debbie Gibson), over and over again.

In college our obsession with rock reached heights that nowadays I find hard to imagine. At times my dormitory friend Vitaly and I communicated solely by whistling tunes—a regression of sorts to mankind's preverbal days. He greeted me with "Good Day Sunshine"; I responded with "I'm Only Sleeping." At a party he took one look and whistled, "You're Gonna Lose That Girl"; I responded with "Another Girl." We did not think much of diamond rings, and we needed no other words to express ourselves.

Without MTV or Woodstock, rock & roll was not an easy obsession to pursue. Albums arrived in the same way as other commodities did—via tourists, students, Soviets returning from abroad. Black-market prices were prohibitive: a sealed *Abbey Road* sold for 125 rubles, or what my mother made in a month.

In Kharkov my cousin Lyonya had a friend nicknamed Zhuk ("The Bug"), a black-market operator, who, Lyonya told me, could "move anything within hours." Zhuk's room was a shrine to Mick Jagger: a full-size, blown-up color picture occupied one wall; other walls were covered with assorted fanzine Stones clippings. Zhuk had his girlfriend bleach her hair and called her Marianne; he also looked seriously for ways to enlarge his lips with clothespins. Zhuk resold LPs he bought from foreign students to syndicates, whose members kicked in twenty-five or thirty rubles apiece for an LP, which then they rented out for taping at five rubles a pop, or fifty kopecks (half a ruble) a track. As Lyonya's cousin, I was allowed to tape for free; as a goodwill gesture, I translated for Zhuk the assorted clippings on Jagger from Western magazines. One of the articles was in Swedish. "I can't read that," I whispered to Lyonya. "Fake it," he said. "Zhuk is a nut, anyway. Don't you want to tape The Jefferson Airplane?"

At school many students had an LP or two, which they were constantly swapping—for one day only, just for personal taping. In my fourth year I acquired an LP of my own, Bob Dylan's

Bringing It All Back Home, a gift from my future wife, Natasha, and I was able to parlay it into a collection of more than fifty tapes. That was the entire reason for going to school in my last years—to swap paperbacks and records . . .

LPs were taped on huge, unwieldy reel-to-reel contraptions. Blank tape was hard to find, but the stores had plenty of tapes with old Revolutionary anthems in stock. I was considered a slob: I was too impatient to erase them first, as my purist friends did, and on my tapes you could hear bursts of the Red Army Choir between the sides of *Sticky Fingers*. Truly, the avant-garde, whether arrived at by design or through sloth, must be the antithesis of purity.

A friend named Sergei toted a thick ledger into which he studiously copied every "yeah, yeah, yeah" ever copyrighted by Lennon-McCartney. He claimed he had been born again—sort of—after hearing "She Loves You." He was a modest, unprepossessing guy: five-foot-two, balding at twenty, he seemed to have no life outside his legendary tape collection, which was meticulously arranged and catalogued. I am curious about it sometimes. How much of it was an obsession with music? with its message? Was the inaccessibility of records and other rockabilia related to, perhaps, some other emptiness in his life? If he came to America, would he persevere in his obsession, or, faced with the glut of music and accompanying trivia, would he cool off? At least, he wouldn't have to take black-and-white pictures of album covers and paste them on his tape boxes.

The questions will remain rhetorical: I lost track of Sergei, as I did of many others. But recently I met Vladimir, a fellow émigré of my age. Relatively speaking, he is an émigré success story—a computer engineer job with CBS, a small apartment building in Brooklyn, a co-op on West Fifty-seventh Street (now, with two kids, he is shopping for a house in Connecticut). On entering his place, I was assaulted by earsplitting rock (ironically, it was "Immigrant Song," *Led Zep III*) coming out of huge speakers. Wife and kids were out, he explained with a blissful expression. We settled in comfortably; it was just like 1971 all over again, and the business that I had come for could wait, at least till the album was over.

As for live music, government control took bizarre forms. In order to perform in public, my cousin Lyonya's band had to clear its repertory in advance with the local Komsomol Committee. Each song had to be presented in an ideologically acceptable manner. "Satisfaction" became an anthem to the British working class; "Paint It Black," an anti-racism protest song; "Stairway to Heaven," a folk song (in Marxist dogma, "folk" equals "masses," who can do no wrong).

Things seem to have improved under Gorbachev. I have seen Soviet-made LPs whose liner notes contain comparisons to heavy-metal groups I have never heard of, with the term "heavy metal" transliterated, which indicates a degree of official acceptance. Billy Joel has toured, and when the Scorpions and Metallica played Lenin Stadium, you could see that the leather-and-chained Moscow fans reacted no differently from those in Tokyo or LA. Yet the concert was a Live Aid–type anti-drug charity event; however laudable its agenda, this was not a regular tour. After all, Lenin Stadium is *the* stadium, with its 102,000-seat capacity, and the decision to hold the concert had to be approved at the highest level of government. To me, the TV broadcast smacked of a commercial for glasnost. This is not necessarily bad: if glasnost made it possible for 100,000 kids to get a jolt of rock & roll, it can't be all wrong. But, at the risk of sounding like an old fogie ("We didn't have Led Zep live in *our* time"), I am not amused by the idea that, after all the brouhaha, the Party is still exercising control, however benevolently. They are looser with the reins but far from surrendering them altogether.

I never went as far as Sergei, who even copied lyrics by The Monkees. But Simon and Garfunkel albums came with lyrics on the back cover, and I was fascinated. I never got to see the lyrics of *Bookends*, and I coerced Jenny, an exchange student from Birmingham, England, to help me. The texts generated more questions: Where's Saginaw? Who's Mrs. Wagner, and what was so special about her pies? What's a turnpike? She explained, but added, "It's only a song; aren't you taking this rather too far?" "No, no," I said; "I think I know exactly what they mean by 'counting the cars on the New Jersey turnpike.' " "*Really*," she said, in her very British way. "*Really*," I said. "Because 'I'm empty and aching and I don't know why.' " Simon and Garfunkel were my Toqueville to America.

With Dylan, Jenny had to confess, embarrassed, that she did not quite get it herself. I didn't mind: the failure to understand some parts formed an aura of mystery around the parts that we did understand.

> *Darkness at the break of noon*
> *Shadows even the silver spoon*
> *The handmade blade, the child's balloon*
> *Eclipses both the sun and moon*
> *To understand you know too soon*
> *There is no sense in trying.*

You may not know exactly what it all means, but so what? The words may lie; your instincts, never. The rude, violent clanging of the guitar string; the obsessive fuck-you nasality instead of saccharine sweetness and harmony; the sarcastic intonation, sounds of despair and longing . . . *How could this be phony?* At nineteen there are no other artistic criteria. Once I heard that, I did not want to hear much else.

Dylan's albums never gained the popularity of Hendrix's or Cream's in our crowd, which was fortunate: it translated into lower prices for me. I would tape Hendrix, but Dylan I had to *own*. The prices were still lethal, yet by the time I left Russia I owned five Dylan LPs (and still have them). Whether I understood individual words or not was less important than the obvious fact that the man had what I had always been upbraided for—*attitude*. I did not know the expression "role model," but if a Jewish kid from Hibbing, Minnesota, could wear his attitude on his sleeve like a badge of honor, why not a Jewish kid from Syzran, Russia? I would not accept for one moment that you needed to be a musical genius in order to stand up to the powers that be, to people who think that their money or nationality or breeding or just plain connections give them the right to look down on you.

After twenty years I have cooled off. I admire the camerawork and special effects on MTV, but the music is monotonous and repetitive, and the setting is more of a circus for eight-year-olds. Perhaps I know too much about rockers themselves—they sell soda on TV, their private lives besiege me in the checkout line, and their deals are discussed in the business pages. Familiarity breeds contempt. Perhaps I am nostalgic about my days of ignorance, when all I knew about Mick Jagger was his music. Perhaps my lack of interest is simply a function of aging. I joke that I don't trust anyone under thirty, and I'm not too unhappy that I haven't died before growing old. But I know that the first time I did feel old occurred as I was driving on I-5 in Seattle one day. Normally, I would steady the wheel with my knees as my hands cradled an invisible guitar and my fingers picked the chords. On that day "The White Room" came on the radio, and after a while I realized that something was amiss: my hands were still *on the wheel.*

I could not help taping *Easy Rider* when it played on PBS. "David, this is too much," my friends smirked; "*Easy Rider?*" "Well, it kind of reminds me of Russia," I said.

At the time the movie came out, I had never heard of Peter Fonda or Dennis Hopper. But I would have dropped everything and run off to see the movie version of *Das Kapital* if its sound-track had featured Steppenwolf and Hendrix. I saw the movie three times, including a screening at a film club. The latter was a brutally hacked black-and-white pirated version; all drug-related scenes, including the opening, had been cut, thus de-priving the film of its moral ambiguity and making it easier to sell the characters to select Soviet viewers. But I saw the complete version, too, twice. The pass to the screening cost much begging and cajoling (I once had to proofread a highborn moron's term paper on the vicissitudes of British trade unions in order to get a pass for *The Godfather*). Whatever the version, how can I overestimate *Easy Rider*'s effect? For us, it had FREEDOM writ large on it. It was possible not to have to hold a job? Not to have to go to meetings? To deck yourself out in the most out-rageous manner, hop on a bike, and drive from coast to coast— or live in a colony—just like that?

Some of my fellow émigrés smirk omnisciently at young Americans' exalted leftiness. But were we any less naïve? Al-though we were used to Soviet movies showing feasts in times of famine, *Easy Rider*'s free and loose ways seemed like something concocted by the USIA for foreign consumption. We argued about it interminably in the wee hours around Moscow kitchen tables: it was easy to accept the reality of convertibles and swimming pools and other signs of economic prosperity; it was so much harder to accept the reality of so much freedom.

Six

I must be Micky Trushin's only advocate. I cannot erase the memory of hearing the opening chords of *Sergeant Pepper* from the hallway. I knock bravely. "Okay if I—?" Micky gestures expansively: *Music is free, man.* He even resets the needle to the beginning, and we listen to the entire record in a silence unmarred by any cough or sneeze. Between the cuts we exchange nods and glances of a spiritual understanding beyond words. We do not introduce ourselves until the end. Names seem immaterial.

Micky skipped most of his classes in his first year and was expelled summarily. Part of his problems stemmed from his romance with Sylvia, a Czech exchange student. Socializing with foreigners was discouraged in the first place, but openly living with one? traveling with her around the country? When he came to the Dean's office, hat in hand, begging to repeat the course: "Trushin? Didn't you shack up with a foreigner?"

Like most expelled students, Micky would not leave Moscow. To go back to Kemerovo, in the middle of Siberia? I understood: for me, being back in Syzran would feel like serving a life sentence. He crashed here and there, taking odd jobs and inevitably getting into trouble with the law—his permit to stay in Moscow had expired. The residence law was a vicious circle: without a job, you can't get a permit; without a permit, you can't get a job. He was an illegal alien among us, and my room in the dormitory was his sanctuary.

One brutal January night he showed up looking like a German soldier retreating from Moscow in 1941: bedraggled, thin, wrapped in half a dozen sweaters. I made tea, put on a Dylan tape; out of his worn-out bag, one of many he toted around, came a well-thumbed illustrated Czech magazine with color pictures of Woodstock. We sat there quietly, sipping rum that tasted like floor polish and wondering whether Cream would ever tour Russia and what grass tasted like. (We had no idea it was akin to hashish. What? Russian riffraff and enlightened hippies use chemically related substances?) With the wind groaning outside, the tableau was pure Peace on Earth—a bit like a Christmas card.

Moments like these never last. Someone alerted the dormitory commandant, Micky's longtime foe, who was only too happy to call the police. They banged on the door and asked for me—he had signed in as my guest. A cop stood by, sweating in a warm overcoat and peering at the shabby room squeamishly. Micky packed, in silence: sweaters, scarves, clippings. His face was a blank. Minutes later he was gone.

After months' absence he always came back, emaciated, mangy-looking, his red, potato-shaped nose luminous. He would crash, ask for money or a sweater in the morning, never for more than "a couple of hours, man, I swear, there's this guy owes me . . ." and disappear.

Micky was a Flying Dutchman, constantly on the move, crisscrossing our lives, traveling in another dimension. His vagabondage imposed a different code of ethics: "To live outside the law, you must be honest," he would quote Dylan with a wink. This code allowed him to cheat, to steal—perhaps even, on occasion, to collaborate with the police (eluding them as long as he did could not have been pure luck). Yet he was a most reluctant existential character, always ready to trade a piece of his freedom—never the whole thing—for a meal and shelter. And, like an inspired con man, he constantly baffled his friends/creditors by popping up out of nowhere and showering them with cigarettes/clothes/LPs.

We students could feel smug toward him; we were not being chased out by the cops into the cold. We could secretly envy his being unburdened by tests and term papers, his ability to go out there and sleep with a foreign girl—something that no InYaz student, chained to visions of Kuala Lumpur and the UN, would ever do. We were unwilling to pay the price that freedom exacted. And, when it came to paying that bill, poor Micky was like a Third World country, barely keeping up on the interest.

Being on record as Micky's host did not bode well for me. "You really know how to pick 'em, Gurevich," my friend Sheriff, a.k.a. Leonid Vorontsov, commented darkly. "These guys run up files a foot thick, like your friend Micky with his Czech, and then burn out quick. You're chalking up a lot of black marks upstairs. Is there a single student expelled you were *not* friends with?"

"Maybe it's the other way around," I said. "Maybe I'm like the kiss of death. Maybe it's associating with me that brings them down. Maybe I am an informer myself."

Sheriff chuckled. "Believe me, I've seen informers—"

"With your Party membership, you would."

"—and you're not one of them. You don't have what it takes."

Sheriff's favorite pastime was commenting on the flaws in my character, and he got away with a lot. He was a well-balanced career man, an Army vet and a Party member, who loved Led Zep, *Easy Rider*, and tall, well-scrubbed blondes. His nickname came from having seen *The Magnificent Seven* fifteen times—it was the only classic Western that had played openly in Russia. He respected me for having seen every Sergio Leone movie at the Moscow Film Festival twice and knowing them all by heart. We would sit around past midnight, sipping the Scotch that he procured through his high contacts.

In the daytime the presence of others imposed a certain awkwardness between us. His Party pals would eye me, in my torn jeans, suspiciously (they always wore suits, the little apparatchiks), then look at him: *What are you doing with that bum?* What could he possibly tell them? That I was helping him with Latin?

Similarly, many of my regular drinking companions eyed *me* suspiciously: *What are you doing, being friendly with a Party member?* If forced to explain, I could have simply said that I like Scotch—but, as long as I chipped in for booze and did not freeload, questions like that were in bad taste.

Much as I liked having a good time, listening to rock, and playing cards, the company of like-minded people was somehow never enough. When people around you agree too much, the simplest, sometimes most inane things tend to ossify into gospel, and your mind grows numb; you need an alternative. Out-and-out Communists did not interest me: they spoke in formulas, their minds were welded shut, and whatever doubts they might have had about their virtues, they would not have shared them with me in a million years. But someone like Sheriff, with a foot in each camp, would have a completely different take on life—and it was this alternative point of view that always fascinated me.

The dormitory days rolled on, soaked with rock & roll, booze, and all-night whist marathons (an early version of bridge, popular in Russia). *"Carpe diem"* was the motto; how did that song go, "Tomorrow Never Knows"? I paid lip service to Sheriff's warnings and hung out with the "bad apples." I remember them: Kolya from Orenburg, Vanya from Leningrad, Dima from Orekhovo-Zuyevo. They were not less of an affront to the system than Micky was: they were regular kids, each of whom had had one glass too many, missed one class too many, and maybe said something he should not have said in mixed company. They all went home . . . One farewell party came after another, our ranks were thinning—but there were always new freshmen joining in. Why didn't I follow the "bad apples" in demise? Perhaps because behind my carefree façade I always had a sense of limits, a way of hedging my bets, of showing up in class before it was too late, of delivering a paper on time. This sense may have had less to do with recklessness than with fear; after each expulsion I would mechanically step up my attendance. Another reason may be that two years of unfettered life without father had given me a head start: I had already tasted freedom from familial law and order; to my friends, this was all brand-new.

My friend Musheg Tsagoyan—who liked to be called Moshe— was hit especially hard by the novel freedom of dorm life. His parents had a stern notion of discipline. Through high school, he told me, he had never been allowed to stay up past eleven.

We met through rock—what else? Moshe taped rock shows from every station in the world, from the BBC to Radio Monte Carlo to Radio South Africa, and could tell you at any given moment how many weeks "Stairway to Heaven" had been on the charts and where it was now. And I had thought *I* was a freak for knowing that "Another Girl" was on *Help* (Parlophone Records), side A, cut 5. I was amused and relieved: here was someone even freakier. This slight, carrot-haired, freckled kid sat for hours chain-smoking amid the chaos that his room was—empty bottles, ashtrays, tapes, charts; his radio blaring, he worked out all the possible hands in whist. He was well liked: a harmless, friendly nut. Which was how he lasted as long as he did—three years—before going off the deep end: no one took him seriously.

Moshe came to class only if a teacher showed concern for his whereabouts. Then he put on a shirt and headed for school. He barely knew his classmates or classrooms, yet his grades never slipped below B. Grudgingly I had to give the sonuvabitch his due. If there had been a Russian chapter of Mensa, he could have probably passed their test without having to interrupt a game of whist.

After Moshe warmed up to me—he kept most people at arm's length—I became the sounding board for his ideas. How about compiling a comparative history of the Jews and the Armenians? (Despite his blue eyes and red hair, he had pure Armenian blood; the Jewish nickname was an affectation.) He was from Volgograd (known as Stalingrad during World War II), where he claimed there were plenty of German weapons from the war still around . . . What about the arms trade? How about making porno films and selling them to Georgians? "Sounds like a great idea," I said. "Shuffle the deck, please."

"You have no imagination," he said.

"I compensate for it by leaving the dorm once in a while. You just sit here."

The single time he left the dorm, apart from an occasional visit to school, was to hurry to the Illusion Theater following the rumor that *Help!* was playing (a false alarm, of course: Soviet theaters—even the Illusion, which was more of a film club—could not play a Beatles movie). Instead, the world came to him. He found it deliriously amusing that, sooner or later, anyone on a binge came to his room. The door was smashed weekly, and the furniture was literally on its last legs: a world of wrack and ruin.

We floated apart. Although after the first year Moscow lost much of its luster for me—there were only so many plays and movies—I still could not be held within the dorm. I went to plays, movies, parties—for entertainment, but also because I was feeling cooped up. My soon-to-be-expelled pals Vanya, Kolya, and Dima hardly ever left the dorm. My motto became "When in doubt, go out."

But there was no nightlife in Moscow, not even all-night places to eat, and eventually we ended up back at the dorm. And I felt uncomfortable visiting my Moscow friends, all of whom lived with their parents.

To these friends, visiting the dorm was like slumming: they saw fun, fun, fun—vodka on the table, girls, the stereo going full blast. They envied us our freedom. They were not around in the morning to clean up the mess. We ate cafeteria food, playing Russian roulette with our stomachs, and did our laundry in the sink (no washer/dryers or laundromats).

When I went to visit them, I occasionally envied them the comfort of clean shirts and home-cooked meals and the refrigerator they could raid after midnight. Used to the dorm's Spartan comfort and general sloth, I felt like a vandal and a boor—back at Sergei's apartment in Syzran. But the thought of someone telling me to turn down the stereo was by now anathema to me. And when their parents went away and they threw parties, I felt ill at ease drinking and smoking in a place where I had to watch out for breaking a glass or leaving a cigarette burn on the chair. To top it all, there was money: my Moscow friends could spend freely; me, I had to think of the time left before the next scholarship payday. My freedoms corresponded to their unfreedoms, and the differences drove me back to the dorm.

None of this bothered Moshe, who was perfectly content to stay put. He thrived on being at the center of things. His file must have bulged with informers' reports of his misconduct, but somehow he always found protectors: first Sheriff, then Gleb Treboy, the *éminence grise* of the Party in the dorm, and himself a whist lover. After Gleb graduated, Moshe became vulnerable. He cloistered himself completely, he was seen taking codeine with his booze, and when he emerged from his room for a whist game, his eyes had a glazed look. Which was exactly what he looked like when I last went to see him. By that time he had not been to school for three months—not one class.

He had moved to a tiny cell: it was meant for two, but his roommate was on a leave of absence. His complexion was pasty, as if he had not seen sunlight for weeks. His movements were jerky but slow and uncertain, though he did not smell of booze. It was in stark contrast with the Moshe who had used to run along the hall yelling, " 'My Sweet Lord'! Number one! Third straight week!"

I had brought some wine; he gulped it down matter-of-factly, washing a pill down and not bothering to explain much.

"So." Moshe grinned his trademark scamp grin. "They sent you to check on me, huh?"

I stared at him incredulously.

That seemed to have convinced him. "You didn't know that I've been summoned to appear in front of the Komsomol Committee?"

I shook my head. "What are the charges?"

"*Everything*. Academic, discipline, antisocial—meaning gambling."

Moshe had long been cleaning up in whist (I was probably the only one who did not owe him), and one sore loser refused to pay. Moshe promised physical retribution. The guy wrote a *telega*, a report to the administration: "Tsagoyan is a known gambler."

"Not that it's news to them," Moshe said. "It's just different when it comes from someone who is not a regular informer."

"What are you going to do?" I asked.

He handed me a label peeled off a vodka bottle. The message was scribbled in barely legible letters on the back: "I hereby leave the ranks of the Komsomol. Go fuck yourselves."

"I'll send it to them," he said. "Registered mail."

I felt sick. I should have come here sooner, I thought; I could have done something. "Moshe, what is the purpose of this? What will it prove?"

"Nothing," he said. "You're really stupid. Aren't you tired of living in this fishbowl? Where every word, every deed—everything—goes on record?"

I shrugged. "How is it different elsewhere? Is that any reason to drop out?"

He shook his head. "You're like the rest of them. Go have a ball in India, or wherever they send you. If you stop by Volgograd, bring me back a carton of Kents."

"Self-pity is not like you," I said. "Do you have to send *this*? You're not Micky; they've got nothing serious on you. Only two more years—can't you do it?"

"Kiss my ass," he said. "Just for practice. You'll need the skill." He turned his face to the wall. The audience was over.

Moshe left school thereafter, never to be heard from again. I should have done more, I berated myself later; I should have torn up the goddamn note, the hell with Moshe's freedom of expression. Right, as if he couldn't write another one; as if he would run out of vodka labels. I should have used sounder logic; I should have talked about life being unfair. What kind of a friend was I? What stopped me, ultimately, was a lack of confidence: I wasn't sure he was wrong. I suspected that in his exposure to the dorm's intrigue, and, later, in his isolation, Moshe had arrived at the conclusions that I was still groping for in the dark.

Seven

We all watched ourselves at InYaz, especially in the dorm—a fishbowl, as Moshe put it. Sheriff was as well trained as anybody. After his second year he was offered a chance to go to East Germany. He turned it down. Why? I was in shock. True, East is not West—still . . . "Sometimes you have to be patient," he said.

He went a year later, as the head of the group. "This way I know who is informing on whom," he explained. "Would *you* want to be abroad, looking over your shoulder twenty-four hours a day?"

In a sense, informing is merely another way of shafting your neighbor. I get goosebumps as I read the accounts of Stalin's Russia—informing as a way of life . . . You want your neighbor's apartment? job? mistress? Write a report denouncing him as a Trotskyite, a Belgian spy, someone who harbors anti-Soviet sentiments. Don't worry about the evidence—the KGB will take care of that.

The Russia I grew up in was a more lenient place. Fifty years of Socialism had successfully conditioned people to keep their mouths shut, freeing the KGB to concentrate on dissidents. But at InYaz time stood still. After all, we were future soldiers in the Battle of Ideas (to say nothing of our military training) against the decadent West. The Party had a right to know whom it could trust . . .

Raf was a Kazan Tatar, a darkly handsome, decent guy with no great ambitions. All he wanted was a little comfort in his life. Accordingly, he picked Arabic for his second language. A tour of duty in Yemen would buy a co-op; another in Syria, a car; then a quiet desk job at Exportthis Importthat.

Raf drank and smoked moderately and preferred Sinatra to Hendrix. His only weakness was women. His main regret in life, he said, was that there were 2 billion women in the world and he could not bed them all. As befits an InYaz student, he was status-conscious: the last thing he wanted was a waitress who would fake pregnancy and force him into marriage. But upper-class blondes (his word for them was "clean," which sounded like something more than mere hygiene) were not falling head over heels for a poor Tatar boy, no matter how handsome. Not a black—not quite a white, either. Might give you a shiner at the drop of a hat. (*That* he would, he told me.) Raf was getting frustrated with his upward-dating plans. Money was the answer, he told himself; once he came back from Arabia, loaded with Italian suits, keys to a Lada sedan in hand—all would change. To that end he would study hard and mind his own business. He would keep his nose clean.

Every summer a group of exchange students from the University of Birmingham spent a month at InYaz. There were parties every night, but Raf bravely stayed away, afraid to be seen stumbling out of a foreigner's room at a late hour.

It must have been one of those summer nights when loneliness fills your mouth with a bitter taste. Somehow Raf's feet walked toward laughter, music, and wine. One of the girls ended up in his room. He did not find her all that attractive, he told me; he was just curious: British girls, what makes them tick?

In the morning he found himself on the horns of a dilemma: If he told her to keep it secret, she'd ask why. Then he'd have to explain to her that everyone is watched, and even if that is not strictly true, one simply has to assume that it is—for one's own good. And if she disregarded his warnings and shared them with a friend? How could he expect a nineteen-year-old English girl to adapt to the rules of another world? How could he be sure?

They said goodbye the night before her departure. He could not be seen walking her to the airport bus. He felt sorry for her, he told me; but what could he do? They just pick up their passports and go. They don't understand how a one-night stand can mess up a guy's career . . .

He told me about it in September, when I came back from summer vacation. He couldn't sleep, he had lost his appetite, and he was smoking two packs a day. The affair seemed too great a burden to carry alone: the macho pride of conquest, combined with self-protective fear. Why did he confide in me? Perhaps he knew what Sheriff did: that I did not "have what it takes" to inform on him.

Time went by, and Raf began to recover. He even started joking about her coming back next summer. He started believing that his warnings must have worked.

Then the letter came, four sheets of exotically semitransparent bluish paper with dainty little flowers on the margin and covered with neat, tiny handwriting. She could not get him out of her head, she wrote; she did not want anything from him; she just wanted to tell him that she loved him and remembered him and was looking forward to seeing him the coming summer.

My first reaction was uneasy respect—and envy, that in two nights Raf could have elicited such a reaction. But Raf's eyes were bloodshot, and his hands were shaking. "I don't understand how I could ruin my whole life with one fuck," he said. "Should I go to the Dean's office and confess? Maybe I should first talk to Vasya Kizilov" (the Party man in the dorm).

We inspected every inch of the letter and the envelope but still could not tell whether it had been opened. I was about to say that the odds of any one letter being read were low—but I had an experience of my own to recall . . .

I must have been twelve or thirteen. One Sunday my father and I stopped by the central bookstore downtown (or simply "in town," as they say in Syzran). The saleslady, who knew us well, was agog with excitement. "Did you see the Indians?" she asked. "From India! They were here—five minutes ago!"

Live Indians in Syzran! Neither my father nor I could bear to miss such an event. We caught up with them as they strolled down Sovyetskaya Street, the main drag, drawing curious looks right and left. My father egged me on: he must have wanted a demonstration of my English skills. They were exchange students from Delhi traveling around Russia, and they were friendly to a nervous kid trying out his fledgling English on them. (Looking back, I can understand their patience: everyone else just stared at them.)

I doubt that anything monumental was said, but later, after I got a letter with a dozen Indian stamps, my father was summoned to the Special Section at his school and upbraided for "unauthorized contacts with foreigners." (He had waited ten years to tell me about it: probably, he had not wanted to sow doubts about the system in a twelve-year-old's mind.) It could have ended badly, he hinted: demotion in rank, expulsion from the Party. At the last moment he got off with a warning for "lack of vigilance."

He looked sad telling me the story, and he offered no comment. Did he castigate himself for having been indiscreet—or was he angry at the Air Force for accusing him, in so many words, of spying for India? I never asked him. To this day I wonder if the Indians were being tailed or our mail was being read.

Now I could not find it in me to give Raf advice—at least, not beyond the usual platitudes: sit tight, play it by ear, and so on. He turned on his side and stared at the wall.

A few days later Sheriff pulled me out of a card game and gestured me to follow him to the terrace, where we could not be overheard.

"When did you talk to Raf last?" he asked. "What did you say?"

"Uh-oh," I said. Sheriff, I knew, was the only other one of us who knew of Raf's indiscretion. "You mean—?

"He spent a long time at the Dean's office today. Do yourself a favor: *stay away*. He won't seek you out himself: he's not vicious enough to earn his new informer stripes at your expense."

"If *that's* what the conversation was about."

"Can you afford to assume otherwise?"

Now it was my turn to worry. I racked my brains to recall what I had said to Raf: disrespectful observations on Party history? on special training? on teachers' politics? on other students? Every dumb joke I may have cracked in his company— and I knew quite a few jokes.

I would have had to hypnotize myself to recall every word I had ever said to him, and it seemed a useless exercise. Kizilov could have me anytime, and he did not need Raf for that.

Among other things, Kizilov was in charge of assigning roommates. At the beginning of my fourth year I found myself sharing a room with Boris and Kozin. Boris was a burly, semicomatose Ukrainian, who listened to the BBC religiously and responded to the reports of world disasters with mournful sighs and apocalyptic prophecies about what would happen when the Chinese/blacks/Jews took over. (My last name did not seem to bother him: because I was his roommate, I must have been a "good" Jew.)

Kozin was about to be expelled, with good reason: most of his energy was consumed in chasing women. By far the most dedicated Lothario I have ever met, he spent his every waking hour planning conquests for the coming week. Raf used a vague notion of "clean" as a criterion, but Kozin was omnivorous: "anything that moves" was fair game.

None of this particularly bothered me. But the year before, Kozin and Boris had fought a war against their ex-roommates, using that peculiarly Soviet weapon, the *telega*.

Although Kozin's roommates, Yuri and Volodya, with their highly affected manners, were reputed to be gay, I doubt that the students, many of whom were fresh from the provinces, had any idea of what homosexuality was. So the two were resented, I think, less on sexual than on sociocultural grounds: both came from rich families (at least Yuri did) and regarded the surrounding prole culture with open contempt.

According to Kozin, Volodya and Yuri fired the opening shot by writing a report in which they painted their roommate's morality in darkly anti-Socialist terms. Kozin fought back: aided by Boris, who had used to be Volodya and Yuri's roommate, he composed a counterreport describing them as vicious pederasts in the employ of the CIA.

The dormitory gossips were filled with delight. People came up to Kozin or Yuri to shake hands and voice approval: "The bastard[s] had it coming." No one seemed to find anything unusual or dubious about the methods.

I had not taken sides then, and I was not about to do so now. All I knew was that I had been put in a room with two proven informers. I went to see Sheriff. "Why me?"

Thoughtfully he ran his hand along his bulging, muscular shoulder, examining invisible pimples. I found it distasteful, but I have yet to meet a blond, tanned, athletic man who did not spend hours contemplating his body and anxiously looking for blemishes. Finally he said, "Vasya [Kizilov] must think you're such a bad boy that you need two informers to keep an eye on you." He chuckled. "Those two are the bottom of the heap anyway."

"Great," I said. "As if my ego wasn't already bruised because I was never invited to inform—"

"I told you, you don't have what it takes—"

"—now you're telling me that, to inform on me, Vasya's scraped bottom."

Whatever Sheriff's opinion of my roommates' informing talents, I complained too much, I believe. It was reasonable to expect at least one informer per room, and I might as well live with known quantities. It was reasonable to expect that your every casual remark would be passed along to the authorities sooner or later, which was bad enough. But the informers I knew of were not the best and the brightest—they needed the Party's hand just to stay afloat, and the thought that this very remark would be distorted, jumbled, and mutilated by a moron who was a student thanks only to the Party's largesse was unbearable. Going one logical step further, if the moron did not like you, he could simply *invent* the remark; surely, it did not take much imagination.

What could you do? Were you prepared to lead the life of

an undercover agent, with your every word monitored? You had to make choices: this person I'll trust this far; that person, that far. The game is exhausting. Someone whom you barely know tells you a risqué joke; someone else, whom you know to be in trouble with the administration, is suddenly sent abroad—with a clean bill of health, one assumes; should you review their respective ratings? A computer code has yet to be written to simulate this process of constant review. But it beats imposing a permanent gag order on yourself. One way or another, it is a form of social Darwinism: this is how the Party selects its best.

From the distance of almost twenty years the game looks both sad and useless. It seems paranoid to allow that I was wrong at every turn; that I misjudged everybody, friend and foe alike. All were vulnerable: some risked expulsion, others wanted careers . . . Is it so cynical of me to believe that Micky, Moshe, Sheriff, and the dozens of others with whom I drank, played cards, and listened to records—that every one of them could have filed reports on me?

Both my roommates were ordinary Soviet students who may never have written another report, before or after their war with Yuri and Volodya. It does not matter in the long run. That was not the primary reason for putting all three of us in one room. Vasya Kizilov was not a tactician in the game of gathering intelligence. He simply deemed all three of us trash—hopeless cases beyond redemption.

I used to think that it would be interesting to pose the question, Did you or didn't you? to any of them after twenty years; this is the stuff of which drama is made. But it is unrealistic to expect that I would ever hold the reports' yellowed sheets in my hands; and, in the absence of hard facts, I prefer to give a friend the benefit of the doubt. If it means letting sleeping dogs lie, so be it. I am content simply to know that I never wrote a report on anybody. Until Gorbachev passes a Freedom of Information Act, this is good enough for me.

Who was Kizilov, anyway? I can still see him walking down the hall, heading for the kitchen in a silent, heavy, bear-like stride. A short, stocky, balding thirty-two-year-old in a track suit, a teapot in hand, his face frozen in a serious, studied expression. He passes me, an eighteen-year-old in torn jeans with a tipsy, prancing walk; my fingers pick invisible chords, and my mouth makes strange sounds into an imagined mike. He does not need to look beyond this façade: he knows a moral cripple when he sees one. We barely acknowledge each other's existence. We have no common ground, common interests, common values.

I knew the bare facts of Kizilov's life. High school—factory—Army service in East Germany—re-enlistment—honorable discharge at the rank of *starshina*, the highest noncom rank. Picked up enough German to barely squeeze through the entrance exams with C's; walked into the Rector's office, laid his Party card on the table. Welcome to InYaz, Comrade.

Now he is too old to play backroom politics with the eager beavers who will step over any number of dead bodies to gain a slot at the UN. The go-getters in Levi's and blazers regard him as a freak of nature: *Where did they find this scarecrow?* But they relax once they see that Vasya has no dreams of the shining castle on the East River, that he would gladly settle for a Soviet-made stereo and a Polish coat. He wants a quiet life with a nice paycheck. He is not too bright, and he needs the time just to keep up, not to jockey for position. (As I said, you needed two foreign languages to graduate, but, like other Party people, he was eventually relieved—by special fiat—of the burden of studying a second language. When it comes to bending academic rules, the Party has no equal.)

With his Party record, he can have any position. He picks Dormitory Commandant, an administrative job that suits him well, especially the title. Used to Army discipline, he has no patience with the punks who party through the night, who pass out on the stairs, who wear torn rags with foreign labels, who swoon at the foreign-language cacophony. At their age he was serving his Motherland—protecting the long-haired freaks from the capitalist threat. He has no illusions about re-educating them, but he must help the Party weed them out. He owes it to the Party, who made it possible for him to go to this prestigious school, and who will provide him with a quiet, undemanding job upon graduation. Where would the Party be without people like him?

I'll concede that Vasya did not hate me. It was, as we say in the US, nothing personal. To him, I was just another overprivileged punk. Were he a character in a novel, I could feel sympathy for him: a simple man of the people, trying to improve his social lot. If we lived in the same apartment building, I would be saying, "Good morning" on the stairs and thinking, Looks kind of dull, but probably not a bad guy. But he was the Party's man, and it was his official responsibility to give the Party his assessment of my character and whether I was to be trusted in the great Battle of Ideas that working in languages is all about. I could not read what he wrote in his reports, but I read it in his face: no, he did not believe that the Party should grant me its trust, whether in picking roommates or in working abroad.

Vasya, wherever you are—tending flowers at your dacha or snoozing on your imported couch or reading *Pravda* with a sense of dissatisfaction—I'm cutting you as much slack as I humanly can. I can even force myself to believe that you did not particularly enjoy filing reports on me. You had nothing *specific* to go on, just your vague suspicions, after all—I never broke the letter of the law. Writing the reports taxed your imagination, taking time away from your studies, and you needed all the time you could get. I don't want to hate you, to impotently visualize you in front of a firing squad; if I run into you on the street, I'll walk on by. Ultimately, you and the Party that you represented so loyally were right to distrust me. Your "class instinct" did not steer you wrong. I would have never settled for the status that you sought—that of a privileged prisoner of the system.

Eight

Komsomol meetings at InYaz were no different in form from meetings at high school: committee elections, attendance, grades, extracurricular work . . . The best way to skip one was to take off early and quietly. But sometimes you just had to attend the last class of the day, and then you had to do some horse-trading with the group Komsomol leader: it was his responsibility to bring you in, dead or alive. "Gurevich, you've missed three meetings in a row." "I'll come, but you owe me four hours." I.e., he had to fix it with the monitor not to mark me absent at two classes of my choice. Komsomol politics is just politics—everything is negotiable.

Some meetings were mere end-of-the-term summings-up, others were kangaroo court sessions. The culprits' personal cases were brought before the Komsomol Committee; then they had to face a meeting. We averaged one Darkness at Noon a month.

While working at Intourist, Student X accepted a tape deck as a present from tourists—a blatant case of moral decay. No one asks the culprit if this is true or false. Or how he was found out.

> CHARACTER WITNESS (*his group Komsomol leader*): Uh, Comrade X had good grades, participated in extracurricular activity, was modest in daily life [a *sine qua non* of each reference].
> THE SECRETARY (*shaking his head*): Inconclusive. Flaws in

ideological work. What do you have to say for yourself, Comrade X?

We eye X's face with curiosity. There but for the grace of God . . . How could he screw up? Everybody takes, but you gotta know when and how. Someone must have informed. His expression is a blank. He is exhausted after days of grilling. All he wants now is for this to be over. "I'm sorry. I won't do it again. Honest."

The Committee recommends expulsion. (Once you are expelled from the Komsomol, expulsion from school follows automatically.) Charge: "Deeds incompatible with Komsomol membership." Votes in favor? An unsteady show of hands. Against? None. Abstaining? None. Doesn't add up? No problem; the Komsomol uses its own brand of math. Anyway, it's already past eight in the evening.

Next case: Student Y wrote a letter to the Voice of America, in which he voiced anti-Soviet sentiments. How was he found out? Blank. What exactly did it say? Well, it must have been anti-Soviet, because if it had not, then he would have written it to Radio Moscow, right? Expelled. Next case.

Some "crimes" never reached the meeting. They were plea-bargained, in a manner of speaking: repentance, then reprimand or warning. But everything went into your file. When the time came for you to be approved for the prized assignment abroad, the file would be studied carefully. The Party had a right to know the odds of you defecting, didn't it?

Again, just like in the old days, it was not enough to keep your own nose clean. An overt refusal to rise and join the chorus of disapproval could be held against you, too. At least, this was how we were made to feel. In a sense, we In Yaz students cringed before the system in a manner more distasteful than our parents' generation did. Under Stalin, failure to denounce the "traitor" was punished by death or years in Siberia; at InYaz it was a setback to your career. But so many of us wanted to succeed . . .

It started out as a rumor (*Pravda* does not carry engagement announcements). Marrying a foreigner was not common at InYaz. You automatically forfeited your brilliant career, for warriors at the ideological front cannot have politically suspect spouses. On the other hand, it is a rare Soviet citizen who marries a foreigner and then remains in Russia. But I had always suspected that Natasha Kuznetsova kept her big eyes open for all possible options. When I was told that she had gotten engaged to a Dutch art dealer three times her age—well, I said, that makes sense. There must be better ways to get to Kuala Lumpur than sweating it out at Komsomol meetings.

Natasha joined the Dutch group in her second year. This raised a few eyebrows. The Translation Department was "men-only"; women were semiofficially barred. The logic was simple: "We train them, and then they get pregnant and retire." I do not recall feminist sit-ins outside the school: in Russia you don't fight the law; it is designed with mile-wide loopholes built in. The curriculum of the Pedagogical Department, where the girls studied, was by and large similar to ours. After graduation, girls with parents in high places were more likely to work as interpreters or translators than as teachers. Yet there were always exceptions, and Natasha was one of them.

She projected a Lolita-like image: a slim, boyish figure; hair cut short; and curled, pouting lips. Her most striking feature was her eyes, which bulged so as to make me wonder about her thyroid. We were on good terms but not close.

Later I learned that Natasha had wangled her transfer from the Pedagogical Department—ostensibly to study Dutch—through the personal recommendation of Natalya Nikolayevna, our third-year English teacher.

Natalya Nikolayevna: long, raven hair, impeccable English suits; the sight of her long, slender legs in class at eight A.M. made us gnash our teeth. Yet NN was a young Socialist cadre to the core. A general's daughter, she had all the right credentials and all the right contacts, which she reinforced by tireless networking. At twenty-six she already had two trips to England under her belt, and she spoke of Albion with ill-concealed awe. She was the image of modern Russia that the Soviets love to project. A closet feminist, too, which was a factor in helping Natasha with the transfer. The two Natashas were such pals, huddling over coffee at the cafeteria. To NN, Natasha's engagement was a stab in the back. Your protégés have no right to betray you.

NN asked us to stay after class. It was important, she said. She walked around the classroom, asked us to open the window, and lit a cigarette. We exchanged glances. Smoking in the classroom? That certainly set the tone. This was serious.

"You may have already guessed what this is about," she said bitterly. "You must have received the invitations to Natasha's wedding reception."

We had. They were beautifully printed: gilded letters on thick, snow-white paper. The reception was to be held at a fancy hotel for foreigners. I ignored the invitation: I did not even have a suit to go to a place like that.

"Natasha is not here today," NN said, "and it is bad manners to speak behind a person's back. However, I assure you that I have repeatedly asked her to come by, and I never got a response. So . . . let's talk. I want to know what you think. Do you approve, disapprove, what? Perhaps you think it's all right for a young girl to go off like this and marry a foreigner?"

She went on about Natasha's immaturity, her naïveté, her bedazzlement by riches. We coughed and nodded: *Yeah Sure No doubt about it You're right.* We had no idea what she was driving at. We were such a bunch of innocents. Not rebels—it never occurred to us to argue, to ask: What right do we, or you, NN, have to judge Natasha? What business is it of ours? That would have been equivalent, in our minds, to leaping up and screaming, "Lenin sucks!" No, our only desire was to be told what to do, and to take off. It was getting close to eight, the liquor stores were closing, and, God, did we need a drink after this. I don't think we liked our classmate Natasha much at that moment. We understood her desire to lead an elegant life on Prinsengracht in Amsterdam, and we certainly did not blame her for avoiding the meeting, but we felt she was going over our dead-tired bodies.

"I am disappointed in you." NN lit another cigarette from the smoldering one. Her long, purple fingernails looked weapon-like. "You sit here so passively! She's been with you for two years—don't you care what happens to her? Alone in a capitalist country, amid egotism and greed, with an old man who will exploit her youth? Do you know what it's like out there?"

No, rushed through our minds; and if you don't let us know where this conversation is heading, we'll never find out "what it's like out there."

"Well—" She regarded us with a look that seemed familiar. "Will you just let it go? Or are you going to let her know how you feel?"

Suddenly it clicked for me. I remembered my mother demanding that I sit down and write my father a letter. "He'll see the light, he'll leave that whore—or else you disown him!" All NN wanted us to do was to write a letter.

"Let's take a break," she said wearily; "Comrade Chernov will come by to talk to you."

Outside we put our minds together. If the Party Secretary of the Translation Department himself was coming, it was a big mess, a grave ideological oversight. Someone had to take the rap. The only thing we could do was to forge the minutes of a formal Komsomol meeting—the idea of convening a real one was instantly rejected—and adopt a resolution condemning Natasha's behavior as unworthy of a Soviet student. Why hadn't NN taken the bull by the horns?

Chernov was not your boorish Old Guard Stalinist. He had polished his act during his five years at the UN. The ready smile shot creases across the wrinkles in his face, making it look like a tortoise shell. In his position—he was the one deciding on UN candidates—this might be a smile one could count on: that of a strict but kind-hearted uncle, to whom you turn if you've gotten a girl in trouble, for example. Who'll give you both a lecture and the money. Coming after NN, he was the good cop.

He removed his horn-rimmed glasses, breathed on them, and wiped them with an immaculate white handkerchief. Then he filled his pipe and lit it in two energetic drags. "Well," he said, his avuncular expression intact, "what do you make of it?"

Two of my classmates, well-known apple polishers, rushed to carry the ball, interrupting each other to play back NN's lines on Natasha's immaturity and naïveté.

"What about the reception?" Chernov asked. "Have you made plans? Rented tuxes yet?"

Huh?

"I'm joking," he said. "I doubt it's black tie. Seriously,

are you planning to attend? I am not trying to intrude, mind you—just curious." Oh, the look in his brown, almost yellow eyes . . .

We students avoided one another's eyes. The implications were clear. At least a couple of people were good friends of Natasha's. Now they could remain either good friends or good students. A fork in the road. I wished Natasha and I had been friends, and I thought that maybe I should go, just to make some kind of point, whatever this point might be. Several subdued "no"s came up.

"And in what manner," Chernov said, "are you going to proceed about this . . . *rejection*? Surely it says RSVP on the invitation. Anyone has it on him?"

No, we all shook our heads. Just the fact of having it on you seemed like guilt by association.

"In any case," he proceeded, "as future graduates of this Institute, you must refuse in a civilized fashion. Rather than do it individually, you should do it collectively—in one fell swoop, so to speak. When Natasha comes to class, explain to her *why* you feel it would be improper for you to attend. You must stress that the decision comes from you, rather than from me or Natalya Nikolayevna. Sometimes, I fear, the disapproval of one's peers has a stronger effect than that of parents or teachers." He flashed a smile at NN, inviting her to share his amusement at such a paradoxical phenomenon.

She weakly smiled back. She was not amused. It had been a long day for her, too. She'd pick her protégés more carefully next time.

"If you go," Chernov went on, "I understand. At your age, you want to have fun. I can't promise you much fun there, though. God knows what kind of people you'll meet. You are fine, bright young men, good students, with every reason to

165

expect excellent jobs and exciting careers. Trust me, you have many fun parties ahead of you, in important places, with interesting people—on better occasions than this reception."

I was hesitating. On one side of the scales were my democratic distaste for stuffed-shirt affairs and my resentment that Natasha had been able to buy her freedom with her body (it is hard to see it differently at twenty). On the other side, I felt an unbearable yearning to stick it to Chernov and NN. How dare they talk to me like that? to push me in a manner so blatant? The scale was unsteady, it bounced up and down . . . This is crazy, I told myself—I have to do something I don't like just to make a point? But, ultimately, what tipped the balance was the one tiny iota of hope that Chernov's speech had deposited somewhere in my heart: ". . . good students, with every reason to expect excellent jobs and exciting careers." He was good; he knew which buttons to push. In my fourth year my mind knew that it was all over, that I had nothing to expect from the system, but my heart refused to believe that the doors were closed, and a seasoned Party propagandist knew how to keep this flicker of hope alive.

The Natasha affair fizzled out. There was no meeting: we never even tried to bother her about it. I'm sure that NN and Chernov put Natasha through the wringer behind closed doors, trying to talk her out of her decision, but she was not Student X or Y: the Komsomol's disapproval meant nothing to her, just as it would mean nothing to me three years later, when I was emigrating. Two of her closest friends attended the reception, and no tangible harm befell them. Nothing happened to NN and Chernov, either: they were too well entrenched in the system to be brought down by a minor embarrassment. All they wanted was to write in their report that "educational work with the group was conducted . . . Classmates voiced their ardent disapproval." Nothing more, nothing less.

Nine

My fourth year was coming to an end. Hardly anyone was left from the old gang; drinking and whist playing were turning into routines; even rock brought less joy. I had no trouble finding new miscreants for company, but deep inside I felt caught in a rut and was terrified of ending up like the others.

Then, on March 8, 1972, I went to a party—with only six people there, it was more like a blind date—where I met a girl named Natasha (you can tell it's a common name). When she smiled, there was a glint of daring in her eyes, a kind of good-natured spunk, that instantly attracted me. Her laughter was light-hearted and natural; I felt at ease in a way I had never felt before. She wore a fuchsia knit blouse, a color that becomes her to this day. When we slow-danced, I reached under it and lightly ran my hand down her back. Her skin was cool and smooth; it drew my hand like a magnet. She responded with a slight tremor that seemed to go direct to my heart. We must have slow-danced for six hours straight.

I took her home and returned to the dorm at dawn. We had not gone beyond passionate necking, but in my heart I was calmly confident that within twenty-four hours we would be making love, that every moment of it would be wonderful, that it would last for a long, long time.

And it all came true. I even remember what we played through the night: *Deep Purple in Rock*, my tape of the moment.

Within a month we moved in together, and in another month

we were married. I was lucky: besides making me deliriously happy, she made sense of my life. For at least the last year of school, I had a realm where I could escape from reality. We had problems: her mother was blind with fury at the prospect of a penniless Jew for a son-in-law. But, other than that, we were the happiest, the most carefree couple around. Natasha took evening classes at InYaz and worked at a library. And from free-lance translation jobs I was already earning as much as she did. We were not exactly raking it in, but we got by. At twenty-one, love can make up for an awful lot of money problems. Then came graduation.

Point Five (nationality/ethnicity) in my internal passport said, "Russian"—a thin cover for my Jewishness that I inherited from my grandfather the convert, and that I never paid much attention to. In Syzran it did not seem to matter. There are numerous Asiatic ethnic groups living along the Volga—Tatars, Bashkirs, Chuvashes, Maris; I was not aware how a Gurevich was different from an Ivanov or a Muhammedov.

We had a sprinkling of Jews at InYaz: Herskovitz, Puhrer, Luxemburg, Hazanov, Arievich, Elbert. At the time, I thought it was kind of funny that we were all scattered, one or two per study group, but later I ceased to find it amusing. Some forms of anti-Semitism are dumber than others: was the Dean's office afraid that two Jews in the group would form a cabal and rule over the hapless gentiles? We had little in common with one another; some came from the élite, some from the middle class. If the Party perceived us as budding Elders of Zion—well, I can only quote Abbie Hoffman's response to conspiracy charges at the Chicago trial: "We couldn't agree on lunch."

The only thing we had in common was grades: not many

C's among us. Yet it was the students with Russian names like Ivanov who, regardless of grades, were recommended for jobs with foreign delegations, from dietitians to rugby teams. When, by the fourth year, the one-year Third World jobs started coming in, I realized that, with my last name, I was not on anybody's short list.

Every day an Ivanov or Petrov, with Komsomol record or without, was being recommended for a job; and yet, despite all the signs, after the "Dutch wedding" meeting I realized that a corner of my brain seemed to be paralyzed by hope. Hope is a natural human trait; once it's gone, you're dead. But it should be directed within yourself, not at others—and never at the system.

In retrospect, I may be too hard on myself: giving up hope is easier at forty than at twenty. At the time, it was easy enough to close my eyes to the unpleasant side effect of having Gurevich for a last name. Especially amid all that conjugal bliss.

And now Gurevich, Puhrer, & Co. were en masse "not recommended for working abroad." For a graduate, a college reference is everything, and if you are in languages, the best jobs involve traveling abroad; my reference was equivalent to being blacklisted. Caste can overcome prejudice: the ones with influential parents managed to bypass it as time went by. But for the moment we were all in the same boat.

Much later I learned that the dormitory informers had described me as "the leader of the Zionist cell." One can only speculate about the train of thought that led to this label: Jewish name—wrong attitude—rowdy behavior? It felt rather flattering: sort of a nickel-and-dime Sharansky. Isn't it romantic?— "At twenty I led a Zionist cell in a Soviet Ivy League school." Why didn't I play it up later in the US?

The trouble is, there isn't an iota of truth in it. Whoever

wrote that report—could have been anybody, from Kizilov to Kozin—was far, far removed from reality. The word "Zionist" was not unfamiliar to me, but I certainly knew and cared more about Eric Clapton than Herzl or Zhabotinsky. Sometimes a search for cultural and ethnic identity starts with an informer's report. *Now* I was interested in Herzl.

The InYaz KGB were not so stupid as to use the accusation born of an informer's ignorance as the official reason for black-listing. The latter, "lack of involvement in social work," was a sham: many students had never attended a meeting, had grad-uated with straight C's, and were now going to India or Yemen. For me, it was less of a slap in the face than for other Jews: they had put in hours of Komsomol work, had hustled with the rest—they were "good Jews." Me, apart from marking time at a few meetings, I hadn't done a thing; now I could gloat. "Hey, Luxemburg, remember the time I was going to see *Casablanca* and you had to go to a meeting?" But gloating does not make you happy or bring you closer to truth.

I was summoned to the Dean's office, where Yudintsev, the Dean's deputy in charge of work assignments—according to rumor, a retired KGB colonel—read it from my file: "Not rec-ommended for working abroad." Looking over his neat gray crewcut (he was a full foot shorter), I was sad and relieved at the same time. Sad, because hope was dead; relieved, because finally the cards were on the table. No longer did I have to strain my eyes, trying to read the subtext; no longer was the message whispered in "you know"s and "you understand"s, punctuated by nervous little laughs. The word from the system came through loud and clear: *We don't want your kind.*

Part Three

Part Three

One

The rift between my father and myself had been growing through the years. It started with money.

Few of us are rational about money. I know people who save pennies by buying generic foods, only to splurge on Chivas. Before my father moved in with his second wife, Natasha, he used to go on stamp-buying sprees, then freeze at the sight of restaurant prices. Later he became tight-fisted. It was my bad luck to be going to college at about the same time.

Like most students, I received a small scholarship; this plus a share of the child support my mother was still getting came to eighty-five rubles a month. About an average dormitory income—just enough to scrape by. But the city is filled with temptations, and not just Levi's: books, plays, movies. Heavily subsidized, they cost relatively less than in America; as with everything else in Russia, the issue is availability rather than money. But even these seemingly low prices can burn a hole in a student's pocket.

Rock & roll took priority. I asked my father to help me buy a tape recorder—a common sight in the dorm. He responded with a long, earnest letter on the virtues of modest living, how little the students had gotten by on in his time, etc. Could I tell him that I had just plunked down thirty rubles on a pair of Levi's? His letter worked. I decided never to ask for anything again.

But when I began getting free-lance translation jobs, I reluctantly took another shot. If you don't want to spoil me, I reasoned, then help me buy a typewriter (the equivalent of my two months' budget) and let me support my "high-living" habits myself. I drafted a business-like proposal devoid of emotion and even complete with sort of a payback schedule.

I could understand his puritanical opposition to the tape recorder: from his Syzran perspective, it seemed like a rich man's toy. (*He* didn't have one.) But a typewriter was different, I reckoned: it was a tool of employment, a means of making money; also, a *gadget*, a labor-saving device, something that my father, with his techie mind, would understand.

At first he agreed, but then I got a lengthy letter with a nauseatingly familiar opener: "Upon careful consideration, Aunt Natasha and I have decided . . ." It felt like a *Pravda* editorial.

This was not like him, I reflected. I could hear Aunt Natasha's whisper between the lines. It didn't take a leap of imagination to re-create her arguments, starting with "He's his mother's son, you know how wasteful they are . . . He wants to be better than anyone else, to show off—whoever heard of having your own typewriter?" (True, no one I knew in Syzran owned one. Nor in the dorm: save for the graduation theses, our school papers were submitted in longhand.) The final argument was spelled out in black-and-white: "You know that typewriters must be registered with the police." This one stunned me: not only was it untrue (perhaps outdated), but even if it were true? Did they think I would be typing dissident manifestos? Way back I may have cracked a few careless jokes— who doesn't in Russia? But I expected my father to know better than to draw connections between cracking jokes and breaking the law.

I ended up renting a typewriter on a job-by-job basis. But communications with my father were now confined to birthday cards. I did not need Aunt Natasha's advice on life copied down in his hand.

In order to keep my future mother-in-law away from the wedding (not that she was begging to come), we decided that all our parents would be excluded. Soon my father came to Moscow to visit. For a brief moment all was forgiven and forgotten. But when I tried to explain my situation with the Institute and the discrimination in employment, all hell broke loose.

"I don't believe it!" He banged his fist. "You should have joined the Party! Then—"

"It's a double whammy," I said. "First, the Party recruits among workers and soldiers—who have nothing to lose but their chains, who have everything to gain by joining. Second, it isn't too keen on the Jews."

"No, no, no! When I joined—"

"You joined in 1941. Anybody could join then, everybody was one step away from death . . ."

I told him I knew of only two Jewish students at InYaz who were Party members. Both were much older and had joined while serving in the Army. It had been a clever maneuver on their part: surely, not many of their fellow soldiers were dying to join, and after months of cultivating—perhaps even bribing— the Party Secretary it was possible to make him overlook the inconvenience of their last names. "Perhaps if I had entered your school, if I had joined the Air Force—"

"Not a bad idea at all," he nodded bitterly.

At InYaz, I went on, the competition was fierce. The entire

Komsomol Bureau had fought tooth and nail to be recommended, but only one, Kafirov, had won the prize. "And they were mostly Russians," I added.

"I don't believe it," he repeated. "I refuse to believe it. If you just went to your Party Secretary, if you sat down with him, talked man to man—did you try to do that?"

That would be Chernov, I thought. Imagine Chernov and my father belonging to the same Party. Chernov may have looked like an uncle during the Kuznetsova affair, but the last thing he wanted was a heart-to-heart with me. And I would have died rather than carry his bags for him (literally) the way Kafirov had been doing for five years.

I said, "In fact, joining is so hard that I'm not really sure I *want* to."

"I'm not surprised! You must have said something, you wag your tongue constantly—they know you're not interested! Do you realize how this makes you look?" Unwillingness to join the Party: in his book, there was no graver mortal sin.

I did not answer. This chicken-and-egg argument was wearing me down: which came first, my reluctance or the Party's cold shoulder? I could not care less. Whatever my feelings about my father's character, I had clung to the illusion that he was smart. But now his pedestal collapsed. I was sad to see him sputter angrily about what I had long considered a nonissue.

He shook his head. "Who could have filled your head with such ideas?" He must have felt he had begotten a monster. Or did he think it was *just a stage*, something I needed to go through before I got back on the track? I wonder if he realized then what a long road we would travel in the next two years.

When I talk about my father with my friend Michael, he says in turn that he was fully prepared to be disowned by his father—whose rank in the US Army was equivalent to my father's in the Soviet Air Force—after Michael announced he was going to Canada to beat the draft. (The Vietnam War ended before he made good on his threat.) Then America must be my Canada, I tell him. But I was never granted amnesty and have no plans to return for permanent residence.

This is an awkward parallel; the only thing it proves is the difficulty of drawing parallels. Blaming the Party for everything under the sun, including the generation gap, will make me sound like the Party itself—which, further, never shied away from taking credit for everything, including the Bolshoi Ballet and the space flights. But I cannot completely drive away the thought that it was an ugly, ruthless political dogma that gave this (perhaps universal) generation gap conflict such a painful edge.

As I visited Kharkov only occasionally, I did not give my relatives there much thought. They were in retail—so what? It was not until I found myself at InYaz that an uneasy feeling crept in. My Moscow friends' parents and grandparents were scientists, professors, artists—intelligentsia. My father was in the military, my mother was a doctor—roots humble but respectable. But Kharkov was another story.

My grandmother had six brothers and sisters, who formed a tight clan. This did not mean love and peace. In fact, at no time were all the families on speaking terms with one another; pacts and alliances were constantly shifting. "Don't you talk to Aunt Bella!" Grandma would say. "You know what she said to Aunt Anya about me?" I felt like a UN peace envoy in Lebanon.

Their collective reaction to my graduation woes differed from my father's. They were down-to-earth, practical people; with anti-Semitism in the Ukraine harsher than in Syzran, I did not need to explain to them why I was not UN-bound upon graduation. They urged me to take Natasha's last name: wouldn't life be a lot easier with a fine gentile last name like Mazurov?

They must be joking, I thought. But my great-uncles Boris and Yuri went on to tell me about a man named Shekhter (a reasonably Jewish-sounding name), who pretended he had lost his passport, and then changed his name to Shakhtar (which in Ukrainian means "miner" and thus could be interpreted as— well, a dubiously Ukrainian name). And then there was my uncle Vladik Khaikin, who obtained a fictitious divorce from his gentile wife so that his two sons would be officially in her custody and thus have the Russian last name of Basov. Later they would join the Party, something they could never have hoped for with their father's last name.

"I don't think it's a good idea," I said, seething. To top my recent discovery of my political past as the leader of the Zionist cell, I had just seen stills from *Exodus* in a film magazine. Leon Uris's novel, with its heavily rhetorical style, was too Socialist Realist for my taste. But the picture of Paul Newman proudly standing on the hills of Galilee—*that* had raised my Jewish consciousness dramatically.

I looked at Uncle Yuri and Uncle Boris: stocky men in their sixties, with gold teeth, wrinkled faces, and eyes that had seen everything. They talked in clipped, cryptic phrases sprinkled with Yiddish words (which I did not understand) and ending nonverbally: their eyes rolled skyward, their hands rose. I recognized this mode of communication years later, in southern Italy. An outsider like myself had to strain to make sense of it.

Uncle Yuri managed the city's largest fish store; Uncle Boris was the manager of a meat warehouse, setting priorities for meat deliveries to restaurants and stores. They did well by themselves: underground tycoons who had never spent a day in jail. They played the system like a violin, these Menuhins of retail who knew that the State never dropped anything in your lap just for the asking. Uncle Yuri, called "The Tsar of the Konny Market," after the store's location, would probably disagree with my opinion of informers. He could not have made Konny Market his bailiwick without the support of the Crimes Against Property Police Unit, who relied on him to supply them with information. In that sense, Yuri was to the retail world what Vasya Kizilov was to the dorm.

They meant well. They loved me. They were proud that their great-nephew attended a Moscow school. They thought my marrying Natasha was a brilliant ploy, one that would procure me a Moscow residence permit. They also thought I was a fool to stick by my last name. Like my father, they were disappointed in me.

The ardency of my reaction was perhaps due to my youth and the recency of my discovery: like any brand-new convert, I wanted to be more royalist than the King, more Jewish than Golda Meir. But zealotry stems from ignorance. At the time, I was blissfully unaware of the past of my Illusion Theater idols—Paul Muni had once been Weisenfreund; Edward G. Robinson, Goldenberg. It is safe to assume that their new names had been imposed on them by stage producers or studio heads like Louis B. Mayer—people who had more than a little in common with my uncles.

Great-uncles Boris and Yuri were the ones who had made it big, but all their brothers and sisters were in retail, too. Great-uncle Berchik ran a bookstore; Great-aunt Pasha, a street stand. My grandpa David managed a tiny mom-and-pop grocery. Russian "managing" is functionally similar to American "owning": he was in charge. The State paid him a niggardly salary, and it was up to him to steal as much as he could without getting caught. You might say that in Russia the taxes were higher.

In old, faded pictures Grandpa David does not look kind: his mouth is thin, almost cruel. My memories of him are different, though vague. He bounced me on his knee, cooing ditties about birds and squirrels. But those were rare moments: he worked all the time. He brought his books home. He sat there through long winter evenings, a slight, nervous man in cloth elbow protectors, wearily running the beads on his abacus back and forth and dipping his pen in the inkstand to enter sums in his books. Then he would join us in front of the TV, and, whether we were watching a movie or a concert, he would be snoring within minutes. We ribbed him for this, but my heart is squeezed when I think of him later, after the stroke: feebleminded, semiparalyzed, unable to control his bowels. In a way, his illness afforded him the only vacation of his life.

"Your David has a heart of gold," Grandma's sisters would tell her, but I sensed this was more than an acknowledgment of his goodness; this was also a backhanded compliment. After all, a good Jewish husband does not merely work hard, stay off the sauce, and refrain from chasing women; he also provides well for the family. And Grandpa David brought home barely a fraction of what Uncles Boris and Yuri did.

Whatever tales of his virtues my grandma fed me later, along with her hot, hearty borscht, I am sure he dipped into the till— I don't see how they could have made ends meet otherwise. Had Boris and Yuri emigrated, they would own a chain of supermarkets by now. But Grandpa David was ill suited to his métier. He lived his life in fear of the police, and I don't know which contributed to the stroke more: this fear, or fatigue from working long hours.

A weak man, he should never have gone into a line of work just because his in-laws were in it. Perhaps it is easy for me to judge: like most Soviet people, I have done time standing in line, but I never starved. When he started out, managing a food store may have been the only way to survive. But did he have to spend his whole life torn between the twin spectres of hunger and jail?

I am no economist; my highest financial achievement is balancing a checkbook (and even that I learned in America). But why couldn't Grandpa have owned the place? He would have worked just as hard, and he would have slept in peace like a decent human being, content with working hard and supporting his family—instead of waking up and tossing and turning and dreading the Crimes Against Property cops knocking on the door (the same agents whom Uncle Yuri manipulated so well, sending them away with cases of Armenian brandy and barrels of caviar).

I hope there is a paradise, politics-free, and he is a book-keeper there, happily clicking his calculator. I suspect he still runs himself ragged and dozes off at the sound of the angels' harps. But finally he is rid of the dreaded beast of Financial Accountability: he can enjoy his balanced books in peace.

Recently I was having dinner with my friend Joseph's family, and somehow the conversation shifted to our grandparents. When I mentioned my mother's family, Joseph's mother was appalled. A doctor, like my mother, she comes from Kemerovo, an industrial Siberian city. "We did not have people like that in Kemerovo," she said with conviction. "I'm shocked to learn that Kharkov was such a *nekulturny* place."

Nekulturny ("uncultured") is a grave charge in Russia. It is a catchall for a wide range of misdemeanors, from not knowing half of Pushkin by heart to blowing your nose on the tablecloth.

I burst out laughing. "Who do you think was running Kemerovo stores—saints?"

She shook her head. "We certainly never had people like that among *our* friends."

I had an impression that she was disappointed. Were Joseph and I twelve years old, she would have forbidden him to play with me.

If *Fiddler on the Roof: The Next Generation* were made, it would show the retailers' children going into professions. The girls, including my mother, went to medical school; the boys (her cousins), to engineering school. Then, settling this freshly seized social beachhead, the engineers married other doctors, and the doctors married other engineers. My mother was the only one to break the mold and marry a military man. The uncles cheered. Their retail profits went into mattresses; on paper, my father was wealthier than they. I doubt he made a penny in his life beyond his paycheck, but his uniform was a perfect cover for opening bank accounts and buying jewelry: how could one suspect that an officer with a bemedaled chest was laundering money for Uncle Boris and Uncle Yuri? He must have hated it, but he cowered in the face of family pressure; he was as weak then as he would be later, when dealing with Aunt Natasha.

I have too many cousins to keep track of them all, but the

ones I know, both in Russia and in the US, are all in business and doing well. My father never knew how to make money, only how to earn a living, and he must have passed on this lack of business acumen to me, his only son.

It was late, very late, one night in the dorm, and a lot of whiskey had been drunk, when Sheriff ventured his thoughts on the Jewish Question. "You know, Gurevich, you and other Jews— you really shouldn't bitch about being passed over for jobs."

I waited for the punch line.

He went on: "God gave the Jews the greatest gift of all— the Midas touch. Who knows more about money?"

I saw no room for argument. Rothschilds, etc.

"My point is, why can't you leave itsy-bitsy stuff like languages to poor, dumb Russians?"

It finally dawned on me. "You want to trade? Starting tomorrow, you'll be a Jew and start raking it in over the barrel, and I'll be a Russian and will be allowed to make a quiet, unflashy living in languages."

"Nothing would please me more," he said, without a trace of irony. "If only it were that easy."

Sheriff had grown up in a less-than-*kulturny* environment, which was perhaps one reason we were close: we had both come from the wrong side of the tracks. It's not his fault that the Jews he had grown up with were variations on my mother's family. At the time, I treated this exchange lightly—two tipsy wiseasses trading lines. Later I came to think that he had voiced what I had long suspected: the Russians do not really hate the Jews, they just want them to know their place. They have no objections to our being the moneylenders. (At the same time, a financially successful Jew is resented no more than his gentile counterpart—a mind-set that owes more to seventy years of collectivism-forced poverty than to anti-Semitism.)

Even Solzhenitsyn, the greatest Russian writer of the twentieth century, shows some ambivalence on the subject in *The Gulag Archipelago*. On the one hand, he proclaims profound sympathy for Zionists, which seems to jibe nicely with his quasi-fundamentalist religious views. On the other hand, when he discusses the widespread use of the death penalty in the thirties, he drops rather patronizingly, "Primordial commerce, the bread-and-butter pastime of the Jew, has also become worthy of the death penalty."

Just like I don't need a famous rabbi for my grandfather Semyon's father or a Russian count for my grandmother Musya's father, I don't need famous intellectuals for great-uncles. I am neither proud nor ashamed of my sometimes crooked shopkeeper relatives: they are what they are. I suppose that, with their ethnically predictable business acumen, they fit Sheriff's definition of "good" Jews. But I don't consider myself a "bad" Jew, either. "Difficult," perhaps.

Two

Micky caused me a lot of trouble, yet it was he, and no one else, who, in my third year of college, got me my first free-lance job: translating letters for the Soviet Women's Committee. I was nervous and tremendously proud: I would be translating important foreign documents for an important government body. On top of that, I would be earning money, and both my father and his wife could go to hell with their suggestions on how I should spend it. Americans, many of whom grow up babysitting and delivering newspapers, may find this amusing, coming from a nineteen-year-old. But in Russia this was nothing to sneer at: grandmas babysit, the post office delivers newspapers, seasonal and part-time jobs are hard to come by, and most young people do not start earning money until they graduate from college. It did not bother me that the job paid peanuts: I was too young to draw the logical connection between the importance of a job and its rate of pay.

As I stood in the hall waiting for Tanya, the staff translator, to return to her desk, I was nervous. I was the only man (more like a boy) amid armies of women: they were much older and seemed quite business-like as they darted through the hall with official-looking files in their hands. They ignored me, maybe less because of my gender than of my lowly status as a free-lance translator. I was just a needy kid who came by a couple of times a week to do the work that the staff had neither time nor desire to do: kind of a glorified janitor.

I did not know what to make of my first letters. They were exotic enough, sent from places like India and Chad, but they hardly seemed important. Their writers described at great length their poverty (which a Syzraner like myself did not find convincing) and their pride in Soviet women's progress. I got lost in their convoluted, florid paeans to Soviet womanhood until they asked for a free subscription to *The Soviet Woman*, the glossy illustrated monthly published by the Committee. As I banged out the translations on a decrepit rented manual, I thought that I would have to spend a lifetime in India to understand the authors—all of whom were men.

Tanya laughed when I shared my misgivings with her. "This is crank mail. Wait till I go on maternity leave. You'll have to do serious stuff."

She meant the Committee's correspondence with its foreign counterparts, like the Women's International League for Peace and Freedom. The Committee is one of the "nongovernmental" "public" organizations that the Soviets love to parade abroad. Its executives fly around the world, from seminar to panel to conference, fighting for peace and breathlessly reporting on the achievements of the Soviet Woman. Their Western counterparts love receiving them, and the Committee execs love inviting their counterparts to Russia. In their letters they recalled what great fun they had had in London/Tokyo/Nairobi and the important resolutions they had adopted there for world peace and the anti-imperialist struggle; now it was time to organize another conference, to appoint a steering committee, and to draft more resolutions . . . Moscow has plenty of places like this, and later

I worked for many of them, both translating mail and working with delegations.

My contribution to the Committee's valiant struggle for world peace and women's rights abroad reached its apogee with the arrival of a letter signed "Angela Davis." I was excited: at the time, Ms. Davis and President Nixon were the two best-known Americans in Russia. It was a rare political rally that did not adopt a resolution to demand Comrade Davis's release.

I decided not to read it in haste: I had a party to go to, which always took precedence over anything that had to do with the Party. Early the next morning the phone rang. It was one of the Committee's executives. Did I have the letter? "Yes," I said, "I was just going to—" She sighed relief. Clearly, I had not been meant to handle it, and for a moment they thought it had gotten lost. "Bring it over as soon as you can," she said.

The letter was a letdown. Ms. Davis was merely thanking the Soviet comrades for their unflagging solidarity in the anti-imperialist struggle and asking that they send her some books with statistics. I had expected her to ask for something more daring, like a hundred Kalashnikovs for the Black Panthers. I was doubly disappointed since it was written in the same boring, wooden language as Party resolutions. Was this the same woman who had bought weapons for a courtroom rescue? Perhaps all Party minds think alike. (Later I could not forgive myself for not ironing the letter: who knows what messages in secret ink might have shown up? Too bad that by then I had left spy thrillers for Philip Roth novels.) Still, I was amused. Imagine Sharansky writing from his camp to, say, the Heritage Foundation and requesting statistics.

The next day, the letter made it to *Pravda*'s front page, bumping aside the usual accounts of record-breaking crops. "In her letter Comrade Davis expressed . . ." I was not amused; my translation was quoted without attribution. But suing *Pravda* was not fashionable in my time.

In the first of many forms that we signed at InYaz we pledged not to take employment involving contact with foreigners without the school's approval. This sounded a bit inane—we had neither skills nor connections for such jobs—and we interpreted it to mean *any* contact with foreigners (perhaps this was the intended effect). Later seniors like me, whom the school had not recommended for these jobs anyway, grew bold enough to ignore the pledge. In Russia the spirit of the law lives in its loopholes.

I started working as an interpreter in my final year. The woman at Sputnik, a low-budget version of Intourist, was not happy with my last name—but other Dutch interpreters in Moscow were too well heeled to take such lowly assignments.

On my first day I was shaky: I had never spoken to a Dutch native before. A week later I was going a mile a minute. But language was only part of the experience.

I had seen and talked to Westerners before, but now I was spending whole days with them—two weeks at a time. Moreover, they were only slightly older than I. First off, I was struck by their appearance. I realized that what was a prestige item of clothing in Russia did not count for much in Holland. Yet *how* they wore it: they pulled on their denims in a totally unselfconscious way, without any regard for how they looked—their looks did not seem to matter to them, period. And how they acted: they did not think twice about sitting on the floor, putting up their feet on whatever was in sight, smoking wherever they pleased; even their body language was different—relaxed, jaunty, seemingly unencumbered by social convention.

Soviets interpreted this simply as bad manners, but I saw it differently: to me, they seemed to behave as though no one had ever told them what to do. It was not a pose; they were completely *natural*. Clearly, unmistakably, they were from another planet, another world, where Kizilov and other Secretaries did not exist—or, at least, held no sway. I do not mean to equate bad manners with freedom. But good manners should stem from free choice; in Russia I thought of them as another aspect of oppression.

My tourists were bricklayers, students, nurses—it was obviously no big deal for them to pack up and go to Russia for two weeks. And, of course, they had already been all over Europe, many of them even to America. The world they described was different from the one seen by the InYaz go-getters: some knew the Jeu de Paume, and all knew bars and rock clubs and nude beaches and places to score dope. Listening to them, I felt I might as well have never left Syzran; I was a medieval apprentice sitting on the stoop near the harbor in Genoa or Hamburg and listening to brave seamen who had sailed all over the big, exotic world. And there was nothing in my current circumstances to suggest even remotely that I would ever be like them.

I enjoyed being with my tourists, and I mixed with them effortlessly. With them I could maintain the illusion of oneness with them, of sharing their laissez-faire attitude. Then they left, and I was—well, back to reality.

I quickly progressed beyond the nickel-and-dime Sputnik tours and started working at more respectable places, using both Dutch and English. No longer a mere tour guide, I was in charge of delegations, specialized groups that visited Russia through outfits like the World Peace Committee, the Committee of Afro-Asian Solidarity, or the Committee of Youth Organizations. In practical terms this meant that I seldom had to take my charges to the same museums over and over again (on the road, local guides took over); I interpreted at rallies and receptions and was responsible for tickets, hotels, meals: I was in charge, period.

The pay was ridiculously low, but my needs were modest, and my expenses were covered generously. I enjoyed traveling in style, seeing new places, meeting new people. I would have been happy to do it full-time. But there was a problem. The usual one.

I got along well with the officials who hired me for temporary assignments. They valued me as a skilled, responsible specialist. Some even hinted that they would be happy to hire me full-time. But we both knew very well that this was impossible. Applicants for full-time jobs are vetted by Personnel, and the Chief of Personnel is always a retired KGB officer who would rather defect than hire a Jew.

On the other hand, I could not free-lance full-time. The Soviet system is dead set against it. Free-lancing means you are not tied to any given "collective," that the State's control over you is drastically reduced. It works simply: if you don't have a stamp from a permanent job in your passport, you are a "parasite" and can be exiled. (This was Joseph Brodsky's corpus delicti. Had his poetry been conventional and filled with praise for the Party, he would have qualified for membership in the Writers' Union and, with the proper stamp in his passport, been freed from the necessity of a job.)

How do you get a job in Russia? Certainly, not through the want ads. You get it the same way you get anything: through a friend who asks a friend who asks a friend. Thus, upon graduation I was steered to an opening in the Scientific Information Section at the Coal Industry Research Institute, where I was to sit from nine to five and diligently translate articles about collieries and strip-mining methods.

At the time—1973—the Coal Institute was scattered among half a dozen different places in Moscow. Mine was a stone's throw from the Kremlin, a large room in a warren of offices in a refurbished wooden warehouse that seemed to go back to pre-Napoleonic Moscow (the emperor had allegedly burned the city in 1812). With its bleak light and a dozen desks set close to one another (the Party had not invented partitions yet), the place had a Dickensian feel. There was another section in the room that had something to do with designing computer centers— never mind that hardly anyone there had ever seen a computer.

Cautiously I came in for a few weeks, looking for the loopholes, the weak spots in the routine. Russian office ways are not unlike American ones, except that the Russians work about a tenth as much. The men left their desks for breaks with the kind of promptness warranted by American unions, except that in Russia they did so every half hour. The official pretext was stepping outside for a smoke (the place was too much of a firetrap to risk it indoors). The women, who made up the majority, went shopping (the only smoker among them had it both ways). They loved the office's proximity to all the major stores. One of them would be dispatched to GUM, the Macy's of Moscow, first thing in the morning, to take a place in the most promising line, for Italian blouses or Czech teapots. To observe the amenities in front of the Section Chief, they developed a complicated coded-message system whereby the one already in line called for another to come to relieve her, or to be dispatched to yet another department of GUM, to catch German linens. In the afternoon they drank tea, lovingly regarded the morning's trophies, and traded stories of warfare in the department store lines.

Our Section Chief, Nikolai Ivanovich, was the true Job of the office. A thin, balding man, he wore dark-green suits and would not sit down at his desk without putting on black cloth elbow protectors—just like my grandfather David. Nikolai Ivanovich had a year to go before retirement and yearned for peace, which the women thwarted with their shopping, absenteeism, and constant chatting (men were more discreet, restricting their talk of soccer to smoke breaks). He did not expect anybody to do much—just to sit there from nine to five.

In an unrequited display of male solidarity, he expected me to be his right-hand man in curbing the women's permanent state of revolt. But I had different plans. Whenever an article arrived for translation, I instantly signed out: "Gone to the library."

"Why can't you do it here?" Nikolai Ivanovich asked sorrowfully.

"We don't have the right dictionary."

"Why can't you order this dictionary?"

"Because it's a foreign dictionary. Who will pay?"

He shook his head in the utmost distress. "I don't know why you need a foreign dictionary."

"Because this is a very difficult article."

"I don't know, I don't know . . ." His expression was one of complete misery. "How long will it take you to do it?"

"*Weeks*, Nikolai Ivanovich. This is really very difficult."

I could understand his frustration. How could he supervise

me if I was always "in the library"? I could not be counted on for meetings, for May Day preparations—for anything. This violated every precept of the Soviet bureaucracy he lived by.

I signed out and was on my way across the street to the Rossiya Hotel to join another delegation.

Three

Dealing with tourists was not difficult. Especially with the Dutch and the Belgians (Flemish is similar to Dutch, and I had taught myself some French for emergencies). They expected a horsecart and a guide who spoke third-grade German, and here I was, with my reasonably slangy Dutch, putting them aboard an air-conditioned bus. They could not have been more grateful; for me, it was smooth sailing. They depended on me, and I repaid their trust. If the food was inedible, or the room unheated, I did not play the flag-waving, hard-ass patriot (as some other interpreters did) by telling them how awful things had been before the Revolution, how the Nazis had raped the land, and how great our Bolshoi Ballet and space program were. I went to the hotel manager. Do you realize how important this delegation is? Do you want me to pick up the phone and call Comrade X at the local Komsomol Committee? or Comrade Y in *Moscow*? This is the only approach that works in Russia. There is no point in telling a Volgograd hotel manager that he cannot put eight grown-ups in one room without a sink. Even my dedicated Socialists were aghast: "You know, in Holland this would be a sanitary violation."

Being stuck between two worlds had a familiar feel to me. It was made easier by the fact that my foreigners were not exactly followers of William F. Buckley, Jr. Most trips were sponsored either by Western leftist organizations or by the Soviet hosts (the line often blurred). All came with a built-in predisposition toward the USSR, sanitary conditions notwithstanding. They wanted to believe—and I played along.

I escorted group after group from town to town, from school to factory to collective farm to Young Pioneer camp to peace rally. Local cadre, stiff in their bulky suits, went on breathlessly about their dedicated labor for Socialism, about Edenic conditions for workers, about endless benefits for women. Guests, sweating in overheated rooms, nodded, smiled politely, took notes, clicked cameras, thanked for the souvenirs. If a less-than-diplomatic question was asked, the host smiled widely, just as politicians do everywhere: "I'm really glad you asked that . . ." And go on about how the union worked *together* with the administration to protect the workers' rights.

My language skills were never challenged, but at times my Marxist-trained mind quickly provided more ambiguous phrasing, or a little extra nuance to make things more palatable for the visitors. Jacques, a retired steelworker from Charleroi, arrived laden with bagfuls of film, tapes, and notepads to record every moment of the trip. A reputed Stalinist, he was much derided by the rest of the group. We were visiting a farmers' rest home outside Irkutsk, in Siberia. Jacques, taping away as usual, found an old crone who mistook him for a Soviet Mike Wallace. She hogged the mike and piled up complaints about their farm chairman, a crook and a lush, who would not have a roof fixed without a bribe. When Jacques asked, beaming, if she would ever consider living in a capitalist country, her eager "*Da*" (she'd go anyplace from that damn farm, she said) was hard to translate as the "*Non*" he yearned for. The local French-speaking escort, a local college teenager, looked terrified: *What will the Moscow comrade do?* Jacques's blue eyes watered, and his calloused, arthritic hands shook with enthusiasm. I felt sorry for him—and for myself, too, if the teenager was going to include this in her own report. "Yes," I said sadly, "yes, I would certainly *visit* your country—*just for a vacation.*"

What's the big deal? An old lady in a dinky rest home and an old Belgian Stalinist . . . in the "big picture," *who cares?* A part of me felt that my translation was terribly clever, but another part knew that ideology and professionalism do not mix, and I had just made an unprofessional choice. So I added, off the wall, a touch of black humor to suppress the nausea rising in my stomach: "Just to see how your proletariat fights for its rights." The local escort giggled approvingly. Jacques was delighted: he shook the old woman's hand for a long time and gave her two packs of Wrigley's. As for me, the Party never knew what an imaginative hack it was missing.

Before I break my arm patting myself on the back: had my employers expected anything less? I was one of them, wasn't I? When I brought a group back to Moscow for a chat at the Committee of Youth Organizations headquarters on Khmelnitsky Street, the executive assigned for the chat took me aside. "What kind of group you got here?" he asked. "*Nashi?*" ("Ours"?) (He was too lazy, or hung over, to look at the schedule.) "Ours" meant Communists; the rest were Socialists and . . . others. The executive had different speeches for the two types. The Communists were told, without further ado, that the Committee was, in fact, the cover for the Komsomol Central Committee's International Section. As far as the "others" were concerned, it represented a broad front of Soviet public organizations, including ones without political affiliation. He said it with a straight face, and I interpreted with an even straighter one.

"Ideological" museums were even more nauseating. I visited Lenin's Mausoleum once. As VIPs, we were smuggled ahead of the long line to see a waxy yellow dummy in the basement. One can only pity a country where, in the twentieth century, political ends are achieved through such blatant superstition and humbuggery. It is as if Madame Tussaud's were to open a branch on the Promenade in DC and stuff it with waxworks of Washington and the Founding Fathers.

I used every pretext to get out of visiting the cathedrals of Communism: the Lenin Museum and the Revolution Museum in Moscow, Lenin's apartment museum in Leningrad—to me, they were the ghosts of Marxist exams past. The guides were junior Party members, who, I think, were deranged or else were failed actors: they would point at an ordinary-looking cot and declare in a dramatic voice, "Lenin slept here." I have been told that America has its share of patriotic shrines, but I have avoided them. I have been inoculated against admiring used furniture.

I have unwittingly wandered into only two places in the West that reminded me of Soviet museums. One was the Mormon Cathedral in Salt Lake City, whose huge spaces are generously filled with pious tableaux from the Lives of the Founders (but, at least, this faith calls itself a faith, and nothing else). The other was the museum at the Alcazar of Toledo, Spain, dedicated to Franco's glorious defenders of the fortress. In Democratic Spain it had few visitors and the same air of religious piety.

In a sense, my "consciousness-raising" was more effective because I was dealing with people sympathetic to Socialism, rather than with Americans, for example. In tourist areas I spent enough time around Americans to see that the facilities offered them never measured up to what they were used to. My rational side realized that this was a normal reaction for people who came from the wealthiest country in the world. But the Young Pioneer hiding in me was still firing off choked salutes, and the little monster was quick to take umbrage at the most innocent remark—for example, that it was impossible to get eggs at breakfast any way but sunny side up. What about Syzran, where eggs at the store are sold out by noon?

My "lefties" were tolerant, and their reticence affected me more than the Americans' outspokenness. Once, our flight out of Novosibirsk was delayed. Late at night we made our way through the airport; the cafeteria was closed, chairs were few, and the multitude of stranded, long-suffering Soviet passengers were camping on the floor with bags and suitcases under their heads. We marched to the elegantly appointed—and deserted—VIP lounge to be served espresso by a sleepy bartender, who had been awakened just to serve us. This seemed normal to me, who had grown up in a society where privilege is seldom questioned, just as it would seem normal to an American executive to march upstairs to the first-class lounge or the airline club. My Socialists did not say anything, but I sensed their discomfort—they were workers and nurses, not CEOs. Yet they, too, said nothing, lest they seem ungrateful. After a while they picked up the blankets they had been given and went to sleep on the long, soft couches. The local Komsomol liaison for the visit sighed with relief and gave me a wink. No need to explain anything; no need to complicate the reports.

But I had a hard time going to sleep. I realized that my job was the only reason I was sitting in a comfortable armchair instead of lying on the floor downstairs, using my bag for a pillow. I could not come up with any satisfactory rationalization: what was it about my job that gave me this privilege? I did not know yet that I was experiencing a faint, tentative pang of what some people call liberal guilt.

On another occasion, in Leningrad, I dropped my group off at the ballet and asked the driver to take me to a friend's place on

Vasilyevsky Island. It was past midnight when I decided to go back. I flagged a cab and asked him to take me to the Smolny Hotel, where we were staying.

"No such place," he said.

"It's right near Smolny," I said patiently. "You must have heard of *that*." The Smolny Institute is a landmark: it housed the Bolshevik headquarters during the Revolution.

"I've been driving a cab for seven years," he said. "There *is* a Smolny. There is *no* Smolny Hotel."

"Fine," I said. "Take me to Smolny. I'll take it from there." I was not drunk enough to argue with a cab driver.

We drove around Smolny Square a few times, and I started getting a funny feeling in my stomach: there was no sign of a hotel. It had been dusk when we arrived; I had gotten into the car straight from the lobby and did not know where *exactly* the hotel was. Naïvely I had thought there would be a large sign—now, cringing at the amount on the meter, I got out. I don't know how long I circled the area, with the snowstorm whipping my face and my shoes sinking in the fresh snow. I was not that drunk. Was I suffering from amnesia? Was it all a dream? Finally I saw a familiar doorway. There was no sign—nothing. The plainclothesman at the door gave me a long look but kept silent.

The rooms at the Smolny were decent by Soviet standards; the downstairs bar featured White Horse and Martel, and Sinatra crooning on a Grundig stereo. One of my tourists was so impressed that he asked me how he could make a reservation the following year.

"Can't do that," I said, still angry about my first night. "It's a Party hotel. Didn't you notice there's not even a sign outside?" Like myself, they had been marched into the bus directly from the lobby. "Unless you know about it, this hotel doesn't exist."

I don't think he understood; but the look in his eyes told

me that there was something totally, irrevocably wrong about this situation.

By now I realize that there's nothing inherently Soviet about privilege: there's a club named Castel on a quiet street off Saint-Germain-des-Prés in Paris, and half a dozen places in New York where Cro-Magnon bouncers keep away noncelebs whose manner of dress doesn't sink to the club's standards. Whether you like it or not, whether you frequent these places or not, you might as well admit that vanity is a part of human nature, and if it needs outlets, they might as well be out in the open. Call it glasnost.

It would be hypocritical to say that every day brought such pangs of guilt as the one I had felt at the airport. Nothing in my background prepared me for guilt: my past was overwhelmingly modest, and, as a Soviet, I was not conditioned to feel sorry for the less fortunate. From my high-school days in Syzran to my college days in Moscow I had accepted the Orwellian notion that some people would always be more equal than others. I was not as obsessed with privilege as my fellow InYaz students were, but I had no qualms about accepting it when it fell into my lap. I traveled in style, wore Western clothes, smoked Marlboros, hung out till the wee hours in foreign-currency bars. From the InYaz minitrials I got the wheres, whats, and hows of gift-taking down to a science. In that sense, it was a typically Soviet job, attractive less for its pay than for its fringe benefits. I was no different from my mother, who got sausage under the counter from her patients. Yet I felt more and more that it was unfair to label these meager economical advantages as "privilege." This may sound like a crude rationalization, but I was not really getting anything beyond the budget of an ordinary frugal Western tourist.

I knew that even those of my tourists who paid their own way were not millionaires or movie stars but ordinary people with ordinary jobs. It was not just a matter of material goods: I knew Americans had more available to them. A friend of mine, whose wife was a clerk at the US embassy, had the rare privilege of ordering American goods once a year, and he showed me her Sears catalogue. The tourists carried a certain air with them, and from their attitudes and casual remarks I was gaining a new perspective on my own society.

Among friends I joked that I was working on Potemkin Villages and should join the Architects' Union. The joke left a bitter taste in my mouth: to some degree I still wanted to be patriotic, but I felt that to all foreigners, regardless of politics, Russia was one big Syzran. I was living in a third-rate country that pretended it was first-rate, and I was helping to perpetuate the lie.

Once, when I was taking a group of tourists around the Moscow subway, with its overblown Stalinist décor, a high-school teacher from Amsterdam said sadly, pointing at orna-mental tiles and mosaics, "All this was done in the thirties? While people were starving to death in the Ukraine?"

Of course, I knew of the famine caused by collectivization; I found the subway décor garish and wasteful, especially its muscle-bulging sculptures; but it had never before occurred to me to connect the dots. That remark brought home to me the alienation of a Soviet citizen: you never think of public funds as being, in part, your own.

To someone who studied history by Soviet textbooks, this was a minirevelation. Such remarks "raised my consciousness," but they also imbued me with a sense of freedom—not at official functions, not at museums; just while riding on the bus or sitting in a bar with my Westerners. It was an illusion, but I felt almost like one of them, and it seemed natural, not like a privilege at all. If it actually was one, then the problem was not with them or with me. The problem was with the system.

Seeing a group off at the airport was the hardest part. Wherever they were going, I could not go. Nor could I go straight home, no matter how tired I was. There was no hard-liquor bar for rubles at the airport, so I installed myself in the cafeteria, poured myself shot after shot of whiskey (a going-away present)—and listened to the announcer: "Alitalia flight 111 to Rome boarding . . . KLM flight 222 to Amsterdam . . . Swissair flight 333 . . ." It sounded like Tchaikovsky, Prokofiev, Mozart. I pictured what my new friends would be doing after they landed: that's all they had talked about on the way to the airport. One missed rijsttafel, another was going to see The Who playing at Vondel Park, a third was going to Paris—all outside my reach. Things that sounded so *normal* for a modern society.

I felt little envy looking at Soviets returning from their business trips, huffing and puffing their enormous suitcases and cardboard boxes through customs. They had gone west to shop; and shopping, to me, was not living.

Later I became friendly with some people who had traveled abroad. They told stories of humiliation wrought by the multiple Party committees required to approve their visas. For us who could not travel, it was hard to empathize with the pain that gnawed at their exhilaration in Paris when they had to pinch *centimes* and forgo the Jeu de Paume in order to buy a pair of jeans for the Party boss who had made their trip possible. Or with the trauma they experienced on returning from the colorful, prosperous West to the bleak Socialist reality.

They mentioned these things in passing, shrugging—par for the course, what do you expect? A week in Paris or Munich, who is to complain? I must have felt *some* envy. But I cannot recall any; instead, I remember a feeling of impotent frustration: it seemed to me that they had been doubly humiliated, first by Party mandarins, then by Western store windows.

Soviets visiting America nowadays are sneeringly called vacuum cleaners for the insatiable way they suck in consumer goods. The older generation is hit especially hard: they imbibed the notion that they live in a superpower, but the Bolshoi's fame and the tales of space superiority are poor comfort at the sight of an American shopping mall. I feel sorry for my Moscow friends who, with one day left in New York, choose to rush to Orchard Street, rather than to MOMA. They need to buy VCRs, to resell them later and so pay back the huge amounts of money they borrowed for their airfare (as I write this, Aeroflot tickets sell on the black market for three times their nominal value). They have mile-long shopping lists, for all hell will break loose if an Uncle Misha does not get his Casio watch.

When I explain these things to Americans, they nod absently; they believe me, but it is hard for them to realize the enormity of the Soviet economic crisis that has reduced respected professors of Latin to chachke hunters. Not to oversimplify, one can cite low Soviet rents (for those lucky enough to have apartments), free medical care (if you know the doctor), free schooling (poisoned by indoctrination). My Moscow friends are doing well by Soviet standards, but in New York they feel so poor; it is hard not to be spellbound by the shiny façade of capitalism. As for museums—some call back to say, "Damn Uncle Misha. I should have gone to MOMA."

Four

Sipping Scotch in the airport cafeteria, sometimes at seven in the morning, was never the end of it. Afterward I would call up a friend or two and drink myself blind, to kill the frustration of having to stay and to blow away the stress. For the previous two weeks I had not simply been strutting in my Levi's and hanging out in Intourist bars as if I were going back to Amsterdam. The fun had an underside: rarely was I free to say what *I* thought. I was a bona fide impostor.

This had to do not just with the Party men and the KGB, who were never far away, but with the foreigners themselves as well. I could not expect them, no matter how perceptive, to be completely attuned to our reality. I had only to recall my dorm friend Raf and his British girlfriend. Also, rumors persisted of KGB plants in the groups, whose job it was to weed out loose-mouthed interpreters. The madness of walking a tightrope did not end with graduation from school; it went on, except now I was a more experienced walker.

I tried not to give in to paranoia. But life was becoming just like school, where I'd had to constantly gauge the level of trust I could grant my schoolmates, without fully distrusting everybody. People who did the latter probably went far in life, but I would not trade psyches with them for one moment.

Most of my direct encounters with the KGB took place in

the beginning, when I briefly worked for Intourist. I was on my first group, at a hotel on the outskirts of Moscow, waiting for the bus, which was late as usual. A short, shabby-looking man came up to ask if I was the guide. "You the driver?" I yelled. "Let's get going!"

He held up a red-covered ID. "I work at the hotel," he muttered, "so if you could help me—"

I froze. Yelling at a KGB officer on my first day. Wrong foot. I was bailed out by my fellow guide (large groups require two), who had been with Intourist for years and was not easily intimidated. "The bus is here," she said, ignoring him. "Let's go."

The man eyed me meekly, expecting support. She turned to face him. She was at least a foot taller, wearing high-heeled boots and an aggressive-looking, expensive leather coat. She looked like she could beat him up.

"I don't have time for you," she spat out. "I'm behind schedule. Any questions, you can call the main office."

On the way to the bus she said to me quietly, "Don't waste time on bums. He wants you to do his job for him so he can go have his morning shot-and-beer. Did you see his nose?"

He did have a red, veiny nose that bespoke a long life of hitting the bottle.

"We report on the Sixth Floor; that's enough," she said.

At the Intourist offices the Sixth Floor was where the guides filed daily reports on their groups. The choice was all yours. You could write, "Everything went well. One suitcase got lost in Kiev." But if you wanted to rise through the Intourist ranks and accompany Soviet tour groups abroad, you filed long, tedious sagas about who had said what on the bus.

On my last day I took a Dutch group to the Kremlin, subbing

for another guide. I was back in the office, ready to leave, when an irate call came from the Sixth Floor: Come right away.

The man was boiling. "Where's your report?"

"But I only did one excursion."

"It doesn't matter. It's equivalent to a full day."

I picked up my notebook (just like special training at school) and headed for a vacant desk. The floor was a hive of cell-like rooms, with desks placed far apart. The guides were scribbling away and gluing their reports to group lists (the Party had not invented staplers yet). I wrote, "No incidents."

"That was quick." He frowned. "You mean, nothing happened? Nothing at all?"

"I showed 'em the churches. They loved 'em. Everybody knows that Russian folk art is the best in the world."

"Did they say anything else? Were you with them at all times?"

What is it with this guy?, I wondered. "They were all well disposed toward the USSR. One woman even cried at the Tomb of the Unknown Soldier. She remembered how she hid an escaped Russian prisoner of war in '44."

This was a terrible faux pas.

"WHAT IS HER NAME?"

"Look, it wasn't my group, I was with them for only three hours, do you expect me to know all thirty names . . . ?"

"I don't care about thirty. I want that woman's name!" He pushed the group list toward me. "See if you can find it."

I stared at the list blankly and shook my head. "If I had known . . . maybe next time . . ."

He glanced at some other papers. "This is your last day." Then he decided to shift gears. "Well, I can understand that. There are a few soccer games tonight. Who's your team?"

"Central Army Club." Once an Army brat, always an Army brat.

"Mine, too!" He pushed a pack of cigarettes toward me and gave me a half hour's worth of fatherly advice. You want to come back and work for us again? Then you have to understand what we're all about. You're a smart guy, not like those bimbos (I never heard a KGB man describe women otherwise). Take this woman who hid a Russian. We want to get in touch with her, invite her back, show her that we appreciate what she did then—we want to get her *involved*—we need people like her.

I kept nodding as cold sweat ran down my back and various thriller-like scripts spun in my head. God only knew what any of this meant, but these people did not deal in charity. It was clear that the woman's good deed would not have gone unpunished—if I had come up with her name. Mentioning the incident was incredibly dumb. I had a lot to learn.

We parted best buddies. I stood for a few minutes outside, catching my breath. I could not believe I had come this close, through my stupidity, to doing something I would have regretted all my life. I had almost *collaborated*.

I did not care if it meant missing an all-summer-long first-class cruise on the Black Sea—I did not have it in me to return to the Sixth Floor. I never worked for Intourist again.

(In January 1990 I read a letter to the editor in *The Moscow News*. A frustrated guide was complaining about the need to compile reports on his tourists. Glasnost and all, things stand still at Intourist . . .)

After that my contacts with the KGB were infrequent. Specialized "delegations," as opposed to general tourist groups, are screened in advance, and, as long as they did not hand out fliers in Red Square to protest the invasion of Czechoslovakia, I was seldom bothered.

I did not think much of the KGB's efficiency. The agents assigned to monitor foreigners were unimpressive at best; the ones I met were like the hotel cop, probably the lowest on the totem pole. They were clerks at heart: the forms should be filled out, the case closed. Once you realized this, they were not hard to deal with; on top of that, they were as lazy and incompetent as any other Soviet bureaucrats. What they were best at was exploiting their omnipotent public image.

They could play "good cop" and tell you how "we depend on each other." I realized soon that it was a bluff: they depended on *you* to do their job properly. They would come ask *you* to provide them with information on the group. The rest, exactly as on the Sixth Floor, was up to you. I am sure other interpreters felt the same way I did, but it would have been highly foolish to even touch on the subject with them.

I was always amused by Westerners' overreaction to the KGB. Those who come to Russia to see the churches need not be paranoid. Whatever you say on the bus, the State's need for your dollars will outweigh your most scathing comments. Of course, if you intend to go beyond your itinerary, to visit a dissident, you have every reason to expect attention. I hear this has changed under Gorbachev, but I would be wary. Lack of harassment does not mean lack of surveillance, and the files must be kept in order: you never know when you'll need them. Besides, the agents must have something to do—what other marketable skills do they have?

———

Drinking did not start at the airport, nor was it confined to bars. It was a part of the job. When receiving guests, Soviets put out as much booze as the table will hold. One could be positive and call this tradition a sincere form of hospitality. With foreigners, it is also a way of putting up a front: reality dims and acquires a rosy glow with each successive toast.

Siberia was especially rough: our hosts started off with vodka at breakfast and went on late into the night. They were used to getting visitors drunk, whether the latter came from Moscow or Amsterdam. "Until you get smashed with us, you won't understand Siberia," they would wink. The trip comes back to me vaguely: surely, there were moments as vivid as the night in the VIP lounge of the Novosibirsk airport or the farmers' rest home, but what stays with me is the memory of vodka and cognac and awful red wine and more vodka. After a couple of speeches the words became automatic: "friendship long live heroic people to Communism hurrah . . ." It is a chant, a liturgy; there are no surprises. You slur a little, but no one seems to care.

Siberians are used to tipsy orators. Keeping up with the locals is impossible: "I'll pass on this one—I'm working here—" "Work? You ever operated a Kraz? [A Soviet-made truck, reputed to be the largest in the world.] *That's* work! C'mon, have a glass, look at 'em falling off—" Brave Rotterdam dockers tried to keep up, out of international solidarity and male pride, and collapsed under the table one after another. The hosts winked: thin foreign blood. I felt like a teetotaler.

In the past some guides had had it worse. Denisenko, one of our college instructors, worked in the late forties with a Canadian Communist delegation. Come breakfast, vodka was on the table, and toasts to the Great Teacher Stalin came one after another. He whispered to the Party man in charge that he couldn't possibly drink vodka at seven in the morning *and* then interpret for a full day. Think again, he was told—did he realize whose health he was refusing to drink to?

At any given point, on or off the job, it was easier to drink than to abstain. I did not get drunk often and was considered a moderate. At InYaz the boys started at ten, when the beer stand opened, then pooled their change to buy a bottle of port when the liquor store opened at eleven. At last they were sufficiently warmed up and ready to get serious and buy a "whitehead", i.e. vodka.

I don't think there was a day in my last few years in Russia when I did not have something to drink, either a few beers in a pub or a bottle of Mukuzani red or a couple of shots of cognac at a bar. My dissatisfaction was mounting: delegation jobs were good for a spree, but after they were gone, I felt even worse. My Coal Institute job was a laugh, as the Section Chief kept devising ways to tie me to my desk, and I kept coming up with ways to get free. At home there was no relief, either.

When there were just the two of us, we were able to keep my mother-in-law at bay. But then Natasha got pregnant; the doctor advised against abortion. We shrugged: *Hell, let's have a baby.* In retrospect, our flippancy in the face of the decision seems inexplicable. I was twenty-two; Natasha, twenty-one. When the boy, whom we named Ilya, finally arrived, we simply had no idea what to do with him. As I took this little bundle of blankets from Natasha at the hospital door and carried it to the cab on the icy path, I might as well have been holding a bomb: all I could think was, What if I drop it? Natasha was not much better. We were not ready, emotionally or financially.

We lived in one large room in a communal apartment, sharing the bathroom and the kitchen with four other families. We had no complaints: the central location, on Gorky Street, was hard to beat. Now, suddenly, there were three of us, but we still could not apply for a separate apartment, as we fit into the nine-square-meter-per-person requirement.

Natasha had to quit her job and take a year off from school; she was frustrated about this and everything else. I was frustrated about my jobs and everything else. I washed diapers by hand in the communal sink (there were no Pampers in Russia, and no diaper services) and pushed the carriage on long walks along Pushkin Boulevard. Natasha did ten times as much. But none of this was enough. We were not holding up well.

We could not possibly surrender this fragile six-month lump of life to day-care, which in Russia meant one nurse for twenty babies. One of our communal neighbors was a blue-collar couple, whose kid had attended day-care since he was two weeks old. He looked thin, pale, and undernourished, with a constant expression of fear on his face. Whether this was because his father belted him at every opportunity or because he had spent six years in the day-care system, we did not know—and we did not want to find out with Ilya.

Natasha's mother was married to a famous Soviet author; she lived in a large Writers' Union co-op, summered at her dacha in Peredelkino, and had money to burn. All we could do was accept her generous assistance with the errands and the baby-sitting. It was a classic Trojan horse.

"You'll never have any money, he's no breadwinner, he'll never get a decent job, why should they give one to a Jew with his politics [I must have made a casual remark or two, which was all she needed to make a federal case], you'll be breaking your back all your life, look at yourself, look what he's done to you!!!" Natasha looked in the mirror, and, yes, she was a shadow of her former self. Her resistance was crumbling. Me, whenever I came home and saw her mother there, I turned around. I should have put up a fight. But if I had pushed her away, where would that have left us?

Money was not as big an issue as my mother-in-law would have had us believe. I gave private lessons and hustled like a maniac for translation jobs, typing late into the night behind a partition so as not to wake the baby. We were not starving. But that also meant I had to leave the house, whether to work with a group or to put in a few hours at the Coal Institute or to drop off a translation or to see a student (no more casual moviegoing). Natasha had to bear most of the daily ordeals that Soviet life is famous for: shopping (standing in lines), cooking (from scratch), and cleaning (by hand). Before, we had struggled through them cheerfully; now they took on gigantic proportions. In a sense, my mother-in-law was right: I was never going to make *big* money—and only that could get us a big apartment and a live-in maid. This may sound like a tall order, but otherwise the services we needed were simply not available, were plainly unheard of: who in Russia would even consider a baby-sitter? Both Natasha and I (till I was four) had been brought up by our respective grandmothers. The grandmother taking care of her grandchildren is an institution just as Russian as vodka and borscht; it was what everybody did. Bringing in *my* mother was impossible: she worked herself and also had my teenage sister to take care of. We were trapped.

As we sat in our previously huge, now shrunken room, inhaling the rancid odors of stewed cabbage from the garbage bin in the back, we felt that the baby was the happiest creature in the place. He was blissfully unaware of our misery. Watching him smile was just about the only cheerful thing in our lives.

We gave him love, but it was always tainted by our daily concerns, from which we could not escape. As for love between the two of us, we could only nostalgize. Blaming each other was easier than making an effort. With her mother around, Natasha never ran out of ammunition; I just felt outnumbered. And I was incapable of screaming battles: the memories of my parents' arguments were still raw.

Five

Up to 1974 I had given little thought to emigration. Somehow I had always presumed that my future job, whatever it was, would involve *traveling*, not *living* abroad. It went back to my hot-dog-reporter dream and, curiously, was a bit like its predecessor, the fighter-pilot dream: a vague expectation, barely grounded in reality. But by 1974 reality was gaining ground.

At school I had had few Jewish friends. They were "nice boys," who would not booze till dawn. But then my gentile dorm friends dropped out, and the ones at school went abroad: Mali, Syria, Somalia. Under the tsars the pale had been tangible and clearly shown on the map; now, together with others "not recommended for work abroad," I was still locked inside the ghetto walls, however invisible.

Sasha's parents had gotten him into graduate school, where he was writing a thesis on C. P. Snow, a politically correct British novelist. He complained of boredom but hinted that in a few years, if all went well, he might get an invitation to visit the novelist in England. Shortly after I left, I read that C. P. Snow had died. Poor Sasha.

Naum settled into a job at a watch factory, translating catalogues and manuals. Ditto for Zhenya, and ditto for Vladik, who took humdrum jobs not unlike mine at the Coal Institute.

They, too, did translations and private tutoring on the side, painstakingly carving out a piece of the Soviet Dream for themselves. They still lived with their families—even families wait up to ten years for an apartment, and it is a rare single person who can get one. They were ensconced in family comfort (I cannot imagine Zhenya's grandma letting him leave the house without a hot breakfast) and saving money, too. Ten years down the road, a co-op; another five, a car; a vacation in Poland, if they kept their noses clean. We would get together, drink a little, play whist, swap books and records, rehash the latest from the Voice of America, and quietly agree: no, we were not living in the best or fairest of worlds, but what can you do? My friends were getting on my nerves.

There was an outside chance that, after years of begging and hustling and cultivating connections, after a hundred-odd group tours, after much stupefying drinking with officials, someone would take pity on me and steer me to a language-related job on this or that State Committee. But why should my future employer take a chance on hiring someone he could not send abroad as part of the job? And why should I beg for an opportunity to be doing something in which I not only disbelieved but was growing more and more to loathe?

By then I had read *1984* (loaned by a sympathetic InYaz instructor, of all people). From the very first scene, when Winston is ordered to reach his toes during his morning exercises, I was spellbound. One thought haunted me through the book: how did Orwell know this so well? To me, in 1973, the book felt too real to be a fantasy. It certainly had a firmer grasp of our reality than any Soviet novel did.

My next step was beyond *1984*. One night, after a reception at the Kremlin's Palace of Congresses, I took the official car and had the driver drop me off a couple of blocks from my friend's place. In retrospect, it was pure paranoia. I had not progressed far beyond my parents' generation, after all.

My friend regarded me critically. Dressed to the nines and reeking of cognac, I looked ready to party, not to read samizdat. But it felt so right: after the ritzy reception, filled with rich food and booze, after translating the speeches that contained not a word of truth, after using the official car to get here—*The Gulag Archipelago* was the perfect dessert.

It was a pale carbon copy, perhaps the fifth or sixth, typed on onionskin paper, but we did not complain. We stayed up all night; he had to take it back in the morning. It felt terribly romantic as the joy of discovery, of recognition, merged with the sinking feeling that Solzhenitsyn was right: there was no hope, it was pointless to pick at the details, the entire system was rotten from top to bottom . . . Every ten minutes one of us leapt up: "You gotta hear this! This is really—" "Nooo! If we start reading to each other, we'll never get done by morning!"

Later, in the West, I read the subsequent volumes, but it did not feel the same. I was lucky to have read it the first time the way it was meant to be read.

In general, though, I lacked the nerve for things clandestine. At school I had to write a paper on British politics. I had no desire to do it and intended to turn it in as quickly as possible, so I chose a subject that left no room for controversy: The Congress of the British Communist Party. Any Soviet student knows how to write such a paper—you copy down the Congress's resolutions and footnote them with politically correct comments.

Then Viktor, a fellow student, enlightened me: "You should apply for a permit for the Foreign Library's Special Fund. They have *everything* there: *Time, Newsweek*—you name it."

I put in a request, suggesting it would be most instructive to observe how the Congress was reflected in hostile capitalist media. My academic advisor signed, the head of the British chair signed, the deputy rector in charge of research signed—all, as a matter of fact. (Three signatures is the absolute minimum required to get anything in Russia.)

Cheerfully I presented the note at the Special Fund at the Library of Foreign Languages and was given a four-page form to sign. Its contents planted the first seed of fear in me. Among other things, I promised not to read materials unrelated to the subject of my research and, should I by any chance run into any anti-Soviet propaganda, never to disclose it outside the library. The vague wording was designed to cast a net as wide as possible—and what were you supposed to do, argue? Surely, a mere questioning of this or that item would have made the librarian's eyebrows rise, and later she would have made a note of it. Small print or large, Soviet citizens are not conditioned to read anything they are asked to sign.

I had no idea what to order (open stalls were unheard of), so, like a good boy, I asked for *The Economist* and *The Sunday Times of London* for the period in question. After half an hour the librarian brought the magazines. She glanced at my request and began to scan the tables of contents. "Just to make sure that you get exactly what you need."

"Thank you very much." I felt my face grow warm. This was not what I had in mind. "It is very kind of you to help me. But I can do it myself."

Fortunately, she had to take a phone call and waved me off. I nervously edged into a seat in the reading room and opened the first magazine. The headline stared me in the face: KGB's FIFTIETH ANNIVERSARY: HALF CENTURY OF REPRESSION. I closed it immediately and swallowed. My cheeks burned. A librarian (perhaps I should just call her a cop) was pacing the aisles, peeking at what people were reading. When I opened the magazine again, the words, increasingly blasphemous, danced on the page, the margins sprouted barbed wire, the pictures of KGB chiefs past snarled at me and called out to the librarian-cop, *Arrest him!* I quit after ten minutes. Disclose it outside? I could not remember a word I had read.

I ran into Viktor later. "I can't do it," I told him.

"You just don't have what it takes," he said.

"Don't you find it fucking humiliating?" I yelled.

He shrugged. "So what else is new."

Soon thereafter they kicked Viktor out in disgrace. He was supposed to be writing a thesis on The Continued Exploitation of American Blacks in the Postbellum South; instead, he had ordered something that interested him more: a collection of Beatles lyrics with surrealistic drawings.

I bummed many a magazine from my tourists later on, but it was nothing compared to *buying* my first *Newsweek* when I arrived in Vienna. I could ill afford the price, but the sheer act of picking it up at the kiosk and paying the vendor made me feel like a human being.

My last two years were an odd period. I did not read Soviet papers nor watch TV (we never even bothered buying a set). Except for my one-night stand with Solzhenitsyn, I did not read anything in Russian. Yet I refused the label of a snob, preferring to think that I just liked quality. I could not even figure out my social station. I had no money to speak of; in my imported clothes (tourists' gifts) I only looked like I did. As for my "social superiors"—the ease with which they obtained the things I had to sweat for provoked a casual stab of resentment, nothing more.

I sneered at the movies in regular theaters, too—between the jobs and the family, there was no time to waste on Polish comedies and East German thrillers. Mostly, I attended screenings at various "creative" unions (Film Workers', Architects', Writers', etc.). Since I was not a member, getting passes sometimes involved outright begging. A friend named Vova, a movie buff par excellence, did not have great contacts for passes, but for a couple of Marlboros he would let me in on what was playing where—valuable info, since screenings were always shrouded in secrecy.

One day he called to tell me that something extraordinary was playing at the Film Workers' Union. "This is good for half a pack, man." He paused dramatically. *Last Tango.*

I sat up. The Bertolucci movie was . . . no one I knew had seen it, really, although someone knew a guy who had seen it in Hungary—well, a cut version. Besides Brando playing the lead, we did not know anything about it. But the rumors promised that you would leave the theater a new person—a complete spiritual rebirth.

I looked at the pile of soiled diapers and a stack of translations. It was perfectly clear to me that twice as many diapers and ten times as many pages of translations could not hold me back.

"I'll be back in—in an hour," I told Natasha.

"Have fun." As in ". . . while I'm putting my head in the oven."

We lived a ten-minute walk from the Film Workers' Union. It was drizzling when I left the house, but by the time I got there it was turning into a shower. One look told me that it was a lost cause. Despite the rain, the sidewalk was crowded with people begging for an extra pass. "Doesn't look good," Vova admitted. "But you gotta try, right? How about it? I take east, you take west?"

Usually we begged for spare tickets in tandem, covering both approaches to the theater. If I lucked into two tickets, instead of one, I would share with Vova; and vice versa. But not today. "This is dumb," I said. "They all come by car."

He shrugged. "So we'll have to hustle. C'mon, man—this is *Last Tango!*"

Car after car arrived. Bumping into one another, rain pouring down their faces, the ticketless buffs grabbed the door handles, pushed crumpled bills at the lucky ones: "Spare ticket?" The passengers, making faces, shoved them away. "This is a disgrace! Where's the police? I can't even open my umbrella!" (They must have been thankful for the rain: it gave them a chance to flaunt their umbrellas with Western logos.) I knew that the filmmakers themselves never attended such screenings: they watched movies at the studio. The lucky ticketholders were store managers, hairdressers, maître d's—whoever the filmmakers owed favors to. If my mother had lived in Moscow, she could probably have wangled a pass (filmmakers have children, too) but at the moment that was irrelevant.

"I'm going home," I said.

"Wimping out? You gonna melt from a few raindrops? This is *Last Tango in Paris*, man!"

"I know," I said. "You don't find it humiliating, do you?"

"You're crazy," he said.

"One of us must be," I said. "Good luck." And I went back to diapers and translations, never to hustle for passes again.

Looking back, I can only wish that I had quit in order to help out Natasha—I did feel guilt, but a movie pass in my hand would have made it vanish. I also wish I could think of a dramatic episode to mark the turning point when I decided that I was fed up with the system. I may have had more dramatic opportunities, but somehow they never evolved into full-fledged situations. It may be logical: I never was a political person. But being barred from a screening of *Last Tango in Paris* as the last straw?

If I were given to seeing omens everywhere, *Last Tango* would be as good as any. Arguably, at the time it was the daring film du jour, and why *shouldn't* being barred from seeing it have compelled me to take the most daring decision of my life? In truth, things are more analyzable, of course: I was at my most despondent, I was a film buff, and *Last Tango* was the single most hard-to-see movie in Moscow. The three just happened to cross.

And what if I had lucked into a pass? Or, for that matter, a comfortable job, with an occasional trip to the West and enough money to keep my mother-in-law at bay? What if I had a Russian name like Ivanov? Or if I could run the hundred-meter dash in under ten seconds, with a minimum of steroids?

Perhaps I am splitting hairs, trying to distinguish between political and economic motivations. All I know is that my Russian misfortunes turned out to be my fortunes. I was lucky to be Jewish, and thus to have fewer problems in emigration than ethnic Russians, who had to marry Jews in order to qualify. I was lucky to have been denied the fruits of the system—to have had nothing to lose. Of course, this is not the complete picture: there was family to think of.

One thought overruled everything else in my mind: I was twenty-three, and it felt like the maximum age when you could still act on your convictions. Past this mark I would become like my friends, who toiled away, cursed the system, and eventually found themselves burdened by their meager achievements, those millstones that would only drag them deeper into the morass. It felt like slow death.

Soon afterward, in late 1974, my friend Irene told me quite casually that a friend of hers was emigrating and she was going to give him her personal data. In Vienna he would give it to Sokhnut, the Jewish agency, and they would send her an invitation to a family reunion (with a fictitious relative) in Israel. Was I interested in getting one?

Irene is one of the most delicate, unobtrusive people I know. Before I had a chance to open my mouth, she hurried to assure me that receiving an invitation did not necessarily force me to apply, that it was just—well, in case I ever thought about it . . .

Yes, I said. Yesyesyes.

I arrived in Rome approximately a year after the Film Workers' Union screening. I quickly discovered a revival house in the Trastevere section. It just happened to be playing *Last Tango*. Seeking omens is a dangerous game, but that night was pure bliss. I bought a ticket and walked into a dinky, half-empty theater with creaky, time-worn seats—my first visit to a Western movie house. Afterward I paced the wet sidewalks of Rome for hours on end, the sax solo of the film's final scene echoing in my head, I'm really *here*, I thought.

Six

In late 1974 my beloved Coal Institute finally completed work on its new building in a Moscow suburb and was closing the downtown office. The newly appointed Section Chief looked like a typical young Party cadre. I found his enthusiasm about the new location distasteful—he raved about the invigorating country air; all I saw was a field of familiar Syzran mud between the bus stop and the building. As he went on about my brand-new office and the great new library, which he would stock personally, I realized that he was aware of my modus operandi and firmly determined to put an end to it. "You might find the one-hour commute [from subway to suburban train to bus] tedious," he said tentatively. It occurred to me that what he really wanted me to do was quit.

I closed my eyes for a moment, fighting my perverse streak. I was quitting, without any doubt: you don't commute an hour to earn *this* wage. But the thought of making the bastard happy was wrenching my guts. "I think I'll love it here," I said. "Good," he squeezed out; "I thought for a moment that the commute . . ." "But this country air," I said, "it makes you think of moving." "I thought you lived on Gorky Street," he muttered; "great location—" "Maybe we could swap," I said (he had already told me he lived nearby the new office); "let me call my wife."

Ten minutes later I came back to tell him I was quitting. "Are you sure?" he asked; "I already told *my* wife about the swap—" "Sorry," I said, "my wife is addicted to exhaust fumes." "Do you have a new job?" he asked. I assured him I did. I didn't say where; I did not know myself—Chicago, Dallas, Miami? For the moment I had no desire to look for one. Tutoring in English was more lucrative than going to the office. As for the employment stamp in my passport, who cares? I'm practically out of the country—I might as well be out of the job!

Oh, the exhilaration of the first step. I stood at the end of the suburban train car, near the door, exposing my face to the icy gusts coming through the broken window. Standing amid the usual ragtag collection of bums (it was the only place where smoking was tolerated), I felt like one of them: we were all on the margin of the system now. One of them, reeking of cheap red wine, waved a crumpled, weatherworn scrap of paper in my face. "Just released, Comrade Citizen," he muttered, sputtering saliva. "Whatever you can spare." Indeed, his head had about a week's growth of hair (Soviet inmates are shorn clean). I gave him a one-ruble note. "I'm due for early release myself." He squinted at my sheepskin coat: I did not look like a cellmate. "Whatever you say, boss."

I told Natasha I had asked Irene to help me get an invitation from Israel.

She reacted calmly. "You're doing the right thing."

"What about you?"

"Am I invited?"

"We're married—"

"Are we?"

We were silent for a moment. Then she said, "I can't go

right now. It would be madness, with a one-year-old. How do you know it's going to work out over there?"

"There are no guarantees," I admitted.

"You go, look around—if all goes well, then—I'm scared!"

She started crying; I joined her. As we held each other, we felt our lives running away from us—in different directions. All we had ever wanted was to be happy, to flutter through life like moths. Why was life so unfair, why did it keep bashing our heads with "lesser-evil" choices? Another moment and we would have wept ourselves into a catharsis, wiping the slate clean. Instead, our crying woke Ilya, now a year old, and he joined the chorus. We had no choice but to pick him up and seat him on our joint lap.

"Isn't he cute, this little disaster of ours?" she said, sniffling. He kept whimpering, mostly out of surprise, because we were already giggling at the tableau of the wailing family.

But there was a look in her eyes: of hate, because he was standing in her way of going off to the New World, and of love, because—well, how could she not love him? I said nothing. I had no right to judge her.

"It's best this way," she said. "Really."

Burned once by the abandon of love, we were so rational now—and so naïve. We thought we were making an adult decision; we were wrong again. But the moment was gone.

"We'll have to get a divorce, of course," she said.

She had already been accepted for a job as an Intourist guide; she was due to start any day. If I applied for a visa and we were still married, she would be out of the job—one she really wanted. The allure of my travels must have rubbed off.

We filed for divorce without delay ("irreconcilable differences"), and it was granted within sixty days. The procedure was a formality. We had nothing to divide, nothing to haggle about. We laughed hysterically all the way home—really fooled 'em, didn't we?—and opened champagne. This was our last happy day together.

Months went by. I was still elated by my freedom from the Coal Institute: only after I was rid of it did I realize how much of a strain that farce had been. I worked hard and went to Riga with a group. Now I could smile secretly as they chatted about Paris and London. My plans were still a secret; no one knew but Natasha.

She traveled constantly now, so Ilya was spending a lot of time at her mother's. I realized I missed his weight against my shoulder, his warm breath against my neck. But at the first signs of spring her mother took him to the dacha outside Moscow. It was a long trip that I, always strapped for time and money, could ill afford; I was never invited to stay overnight. The little time that I spent with Ilya was thoroughly poisoned by my mother-in-law's ranting: Jews this, Jews that—Sakharov was a Jew, Solzhenitsyn was a Jew, if Stalin were only alive . . . She was deeply offended at being called an anti-Semite. There are *good* Jews, she protested (her friends in retail); and there are *bad* ones, the ungrateful ones (we know who *they* are), who did not appreciate what the Party had done to save them from the Nazis. I knew that arguing was pointless, yet I often lost my cool, which made her ecstatic; like my own mother, she thrived on screaming. My visits grew less frequent. Natasha shrugged: "You have any suggestions? Just be thankful that the child is breathing the country air."

"*Invigorating* country air."

"Exactly."

The invitation from Israel still did not arrive. What could have gone wrong? Had Irene's friends gotten drunk celebrating their freedom and lost the piece of paper with my personal data that they were supposed to give to the Jewish agency in Vienna? Had the desert wind in Israel blown it off an official's desk? Had the invitation from a mythical relative been intercepted by the Soviets? Had my neighbors stolen it from my mailbox? Hedging my bets, I asked more people to take my data to Vienna. Unemployed, according to my passport, I was half-free from the State—and just as vulnerable to its pressures.

Until one day it arrived: a handsomely beribboned document. My uncle in Haifa was yearning for a family reunion. How could I possibly let him down, no matter how mythical he was? The real uncle I was going to see was Uncle Sam, of course. But, since the official pretext for leaving was a family reunion, the true destination had to be kept secret. The web of lies spun by the Party held me fast to the very last day.

I looked around the local militia precinct uncertainly. This was brand-new to me: no more making calls and asking for referrals. For the first time in my life I was going to challenge the system openly.

There was no reception, no information desk, just a list of rooms with half the items crossed out. Yet it took a passing officer one look to place me. My intentions must have been written all over me. "Second floor," he said. "Room 22."

As usual, I was prepared for the worst. There would be hectoring about betrayal of the Motherland, perhaps even yelling and table-thumping; a curt dismissal was all I could pray for.

But the official was a good-looking, slightly plump young woman, business-like and polite at the same time. She explained the procedure, handed me the long list of papers needed, and even told me to call her if there were problems.

"You know," I said to her at the door, "if there were more officials like you, fewer people would be leaving."

She laughed. "Good luck."

Indeed, this treatment was so unlike anything I had experienced in dealing with the bureaucracy that I was in a daze for the rest of the day. Perhaps this was where the system made a curve. I could visualize the up-to-date memos: "Get them out!" A splendid sign, of course. Or had I simply run into a miracle?— a genuinely nice person within the police apparatus.

After a lengthy celebration that same night I arrived at a third possibility, a personalized version of the first one: they were set on smoothing *my* way because they wanted *me* out.

Like other paranoid theories, this one made some curious sense—or none at all. It was self-aggrandizing (they were bent on getting me out) and self-abasing (I was of no importance) at the same time. I loved its ambivalence. The theory became my emotional mainstay in the months to come.

Seven

According to the emigration procedure, my parents had to release me before the State did. Ostensibly, the reason was financial, to prevent prodigal children from abandoning their parents;
in reality it was, of course, to put more pressure on the applicant.
I kept hearing about prominent fathers—generals and professors—being threatened by their superiors if they signed releases
for their children.

I typed up the forms: "I, _____, have no material claims
on my son, _____, and do not object to his departure abroad."
As the application experts (Moscow teemed with them) recommended, I left out the word "Israel," to be added later. The
signature needed to be notarized; if the local government
officials saw "Israel," this would create unnecessary problems for my parents. At least, this way they could keep it under
their hats.

I hopped off the train in Syzran early in the morning and
followed the familiar route to my father's school. It was a warm,
sunny day in May; even the mud had dried up. This was about
the only thing I noticed. I glanced at our old apartment as I
passed it. Some old blankets were being aired on the terrace.
But I paid no attention to the streets of my childhood, did not
stop by the old school, did not try to find anybody. I was
concentrating.

I realized that this was going to be the single most important encounter of my life. I was certain I was facing an initial rejection. My father would not let me off the hook easily. And his refusal to sign could postpone my departure indefinitely. Just as I steeled myself to resist the distraction of my school memories, I was not going to surrender to my emotions. Now was my big chance to act like an adult: whatever I felt at the sight of him had to be put out of the picture. This was a chess problem: emotions had no place in it. I played and replayed the gambits, the defenses, the endgames. I envied Nabokov's Luzhin, capable of exploring the consequences of every move in a second.

As I walked through the Air Force base, I could not help noticing—especially after seven years' absence—the abundance of posters and slogans. I cringed like a vampire at the sight of a cross.

Father's old office was empty. An officer walked in and asked who I was looking for. A civilian looked suspicious enough, but an unshaven stranger, in a leather jacket and worn-out Levi's, ten times so. I introduced myself. He regarded me curiously. My name seemed to have rung a bell. Not every officer's son went to school in Moscow.

"Well," he said finally, "er . . . you see, your father has retired. Two days ago, actually. We had quite a party for him."

I looked away. Someone had just tilted the board. I might as well junk all my strategies and start over from scratch. It was a whole new chess game.

Since his unsuccessful urging of me to join the Party two years earlier, we had limited our correspondence to holiday greetings. I knew he had recently received a new apartment—finally, after eight years. I had his address but no idea how to find it. After many inquiries and two wrong bus transfers, I finally got there.

The courtyard of my father's building was even worse than

our old one. That one, at least, had felt lived-in: a tiny rotunda, a table for domino players, a few paved walkways. This one was brand-new: plain mud.

I sat on a bench with a broken-off back and tried to think. My father was bad enough, but Aunt Natasha, his wife, was a stone wall. There would be talk of family name, shame, Stalin nostalgia, more shame, repercussions . . . I put out the cigarette. There was no sense in delaying it.

I knocked on their door; no answer. I panicked. What if they had gone away? He was retired now, he could do that. (Of course, he had no telephone for me to call him in advance; I doubt anyone had a phone in a brand-new project.) What was I to do? Write a note, stay overnight—where? There was just one hotel in town, and you could not get a room there unless you were on a business trip. I could locate an old school friend and then spend a day or two with him, lying through my teeth? Or take a train back, write my father a letter, then come back? I walked slowly downstairs, cursing The System. By now, in my frenzied mind, The System was responsible for everything, including the weather (the Party had always said that: I must have come full circle).

I almost bumped into my father as he was climbing the stairs. We looked at each other, and my chessboard flew out the window. He was smiling at me—widely, guilelessly. He was the happiest father in the world.

It was a tiny studio apartment cluttered with junk furniture; I recognized some trinkets on the walls from my grandfather's house. The kitchen was barely large enough to hold two people. And a *coal stove*, in a brand-new building. Where did he store coal? A sick feeling rose in my stomach. Was this any way for a retired Air Force colonel to live?

As I watched him putter about, making tea, I got sicker and

sicker—with him, with myself, with everything. He had aged badly: his hairline was halfway up, his wrinkles had multiplied, his whole body seemed to have shrunk. An old man, trying so hard to please me—I had spent time and effort drafting strategies to beat *him*?

He made cheerful small talk about the retirement party, the boat he was buying to go fishing. He asked me about Natasha, about Ilya, about work. I answered mechanically, looking out the window. It was all a wasteland, spreading to the horizon, where a tiny sliver of bluish gray was visible: the Volga. I needed a drink badly. I could not go on. Until he mentioned that Aunt Natasha would be back from school, where she taught home-making, in the afternoon. *That* shook me up. I looked at him directly for the first time since I had walked in.

"I thought you and Natasha and Ilya might come in the summer," he said slowly. "Spend some time on the beach together." *What is it?*, his eyes begged for an answer.

Jesus, the beach. Don't you know? I came here to hurt you, to leave over your "dead body"—as I expected you to say in one of my "game plans." I rose and paced the room—two steps each way.

"What is it, son?" he said in a small voice. "You have family problems? Natasha? Ilya?"

"No, I'm just tired—"

"Do you want to lie down? I'll make the bed—"

"I'll be fine." *I can't do it.* Not while looking at him. Then all I could think of was the beach, a nice sandy beach, and him teaching Ilya to swim as he had once taught me.

"Aunt Natasha and I were just talking about you . . ."

Magic word. Now. Before she comes back. And then get out. But no hurting.

"Listen," I said, "I'm getting this new job with the State

Committee for the Peaceful Development of Natural Resources—"

"This is great! I told you! How did you get it?"

"Friends. So I need your signature on this. Paperwork."

He read it intently. "This is odd. I never heard of anything like this."

"New regulations."

He hesitated, then signed. He wanted to believe. He was confused. He was no dummy—God only knew what was going through his mind. "Are you telling me the whole story?"

"The whole and a half." *I never lied to you before, and all I got from you was shit.*

I explained that we had to have it notarized. We set out for the project's housing office in silence. My knees giving way, I watched the woman at the office stamp the paper and sign underneath. Then I folded it carefully and put it in my pocket. I caught him looking at me. He had an odd, numb look in his eyes. *He knows*, it rushed through my head. I realized I could not go on for another moment with it.

"Dad," I said, when we were outside, "I hate to do this— but I really have to be in the office early tomorrow morning. I took just one day off." *What's another lie?* It meant I would have to take an afternoon train. We rode a bus to the station. I took off my jacket. My T-shirt was soaked.

He broke the silence. "It's not that warm. You'll catch a cold."

Rather than argue, I put it back on. Good boy.

I don't remember much of the rest of the ride. As I was buying the train ticket, I sneaked a look at him. His face was devoid of emotion. This indicated his worst mood, I knew. I opened my second pack of cigarettes. It was not even three o'clock yet.

233

"You smoke too much," he said. I let it go, and he said in the same, suddenly stiff voice, "I'm even afraid to say what my worst suspicions are about this visit."

"Afraid" is the operative word here, I thought; just like you, Dad.

On the platform he hugged me. It was obviously the strongest hug he could manage, which was not much by now. Then he gave me a wet kiss, another one; his tears were pouring down my face. "I can't help thinking," he whispered, "how you won't even come to my grave."

"Dad, please—"

"Just remember," he now rushed through, as if afraid to forget. "I did my best, it didn't work out all the way, things seldom do in life—but I gave you all I could—"

"I know you did . . ."

I stood on the steps of the car, watching his figure shrink in the distance. In our family Mother was the only one who used the word "love"—as in "If you loved me, you would sit down and write him a letter!" or "If he really loved you, he would not have left you for that whore!" Yet I knew he loved me, though he had never said it in so many words; I knew I loved him, too, and I had never said it, either; I also knew that, in our case, love just wasn't enough.

Eight

As I boarded the Kharkov-bound train to see my mother, I did not have much to cheer about, but, at least, I was not as nervous as when I had gone to see my father. No more chess games; I was going to tell a bold, blatant lie. The first one had been the hardest; now I just had to stay the course. My rationalization about causing my father and myself needless pain applied to my mother tenfold.

Surprisingly, she looked better since I had seen her last. Now she worked as a school doctor: light work load, easy hours. After the chaingang routine of the Syzran clinic, it was like a vacation. Perhaps the physical distance from my father had calmed her down as well. My arrival was a signal to action: my fourteen-year-old sister, Mila, was promptly dispatched to the store with detailed instructions: See such-and-such salesgirl, she'll know it's for me, she won't water the sour cream; stop by the meat section, they'll know who you are and give you *lean* sausage; and call Uncle Boris, we'll have to get your brother a jar of instant coffee before he leaves. Mila made a face—just like me at her age—but went off. My grandmother was already frying eggs and potatoes in the kitchen. Sitting in the eye of this hurricane, I felt like Gogol's Inspector General with a guilt complex. I doubted I could hold the food down, but telling

Grandma I was not hungry was never any use—she would think I was sick and put me to bed.

At the end of the meal, Mila, her smirk unchanged, started clearing the table. Letting the Prince of the House help was unthinkable. I got out the paper. Mother nodded: "I know all about it."

The eggs-potatoes-sausage mass stopped dead on its way to my stomach.

"*He* sent me a telegram," she said calmly. "Saying, 'Don't sign am reversing my decision.' "

"I don't—" I was going to say, "I don't feel so good," but that would have sparked a three-hour discussion of my health. The air was stifling; the windows, as usual, were shut tight: Mother was maniacally afraid of colds. I had never fainted before, but it seemed I was about to. No, I couldn't do that: she would call an ambulance. Out of the corner of my eye I saw a dusty carafe with homemade wine on the shelf; that would help. But it was not even noon yet; I was risking a lecture on alcoholism.

"For once, I agree with him," Mother said firmly. "I'm not signing. I know exactly what this is all about."

The room was swimming. I grabbed a knife and nicked my finger under the table. Nothing dramatic: letting off geysers of blood would have been as bad as fainting. Another nick. The pain shot through my hand; I bit my lip to stifle the "ouch."

"Like Schtirlitz," Grandma nodded with a solemn expression.

Schtirlitz is the hero of *Seventeen Moments in the Spring*, a hit TV miniseries, a Soviet spy who rises to the top in Hitler's SS. To Russians, he is what James Bond is to the rest of the world. He is played by Tikhonov, Mother's favorite actor. She must have known every episode by heart. Now she and

Grandma had concluded that I was going abroad on a spy mission.

"I knew it all the time," Grandma said importantly, "since the day you went to that school. *Now* they don't mind you're Jewish." Her look said it all: when the time came to pick the best to risk life for *them, they* wanted *us* to help.

I'm not made for this, I thought. I was not going to faint, although the handkerchief in my pocket was becoming moist. But neither did I know what to do—laugh, cry? Tell another lie?

"What if they decide they don't want to swap you if you're caught?" Mother asked.

"You're too young for this," Grandma said. "You have all your life ahead of you."

I looked at their expressions and felt like telling the truth. I could not play around anymore. I was not that quick. Instead, I said, "Your fears are premature. Believe me, no one would send me on a mission at twenty-three without my parents' *specific* approval." *Aha, aha, I am wading ashore . . .* "I know from a very good source that if you are on a classified mission and under thirty, they have to check with your parents. At which time you'll be interviewed personally."

They paused. I was listening to my heartbeat. Grandma was shaking her head skeptically, but Mother was nodding . . .

"Did you tell your father that?"

"Yes."

"Then I know exactly what is going on." The fear receded, and her face assumed the familiar expression of wounded virtue. "It's *her*. The bitch. Your 'Aunt Natasha.' "

"You know," I said slowly, "you're absolutely right."

"Finally!" she cried out in triumph. "After all these years! The things I had to go through to hear this! Do you understand what she is really after, that anti-Semite? She's out to get *us*, all of us; and your poor, pitiful father is nothing but a weapon, a tool in her hands! That woman is pure evil! How he could allow that beast to stand in the way of his son's career! And you still call that piece of shit your father?"

My spying career over, I sneaked a look at my finger. The bleeding had stopped. My poor, pitiful father, I thought. What kind of an idealist was he, to share his fears with his wife? What kind of a weakling, to seek support in a woman who lived in fear of anything that did not fit into her tiny world? What kind of arguments could she possibly have used to make him change his mind? The System, I thought obsessively—with his Party-bred idealism, my father did not represent it; The System was every dark, medieval Aunt Natasha. It was she who had forced me out, not my father. I could penetrate his Party shell. If he were The System, then we could still be summering on the beach.

Mother, in the meantime, was becoming her own self again, the one I remembered from my high-school days. She gestured wildly, banged her fist on the table, lapsed into obscenities. Grandma, unable to stand it, left the room.

"What are you waiting for?" Mother shouted. "Here!" She slapped a blank piece of paper on the table. "Here!" She handed me the pen. "Are you going to write him now or not?"

"Mom," I said, "we really have to make it to the housing office before it closes for lunch."

"Aha," she nodded slowly, "I see it now. Finally! After all these years—I always suspected—you proved again—after all he's done to you—"

Mila was trying to hold back, but her eyes were wet. I realized that she was far worse off than I. At least, I had some good memories of our father to fall back on; all she had were our mother's hysterics.

"I am not signing anything," Mother said. "Not until you write the letter. Tell him what you really think of him."

I pulled the paper toward me and picked up the pen.

What kind of fool was he, to send that telegram? Did he really think that he could force me to see the light, mend my ways, and settle into the humiliating routine of slavery? Did he fully realize the consequences? I felt like crying. I was not made of Dostoyevskian stuff; I did not have it in me to forgive him, to love him, to honor him—not if I was going to keep my self-respect. I simply could not balance the two.

I set the paper aside. "I'll do it later, Mom. I can't concentrate right now: I keep thinking of the housing office closing in twenty minutes."

"Will you do it? Swear on my grave."

What was next?, I wondered. Signing it in blood? Just an expression. But, then, after Father left, she had gone to every fortune-teller in Syzran. She went to witch doctors, looking for the potion to bring him back. This came to me later, through her friends' hints. She hid this from me, knowing what my reaction would be: "Five years of college, Mom—and you dabble in black magic . . ." She would nod importantly: "You smartass, you don't know everything; if it were just abracadabra, people wouldn't go to them . . . People *know*."

The lie—did he think that my lying justified his reversal? Perhaps; but now, more than ever, I felt I had done the right thing by not telling him the truth. It was not a pleasant feeling; things should not be this way. By now I was up to my neck in lies, I had no strength left . . . what was another lie?

"I'll do it."

She carried on all the way to the office. She wanted to know how he looked, what his apartment was like, what Aunt Natasha looked like (she refused to believe I had not talked to her). But she was not really interested in any of these things; she just wanted me to confirm her projections that his life was over, that he was living in misery, that Aunt Natasha looked like a toad and lorded over him completely. I played along; none of it was too far from the truth. Communication was hopeless. If I had merely hinted that she was spending all her time talking about him, rather than about me or my family, she would have been furious: "But this is for *you*! You need a father! And what about Mila? How do you think she feels without a father?"

I was sinking deeper and deeper into the bog of her madness. It must stem from love, I thought—no medical condition, no work exhaustion, can create this kind of obsession by itself. Love alone can do it. Love is capable of anything.

Mother went to her school; Mila and I took a streetcar to Uncle Boris's for instant coffee. The food warehouse was a dark, cavernous place; workers in soiled white smocks were lugging carcasses around. Uncle Boris was on his captain's bridge behind the glass partition, signing invoices, talking on the phone, and dragging on his cigarette. He came down, short and stocky, armed with a clipboard; he was wearing the same smock as his workers, but you knew who was in charge. He talked in quick bursts; the workers seemed to get it right away. Way back, these Ukrainians would not have thought twice about handing him over to the Nazis, I reflected. Now they seemed to adore him, and with good reason: he knew exactly how much each could steal without getting caught.

There was nothing unusual in the fact that he had access to instant coffee, unavailable at the store: whoever controls the meat controls all the food. Besides the coffee, he gave me a gallon-sized jar. "For Grandma. Careful, don't spill it." I knew better than to unwrap it in plain sight. "How's Mom?" he asked Mila. "The usual." He nodded sourly. "She's crazy, but what can you do? She's your mom." He excused himself, then came back. "Almost forgot. Manya has retired; you'll need this." He scribbled a quick note on the scrap of paper. "The new girl's Jeanna, she's at window ten. She'll know."

"What was the note for?" I asked Mila when we left.

"For the train ticket. How did you expect to leave?"

Uncle Boris was in full charge of his life, and he was making everyone happy: the State, his workers, his family. I remember many a quiet knock on the door; Grandma would shoo me away, and a worker in a blue smock would hand her a newspaper-wrapped package. "From Boris Solomonovich."

I envied Uncle Boris. He accepted life at face value, making no fuss about it: if stealing is what it takes, then let's steal, and, instead of feeling guilty, let's be smart and not get caught. I envied him because he exuded normality. Next to him, I felt like a freak. Perhaps my decision to leave was a freaky one, too; Uncle Boris surely had no reasons for leaving.

Where could I get some of his normality? The two visits to my parents—and this one was not over yet—left me exhausted. I realized the importance of my decision, for both me and my family, and I was not shying away from the emotional consequences. In fact, I would have given my right arm to be able to simply face my parents and say, "Look, I can't stay. There is absolutely nothing in store for me here. Why don't you just sign this and give me your blessing for a new life? Isn't it already hard as hell for all of us, without these games?"

But I knew my parents too damn well to try out this solemn, classical script. What was going on was even worse than a chess game; it was a farce, with Schtirlitz, Aunt Natasha, et al. I felt utterly inadequate to it. I had gotten this far on luck, rather than quick wits, but how far can you ride on luck?

The picture was coming together: for me, there would be no direct road to freedom, no marching with my head held high, no singing hymns in a clear, ringing voice. There would be getting tangled in the undergrowth and stumbling and falling and rising and getting tangled again. Breaking free was a nasty business. What had happened so far was bad enough, and how did I know if this was the worst?

In retrospect, it is plain to me that, in trying to get free of the system, I was behaving like its prime product, cranking out one lie after another. I had not been brought up to cast doubt on the means that led to "noble" ends: the entire history of the Bolshevik Party, with its tactical twists and turns, was supposed to be continuous proof of the motto. I had not been taught that the means may taint the ends. After many years I still don't have a clear-cut answer as to whether my behavior was moral or not. But my every justification for it still sounds like a hollow rationalization to me.

An hour before the train Mother reminded me about the letter. Fortunately, she was in a calmer mood.

"Mom, it's no good. I can write whatever you want, but he'll never get it. She watches the mail." Another lie to avoid a conflict. Another lie that could well be the truth. The longer I stayed around my mother, the looser my grip on reality.

I talked them out of coming to the station, but Mother and Mila insisted on walking me to the streetcar stop. Grandma, with her bad legs and short breath, accompanied us as far as the gate, then waved Mother and Mila on.

As we hugged, Grandma broke into sobs. "I won't see you again; I just know it."

Both of us were shaking now. I might see my parents again one day, but with Grandma there was no fooling myself. For the first time since making the decision, I saw the word "never" writ large.

Tremors shook her entire body. "You'll try—you'll do your best—to come back—just once before I die."

I nodded, sniffling, unable to say anything. There was no lying to Grandma.

"Mama, Mila—who will take care of them?" she muttered through her sobs, then waved: *Go already, you'll miss the train.*

I walked off, unsteadily. I was the apple of her eye, her wunderkind, her trump in the ongoing contest among sisters about whose grandchildren were the smartest. Barely literate herself, she was the one who had taught me to read when I was two and a half, and from then on no one took greater pride in my precocity, my school grades, my Moscow school. She never acted surprised. "*A yidishe kop,*" she would say with a small shrug: *What, you expected anything less? You think the real Schtirlitz was a Russian?*

Then and there I knew that, whatever I achieved in the New World, it would be too late for her to know. I wouldn't be around to close her eyes; I wouldn't be at her funeral; I'd be lucky to find her grave.

I caught up with Mother and Mila near the streetcar stop, and the full weight of Grandma's last remark landed on my shoulders like a ton of cement. I was not just leaving; I was leaving *them.* Father could fend for himself, however imperfectly; what about them?

They were both wet-eyed, but Mother was chatting away about her plans for the summer, while Mila's large, gray eyes were staring at me directly. She seemed to know, just like Grandma did. She was ten years younger than I; what were my memories of her? That she had been a nuisance I had to baby-sit when I would rather have been playing soccer? Grandma took her to Kharkov when she was four. We had grown up far apart, in place and in time; I never gave her much thought.

Now, of all the people I was leaving behind, it was she for whom I felt sorriest. I was the one who had already gotten away once, at seventeen, and now I was doing it again. She was the one who would have to endure the daily "write him" routine. Write whom? He barely knew her. What was I doing?

The streetcar came. We hugged. "Write, write," Mother pleaded.

"He always says he will," Mila said.

It's not too late, I said to myself. I don't have to use the invitation, nor my parents' releases. And then what?

Before, it used to be my mother—the school—the system—that I felt were imprisoning me. Now I was bound by my own decision, hand and foot.

Nine

After the parental releases, the next hurdle was a character reference from the job. Here the only course of action was to persevere. I could not expect my ex-employers to issue it on the spot: it was a black mark for them, and they were instructed by the powers that be to resist at all costs. My request slowly moved through the channels and sluices, accruing reluctant approvals like barnacles, and now and then running aground. Assorted Secretaries went on important trips, were felled by mysterious germs, took time off, and required others' signatures before daring to attach their own. There were long phone calls and commutes to the new Coal Institute building. I was not enjoying the invigorating country air.

The reference requirement was meant to discourage applicants, to make them think twice before filing. Despite its sheer idiocy, patent to those who grew up in a free country, few questioned its necessity. That its text was a standard formula did not matter. Nothing in Russia is obtainable without a reference: jobs, apartments—why should an exit visa be different? I have met émigrés who had their references notarized and tried to unload them on prospective employers in this country.

Other papers were easier to get, but only compared to the reference. At the word "Israel," officials' faces fell and a chorus of "*zavtra*" ("tomorrow") filled my ears. I put in enough hours in reception rooms to doubt my pet theory about the system's determination to get rid of me. I brought along an Italian textbook (Rome was the way station for Soviet Jews) and chanted my mantra: "*Aspetto, aspetti, aspetta . . .*"

As I had had myself expelled successively from the Komsomol, the union, and the Army Reserve, now I was extracting myself from the system, step by step. No longer did I belong to these esteemed entities, which I associated with nothing but humiliation and boredom. Paraphrasing Chekhov, I was squeezing the slave out of myself, drop by drop. There were gallons more to squeeze.

Finally, on a sunny June day, I returned to the precinct and proudly placed the stack of documents on the young woman's desk. She ticked them off, one by one, and then asked for my passport. I had almost forgotten. The internal passport, its cover colored dark mustard green. The last step. Meekly I placed it on the desk. The walls of the office vanished to reveal an abyss. I caught my breath. Without changing expression, she slammed the Canceled stamp across page one. Now it was irreversible. The twenty-three years of my first life came to an end.

My relief that all the documents were in order, that my labors were done, that now I could do nothing but wait, was submerged in the uncomfortable feeling of nakedness a Soviet citizen feels when stripped of his passport. (I had déjà vu ten years later in the US, when I lost my wallet and my credit cards.) My new freedom was that of an escaped slave: no longer did I toil for the master, but the law was still on his side. In a scrape with the law, any cop could have me for breakfast.

One day I got a call offering me a one-month trip across Siberia with a delegation. I broke up: here was the system at its best, one hand unaware of what the other was doing—an excellent sign that no one was checking on my free-lancing. In a twist, the State's insistence that one hold a steady job turned in my favor. Although the trip would have been a welcome distraction from the nerve-wracking wait, I declined. The caller was a Party functionary—perhaps a bastard in his own right, but he had treated me well. To accept the job and possibly cause him problems would have made me a worse bastard than he could possibly be. It was also a precaution: nothing might have happened. But such precautions made up my daily life. I stopped free-lancing for the Committees and made money by giving lessons and selling off my books and stamps.

My social life changed completely. It was not that my friends panicked about their brilliant careers: they were smart enough to realize that having drinks with me was not the same as disseminating samizdat. But they, at least, knew where they would be a few months from now; I couldn't say the same about myself. The longer I waited, the deeper grew the chasm between myself and those who were staying.

Suddenly, all over town I was meeting people who were battling the system: waiting for invitations, gathering papers, waiting for visas. This informal network included people from different backgrounds who did not have much to discuss but their common goal. "In Vienna the place to stay is . . . You must bring your own linen, in Italy they only have unfurnished rentals . . . In the US the smaller the town, the more generous the Jewish community . . ."

At first this "special-interest" group was a relief, but soon it began to seem not unlike my first year at InYaz, when I had lapped up the tales of Arabian travel on behalf of the Defense Ministry. Now, if I muttered that I planned to stay in Rome, I was instantly scorned: "Do you know what things cost there? *Everybody* lives in Ostia!" (a small town forty minutes from Rome, where most immigrants stayed). The "*everybody*" stung;

again, it implied that I was "setting myself above the collective," no matter how benevolent the latter was. Again, I was feeling like an idiot. Growing up was a remote prospect.

The talk of cutlery and linen drove me back to my "staying" friends, but they were making plans for their summer vacations. I had to stay in Moscow and wait, wait, wait.

The longer I waited, the more of a wreck I became; family life followed suit. Natasha traveled, we saw less and less of each other, and separation did not make our hearts grow fonder. But we were still pals. Once, she brought home the loot from her tourists, and we had coffee, American-style: Sanka, Cremora, and Sweet'n Low. We rolled on the floor. "What kind of country are you going to? Coffee that's not coffee, cream that's not cream, and sugar that's not sugar!"

But we were already seeing others. It's hard to say which of us started; at the time, it did not seem to matter. We laughed about our new "open marriage"—or was it open divorce? I was uneasy with the arrangement: the marriage was already strained enough, and, instead of nursing it back to health, we were blowing it up, just out of perverse curiosity—how far could we go before the bubble burst?

We should never have gotten married. At twenty and nineteen we were as unprepared for that as we would be for a baby a year later. What did we know about life, about others, about the thin ice that forms after the first year or two? In America we would have tried living together first; in Russia the residence permit system required that we make it legal. In America we might still be married. At least, this is how we feel nowadays. The Soviet system provides us with an ironclad alibi to fall back on for the messes we made of our lives.

The bubble burst in a very Soviet way: over the living space. Inevitably, with only a single room between us, one of us would need to bring someone else over. "Scheduling" began; soon we could not bear to see each other. Eventually we descended into ugliness the likes of which I had never seen between my parents nor experienced myself afterward. We were little kids playing with matches in a woodshed; some of the burns we got have not healed to this day.

I was back among the applicants, sitting around smoky kitchens, listening to stories. Someone had gotten a visa in a month, another had been waiting for nine . . . We peered into the fog, trying to fathom the State's ways, to detect a pattern, and found none.

A friend dragged me out of the house for my twenty-fourth birthday. We took a suburban train, had a picnic in the woods, knocked off a couple of bottles of Mukuzani red, made love. She understood that a regular celebration would have been hard for me: sitting at a regular table and forcing grateful smiles at interminable toasts. But the euphoria of freedom from the Komsomol was soon replaced by the misery of self-imposed isolation. I sat in the room playing solitaire, leaving the house only at night. I could not face a soul.

What kind of gamble had I taken?, I wondered, shuffling and reshuffling the deck, and cheating blatantly. We were all wards of the State, its Oliver Twists, always asking for *More!* Yet we preserved a certain latitude that I had relinquished in a bid for freedom. My earlier theories were in a shambles: my brain could not accommodate the endless "on the one hand"s and "on the other hand"s. I abandoned the rational element and, gnashing my teeth, accepted the absurd: the State did whatever it wanted to do. It was turning the tap on and off, to wangle maximum concessions from the Yanks. "Ship fifty yids by Monday," someone said; files were rushed from desk to desk, and no one cared how long you had waited or what secrets you knew. My file just had to be the thinnest: what had I accomplished at twenty-four, how much baggage had I accumulated?

A couple of weeks after my return from Kharkov, I had made a tactical move: I sent my father a carefully worded cable. The application has been rejected, it said; you can breathe safely now. In Moscow anyone could have told him that applications did not get rejected in two weeks, but it was a sure bet that he had never met an applicant. I never heard from him again. Another lie that must have worked. Or did it? Did the authorities contact him and my mother and let them know that I had lied to them about my objectives?

On the job I had attended hundreds of official functions. Had SUT—Someone Up There—recognized my picture on the visa application and wondered why I had never listed my jobs on it and what I had to hide? At the time, I had never heard of any InYaz alumni who had left on an Israeli visa (if they moved to the West, it was by defecting while stationed abroad). Could SUT be still investigating the importance to national security of those military maps? Was SUT going over the informers' reports? I could just see the illiterate, moronic twaddle about my passion for decadent music, my disrespect for the Party, my conspiracy to dislodge the government and replace it with the Elders of Zion. (I open the *Times* every day, looking for Gorbachev to introduce the Freedom of Information Act; I'll be on the first plane, I'll take my number in line, though it will be much longer than the one to see Lenin's mummy, and I have lost my Soviet knack for handling lines.)

Did my father's twenty-five years with the military make me

invaluable to the CIA? Could my mother-in-law have written a report of her own in the Zionist-conspiracy vein? Why not my apartment neighbors, who were gunning for our room? They had heard me speak English on the phone, which is as good as espionage. Anyone I knew could have done anything—either to ingratiate himself with the State or to protect himself from its ire. After all, under the KGB's magnifying glass I showed a lot of blemishes.

Living in Russia is already a tightrope between sanity and madness; I felt I had slipped into the latter. Sleeping was out of the question. Listening to what sold best, linen or cameras, on the Termini Market in Rome drove me further into insanity. I was haunted by the thought of a rejection—it would be a disaster. Except for private lessons, I had cut myself off from all jobs. My family had gone down the drain. I even had no guaranteed place to live, as Natasha had good cause to officially kick me out. I paced the room, terrified; the neon lights of Broadway were dimming . . .

Yet finally the postcard came, requesting that I pick up my visa. There were last-minute snags, a few more papers required. For example, I needed to pay an exorbitant nine hundred rubles for "renouncing Soviet citizenship" (as if I had ever asked for it); but I was already walking on air, adrenaline pumping, veins throbbing with the expectation of freedom . . . The fears multiplied—rumors circulated about people being turned away at the last minute—but I was used to that. Until the plane landed in Vienna, I kept telling myself, I could not afford to relax.

Natasha and I ended up in our most violent shouting match ever: no earthshaking reason, just one word leading to another. This made my getting to see Ilya seem like wishful thinking. I left Natasha every ruble I had, thinking, This is the last straw; whatever happens, I never want to see her again. She hated herself for being afraid to join me, I realize now, and hated me for not forcing her to come along.

I decided against going to see my parents. It was both cowardly and prudent. I did not have it in me to relive the dramas of six months earlier. And the fear of some kind of last-minute stunt, especially on my mother's part, was all too real. I wrote her a six-page letter; but nothing to my father. His telegram still stung.

After attending so many farewell parties, I now hosted my own. Never before had so many people been packed into our room. Some were regulars at such parties, their visa applications moving through bureaucratic channels; but most had nothing to do with the emigration movement and came only because *I* was leaving. Of the latter, some were apprehensive about mixing with such an obvious "black sheep," but after a few glasses of vodka, all caution was tossed to the winds. I'm sure that many of my guests never saw one another again, but for a few moments we were all one—drinking, laughing, crying, wondering what kind of country we had been born in. And what other country took such a heavy toll on ties between people.

At last, on a September morning, I sat in Sheremetevo Airport's transit lounge. I was wasted after the party and tipsy after the early-morning champagne, the last toast, in the same cafeteria where I used to tipple my Scotch in solitude. As I watched the planes take off, my heart was bursting out of my chest and overtaking them. But still my fears would not leave me.

I did not feel like an escaped prisoner who had scaled the wall, shimmied down the water pipe, crawled under the wire, and was now waiting for the getaway car. Perhaps I had not been abused enough by the system to earn that sensation. I felt more like a burglar leaving a mansion in the dark of night, bag filled with loot and every step carefully calculated to avoid tripping the wires. I dreaded bumping into any of my Committee bosses on their way to greet or see off a delegation; I was not sure what I would tell them. The rational part of me doubted they would sound an alarm, but I hated to complicate my Independence Day. I was tired of plot twists and subplots in my life script. I wanted this to be a clean, uncluttered getaway.

Things did not pan out quite that way. First I ran into an Iranian stage director with whom I had once worked. He was changing planes to go to a theater conference in Europe. I don't think he quite understood what I was about to do, just as he did not understand much of what he had seen in Russia. Then I ran into Ali, an Arab student I knew from the dorm days. Now he was working for the Yemeni embassy and had come to meet some dignitaries. Still warily sticking to my cover story, I told him I was going to Israel. Ali sighed. "I hope we won't end up shooting at each other." "I hope not." I had gotten through passport control, having left my friends behind; now it was an Arab friend who first wished me luck in Israel.

Aboard the bus to the airplane, my fears were vanishing quickly. All that remained was the joy of breaking out. Not until the bus crossed the airfield was I stabbed with despair at leaving my family and sadness at leaving my friends. The rational part of me argued that one day I would be crossing the airfield again, armed with my American passport; but I knew it would take a long, long time, and I would not be returning to what—and whom—I was leaving now.

Interlude

Despite my Zionist-leader status in the dormitory informers' reports, I did not get to Israel until many years later—and even then, I went with an American passport. Upon arrival in Vienna in 1975, I firmly declared I was going to the States. Israel was an abstraction—I did not speak the language, I did not know a soul. America was a reality—I felt I had known it that well.

From Vienna I was transferred to Rome, where I spent about four months waiting for my US entry visa. Finally it arrived. My first destination was St. Louis, Missouri. It was not quite a matter of choice—it was offered, and I took it, for the simple reason that I'd never been there.

A volunteer from the Jewish Community Service met me at St. Louis International. On the way to my new apartment, we passed a large building with the sign A&P. "This is a supermarket, right?" I asked.

She turned to me. "How did you know that?"

I shrugged. I did not know the answer. I must have read it someplace—Updike, Roth, Pynchon?

While I hung out in Rome, my American friends repeatedly assured me that my fluency in English placed me well ahead in the game. True, I had no trouble communicating in standard English, which helped me leapfrog over textbook pains of adaptation. I have never been on welfare or sold hot dogs or driven a cab: two weeks after my arrival, I had enough free-lance translation jobs to live on.

The advantage had a downside. Selling hot dogs can be a humbling experience for those with college degrees; being on welfare is even worse. But such experiences generate a powerful, teeth-gnashing urge to make it, to get your own piece of the American Dream—at least, judging by the Russians I know, whose Horatio Alger stories make me feel like an underachiever. Sometimes I feel as though I turned my good fortune with English into a misfortune; things came too easy, I never had to strive. Happy-go-lucky is a dangerous attitude for an émigré to adopt.

And Fluent English, even laced with idiom, is a dangerous thing—like any "little learning"—if it is not backed by an understanding of the country's ways. The American books I'd read in Russia had helped my English, but command of the language alone creates an illusion of seeing the inner workings of society, which may lead to misunderstandings.

It took me a while to learn the nuances: for example, the "I-wash-my-hands-of-you" undertone of "Suit yourself." I'll never forget the first time I heard the jocular "Aw, get outta here"—I actually headed for the door. The person I was talking to had, in effect, been taken in by the fluency of my English and overestimated it.

Or the night I was walking a girl home from a party. She asked me what I thought of her. "You're all right," I said. Surely, Bogart would have said that (at least, instinctively I kept the "kid" out).

" 'All right'?" she said incredulously. "That's it?"

I had a feeling I would be sleeping by myself that night.

———

All the command of idiom and nuance in the world is no substitute for a native mind-set. If freedom in general is the most
important element of this mind-set, then the freedom to exercise
choice is, I think, its most visible manifestation. Take your neighborhood supermarket. In a recent *New York Times* piece a
psychologist noted that the exponential growth of consumer
choices facing Americans causes fatigue and uncertainty. It does,
huh? Imagine a Russian at the A&P for the first time. What *are*
"anchovies," anyway?

In this sense, my twenty-four years in Russia left me woefully
unprepared for the crushing burden of freedom in America. I
have already told of the vicissitudes of buying Western products,
from Levi's to LPs, there; here the constant need to make choices
has borne on me heavily from day one. It is not merely the
torment of spending your last few dollars on a paperback or a
tape. Living in the West (assuming a minimal degree of prosperity) is a nonstop series of choices: where to live, where to
work, what school to go to and what courses to take, what car
to buy . . .

Compared to émigrés, native-born Americans facing these
choices are infinitely better equipped to make them; they routinely balance their needs with checkbook-imposed limitations.
An American buying insurance for his car will use a combination
of objective and subjective factors: relative cost, the broker's
reputation, etc. By contrast, a Russian in Brooklyn, with his
limited English, is likely to turn to a Russian-speaking broker.
I never had to do that. But I don't have an American's facility
for handling such choices, either. As I said, my fluency in English
led people to believe I understood more than I actually did.
Freedom of choice repeatedly hit me on the head and sent me
reeling. There is no one to blame; I asked for it, didn't I? As
the Russian saying goes, *"Za chto borolis, na to i naporolis"*

("We got screwed by the very same thing we had fought for").

I am getting better, though. Back to the store, where freedom of choice is easier to illustrate than in the voting booth. A friend who had me as a houseguest asked me to stop by the grocery and get some cottage cheese on my way home.

"Cottage cheese, Kathy? Large curd? Small curd? California-style? Garden-style? With pineapple? With chives? A pound container? Half a pound? This is not Russia, where all you do is make sure that you have your cottage cheese ration card on you."

"You take this country too seriously," Kathy said.

People often ask me whether I consider myself a Russian or an American. It's a tough call, I say, realizing the imprint that the years in the West have left on my psyche.

I was at LaGuardia, putting my friend Irene's mother on a flight to LA. She told me she had to call San Francisco the next day to register with the Soviet consulate there.

"Why?" I asked, suppressing laughter. I was oddly reminded of vacations with my father. As a military officer, he had to register at the *voyenkomat* (military commissariat) at every location where he planned to spend twenty-four hours or more. The procedure was performed with farcical gravity, but it could be rationalized: nuclear war, mobilization . . . (Americans, I'm told, took their fallout shelters pretty seriously at the time, too.) "Why would you bother?"

"But they *have* to know where I am," she insisted.

"Why?"

"Just . . . *just in case.*"

I gave up. The Russian language is rife with expressions of uncertainty: "*na vsyaky sluchai*," "*malo li chevo*" . . . If Allstate or some other insurance biggie ever cracks the Soviet market, I'll rush to buy stock.

"Besides, it's the law," she said with finality. "It says so right here." She proudly displayed her red Soviet passport, where the last-page do's and don't's included an unequivocal order to register at the nearest consulate within twenty-four hours. "Don't you register with your embassy when you go to Paris or Madrid?"

I shook my head. True, the State Department does *recommend* that we register with the embassy if we plan to stay in the country for a long period, or if the country in question is a dangerous area. Does this mean that the Soviets regard the whole world the way we regard Iran or Lebanon? What disturbed me was that, after years of being denied a mere sixty-day tourist visa to go see her only daughter, this well-educated, liberal-minded woman still firmly believed in the State's wisdom and its best intentions toward its citizens.

I have often heard Americans say, "Whatever the government touches, it turns to shit." True or not, the statement sits well with me. Americans are more skeptical about their government than are people in any other Western democracy (Italians and Israelis come close), which made it easy for me to transfer my feelings about government from Russia. I am aware of the vast differences between the two governments, but the populist streak in the American character has enormous appeal to me. I don't know how long I could stand living in a country like Sweden, with its much-vaunted living standard and social benefits. The paternalism of European governments is anathema to me.

In France in 1984 a friend told me that, along with several other Soviet dissidents/French residents, he had been sent outside Paris on the eve of Brezhnev's visit.

I could not believe my ears. "Why?"

"To avoid possible disturbances," he explained calmly.

My friend tends to exaggerate, and I still don't know if I should believe him. Yet some French people I talked to find his story not only believable but quite normal (he does, too). "Wouldn't your government do the same thing?"

"It might try," I said cautiously, "but I think there would be a public outcry if it did."

Aside from politics, where I cherish the freedom to disagree with my government, my impassioned defense of our freedom to succeed or to fail causes my enlightened European friends to smile. "You're trying to out-American the Americans." I smile back politely. I can play poker or watch the Super Bowl or drink till morning with my American friends, and sooner or later one of them will say, "Don't you guys in Russia . . . ?" Or, "See, David, in America we . . ." Or, "You're so American" (at times sarcastically, but more often meant as the highest compliment a native-born can hand down). Being a foreigner is not unlike being Jewish: if you forget about it, someone will remind you.

I used to bristle, but now I take it in stride. I realize that I can live in this country for another fifty years and still hear people make these remarks. However supercilious and patronizing they sound, they are right, in a way. I will never be like them—and I cherish the freedom to stick to my hyphenated appellation and bear it proudly.

On the other hand, my friend Irene, too, recently called me "overassimilated" when I suggested that a visit to a family counselor might help prop up her marriage. In her book, a family counselor is as bad as a shrink. (Of course, until recently Soviet psychiatry's main claim to fame was "curing" dissidents, rather than helping families; the latter was the function of the Party Committee.) A Russian should need a shrink? Perish the thought! That's for Americans, who "*s zhiru besyatsya*" ("go crazy from too much fat")! She was not talking about the American diet, which is actually much lower in fat than the Russian one. What she meant was: We have spent too much time standing in lines for bread and milk, and we don't have a single problem that a roof over our heads and a little food in our stomachs cannot solve.

My American friends would sneer at this as a prime example of first-generation immigrant thinking, and I agree. But I understand her only too well. We both remember Syzran; it will never cease to loom large in our lives. Our Russian experience puts our New World achievements and failures in a unique perspective. It is the dash of spice in our daily diet of freedom.

Part Four

One

On a July afternoon the KLM airliner came to a stop at the gate in Moscow. I was fidgeting in the aisle, shifting my bag from shoulder to shoulder, thinking that, before I saw one friend or relative, I would have to face the "uniforms," the wooden faces of the regime I had left behind fourteen years before. There was little reason to worry: thanks to glasnost, hundreds of fellow émigrés had already traveled back, and I had never heard of one case of harassment. Yet, out of habit, I expected the worst.

The airport was a dark, cavernous place. Summer was sizzling outside, but inside it felt chilly and damp; it reeked of gasoline and other, unfamiliar—forgotten?—odors; wet wool, perhaps. Away from the surgical cleanliness, the neon lights, and the humming air conditioning of Western airports, this was the most foreign that I had felt in all my years as a Westerner.

The youngish Customs Inspector, with a tiny mustache and a seen-it-all expression, noted the PC for my family (for which I paid a whopping duty) on the declaration form. Not bothering to open the suitcase, he said, "Well, what else do we have here?"

"Oh, just junk," I muttered. "You know—lipstick, soap—" and I almost choked. Fourteen years ago he might have bristled: *Soap? Are you saying we have no soap in the USSR?* Now he just chuckled. "Soap, hee-hee . . . We sure need soap around here." He stamped my declaration and waved me through.

———

My visit had been preceded by mountains of paperwork and months of expectation. For years the Soviets insisted that foreigners stay only at hotels. With the Soviet hotels' exorbitant rates (unmatched by quality), this meant I could come for a few days at most. Under Gorbachev that requirement was lifted: I could be invited by a relative and stay wherever I wished. Immediately I started on the paperwork. It took a few months, made more difficult by the fact that I was applying for two destinations—Moscow and Kharkov—but eventually I got the visa.

It would be less than sincere on my part to say that I had spent every waking moment in the West thinking about my family. "How did you have the nerve to leave by yourself?" people often asked me. I shrugged; I did not consider it that big a deal. I had been on my own, away from family, since seventeen.

In the West the question was asked out of politeness; I lived in "singles cities" like New York and Los Angeles. It was not until my visit to Israel in 1984 that I began seeing my decision in a different light. "You left without your family?" people asked. "How can you live by yourself?" Their faces showed genuine amazement. They made me feel like, if not a cripple, then an aberration of sorts. This set me thinking. When glasnost burst out, I was ready.

It took me a long time to start getting over my resentment of my father's attempt to block my departure. I sent him a couple of cards from Los Angeles, then a letter from Seattle; he never responded. Through Irene I knew he had received them: he mentioned it to her mother, who still lives in Syzran. I knew that he cared: he pelleted her with questions. I could only speculate that he was afraid of the Party's reprimands and would not let me come between himself and his Party card. Thus, when

I began preparing my papers for the trip, I did not include Syzran in my itinerary.

I corresponded irregularly with my mother and sister. Each letter from them lay unopened in my desk for days: I had visions of fires, car crashes, malignant tumors. I knew the quotidian details of their lives: where they lived, what school Mila went to, what hospital Mother worked at. But I found it hard to explain what I did and how I lived. In a sense, I was as far from Kharkov as when I had lived in Moscow.

This came home to me with particular acuteness when I received pictures of my grandmother's funeral. The faces on the black-and-white snapshots were old, haggard; the clothes were worn out, shabby; the background suggested a muddy slum. The sight of an open coffin brought back memories of Lenin's Mausoleum—Paganism, I thought. Grandmother's face was stern, unforgiving. I sat a melancholic, agnostic *shiva* by myself, with a bottle of Scotch for company.

Most letters from them were ill-disguised shopping lists. I regarded it as par for the course: familial feelings are one thing, but in their shoes I would surely have a long shopping list, too. I sent parcels: jeans, sweaters. Many got lost, apparently sticking to the hands of Soviet postal workers.

The situation with Natasha and Ilya was complicated. When she tried to leave Russia, a few years after me, her mother would not grant permission unless Natasha left Ilya behind. In effect, her mother held him hostage, to ensure that Natasha would help her in her old age. I was not surprised that Natasha chose to leave, in the hope of eventually bringing Ilya over. Who was I to blame her?

In America she and I stayed in touch, though we met rarely. The sight of me, she confessed once, reignited her guilt; likewise,

I said. We lived separate lives. She would sometimes cry on my shoulder between her affairs, until she remarried. She sent parcels to Moscow, sometimes inviting me to pitch in. For me, the channel of communication was closed; her mother controlled the mailbox and the telephone. She even told Ilya I was dead. I was dumbstruck—but unsurprised.

Now her mother had finally decided it was best for Ilya to be with his parents. Natasha got a visa back to Russia as well. My ticket was for an earlier date; in order not to upstage her, I agreed to go to Kharkov first and then return to Moscow so that we'd meet the boy together.

Mila and my Moscow cousin Leonid met me at the airport. The hours between the plane landing and the boarding of the Kharkov train flashed by in fast-forward. As I rode into Moscow, I began to recognize, with an effort, the landmarks of my college days: Dynamo Stadium, Mayakovsky Square, my old apartment building in the distance.

Suspended in the air, which was bluish with exhaust fumes and hard to breathe, the city seemed drained of color. In stunning contrast to clean and bouncy Amsterdam, where I had spent half a day between planes, Moscow looked grim, rundown, like the ruins of an empire. Perhaps I'm too inured to garish Western billboards, I thought, resolved against all odds to be positive; at least, the once-ubiquitous posters affirming the Party's hegemony were gone. Who's in charge here?, I wondered.

Mila and I deposited our suitcases in the compartment and stepped outside for a smoke. The platform swarmed with people lugging suitcases, bags, crates; Olympic-class weight-lifting miracles abounded. How will all of this fit inside the train?, I wondered. I felt as if I had never left. It seemed that nothing had changed, that the entire country was barren, that Moscow was one big department-store-cum-supermarket.

"Look." Mila nodded toward an elderly woman in a simple print dress, dragging two hefty burlap bags. Diagonally across her chest were rolls of toilet paper, strung together like bandoliers on a Mexican *bandido*. "Aren't you going to take a picture for your article?" (*The Boston Globe* had commissioned a piece on my trip.)

Mechanically my hand reached for the camera I had bought for the trip. I ran my fingers across its satiny black body but could not bring myself to press the button. I, who was assaulted by toilet paper commercials daily, had no moral right to take this picture. It was too condescending. "Nah," I said. "They got plenty of pictures like that."

When I returned to New York, I polled my photographer friends. Many agreed that, yes, a picture like that would merely overstate the obvious. Many also admitted that they would have taken it anyway and let the editor decide. Listening to them, I realized that American editors who distrust Russians writing about Russia do have a point: we will never be able to shed an empathy that inevitably gets in the way of "objective reporting."

Aboard the train, Mila (now twenty-eight) and I talked into the night. She had just broken up with her husband and was now planning to emigrate with her three-year-old son. I tried to impress upon her the enormous problems she would encounter upon arrival. Working in a library, she had no transferable skills, and she spoke hardly any English. I had little money myself, and, with so many Soviet émigrés arriving, Jewish community funds were running dry; she was bound to end up on public assistance. I knew that system intimately, having interpreted there for years—was she prepared to deal with its frustrations? Shouldn't she try to make up with her husband, a programmer who could earn money after some retraining? Most of all, I was concerned about her attitude toward work. She was used to the easygoing nine-to-five of a Soviet office, where the pay is miserable and nothing much gets done. There are jobs like that in America, too, I admitted, thinking of the government offices I had seen; but they are reserved for citizens, and you need quite a bit of English to pass the test.

None of my arguments was working: I could tell by her pouting, resentful expression, her shaking voice, her big, gray eyes swelling with tears. Everything I said was interpreted one way: *He does not want to help me.* Nothing I might say could mar the image of the Land of Milk and Honey.

I can't blame her, I thought, inhaling cigarette smoke along with the stench of the nearby restroom (the No Smoking signs had forced us to find refuge in the space between the cars). If someone had been telling me these things when I was planning to leave, would I have listened?

"I'll do what I can," I said. It was already morning in New York, and I had only had half an hour's sleep on the plane.

In Kharkov I easily recognized my mother's brother, Uncle Vladik, on the train platform. His hair had turned to steely gray, but at fifty he was still a large man, broad-chested and -shouldered, ignoring his ulcers, bad back, and other ailments, and refusing to act his age. Now he brushed me off, grabbed my largest suitcase, hoisted it onto his back (no porters or carts at the station), and carried it across the square to his old, battered Moskvich. I knew from experience that it was useless to argue.

We could have easily come to blows—not what you'd want to do within minutes of arrival; not after fourteen years away.

Although born in Kharkov, I never knew it well. From visits to my grandparents I remembered broad avenues and trucks rumbling by; the center of town, with its massive, imposing stone buildings; and our neighborhood, Plekhanovka, with small brick houses and wooden fences along the cobblestone streets. The quiet was broken by an occasional clang from a streetcar returning to the depot, or a splash of water from a pail: few houses had indoor plumbing.

Plekhanovka is no more, I learned on our way home (Uncle made a detour). It had been bulldozed to make room for the new subway. Kharkov, a city of 1.6 million, needs its subway. I rode it and found it cheap, clean, and comfortable. Yet the site of our old house between the subway station and the new apartment complexes is an eyesore: a chunk of wasteland, covered with weeds and riddled with puddles.

My mother, sister, and nephew live in a housing project similar to the one where we lived in Syzran. Uncle slowed down as he maneuvered the car among the gaping potholes and the industrial debris. I was not entirely unprepared; my memories had been revived in New York by the recent Soviet movie *Little Vera*, which takes place in a city like Kharkov.

But that was a movie. Now I was looking at the no-man's-land of Russian courtyards up close: paint peeling off the obviously new buildings, mud everywhere, tropical-size weeds, open bins overflowing with garbage, rusty scrap metal scattered around, a line outside the grocery store. Life was as different from celluloid as the smell of rotting garbage outside Uncle's car was different from that of hot-buttered popcorn in the New York theater.

Later, riding through the city, I would see other housing

projects, including Pavlovka, where my uncle lives. They are an Orwellian nightmare, miles of identical gray boxes separated by enormous puddles and weedy lots. Apart from some benches and an occasional sandbox, landscaping appears to be a bourgeois luxury unneeded by Socialist workers. On the other hand, I thought, who am I to belittle indoor plumbing and central heating? Besides, too much public housing in the US does not look any better . . .

The Kharkov roads were an adventure, too. Picture an avenue five lanes wide—and no lane dividers, which makes driving a quasi contact sport. Picture potholes that can devour trucks, turning driving into slalom. Picture slightly elevated streetcar tracks running down the middle of the avenue, with many turns onto side streets, which wreak havoc on a tin can with no suspension to speak of.

"This is like Mexico," I told Uncle.

"You've been to Mexico, too? Was it hard to get a visa?"

He made a U-turn that could not be legal even in Mexico, and brutally muscled his way to the right side. "Wouldn't it make sense to paint lane dividers?" I asked.

He whistled. "You know how much paint that would take?"

I never claimed to understand the workings of Socialist economy.

The "reception committee"—my sister, my aunt, my cousin's wife—were fussing in the kitchen when we walked in. My mother, who had had a bad fall a couple of months earlier, was hobbling around on a crutch, giving instructions that were ignored, and raising the general level of excitement. The table was already loaded so thick with food that I could not see the cloth for the plates. It was ten in the morning, a time when I can barely get down a bagel, and I could smell pork chops frying in the kitchen. And vodka—this was Russia, after all.

Finally we raised our glasses, and I had a good look around me. Uncle's wife, Lyalya, still wore her hair in a beehive unchanged from the sixties. Their daughter-in-law Irina was new to me. Vladik and Lyalya's younger son, their granddaughter, my nephew—they had all grown up while I was away. I knew their faces from pictures, but their names were still bouncing in my head and did not match up with the people. I was a stranger; I did not live with them, did not share the daily struggles that had dug these deep wrinkles in their faces. But the faces were lit by a warmth that enveloped me and brought a lump to my throat. We drank in completely un-Russian style—without long, flowery toasts, which would have been so redundant.

Vodka can build bridges, but they are shaky and ephemeral, never quite connecting in the middle. It was not easy to tell them of my life in New York. To them, "free-lance" translates into "unemployed"; not having a car, a fact of Manhattan life, translates into downright poverty ("No car? In *America*?"). One might point out that I would have similar problems communicating with, say, a fellow airline passenger coming from Chile or Brunei. But I did not come from Brunei. I came from *here*, where my ups and downs were taken to heart and every misunderstanding acquired an exaggerated dimension.

On the other hand, "writer" sounded not only glamorous but lucrative (they thought it was similar to having a membership in the Soviet Writers' Union—a sinecure). And my living in the environs of Times Square was hailed ("a central location," still enviable in Russia). Most important, I had my health. "You look fine," they kept saying. (That was to become one of the motifs of my trip. Coming from amid the stress and madness that form the New York daily strife, somehow I looked younger than most of my old classmates. Which gave me pause: in the United States, what did I know about strife?)

After what seemed like hours, emotionally and physically exhausted, I slid away from the table and, aided by Mila, set out to play Santa Claus. There had been few specific requests, and a lot of guesswork had gone into my shopping. But the yell of joy from Irina at the sight of her ten-dollar swimsuit blew my anxieties away in a second. The cosmetics, the candy, the pantyhose—how easy it is to be a rich Uncle Sam in Russia. Yet a tiny part of myself stubbornly resisted basking in the warmth of gratitude, a small voice injected a note of bitterness: how dismal life here must be, for people to swoon at a one-dollar makeup kit.

My relatives' appreciation had nothing to do with shiny MADE IN USA labels (nor MADE IN CHINA, as it happens). The items I had brought—shampoo, makeup, pantyhose—were not available in Russia, period. I have done enough soul-searching not to treat this small voice of mine lightly. I read the same frustration in the wrinkles on my uncle's brow when later, despite my cousin's protests, he rifled through my toilet kit. My uncle is a Party member in good standing, who knows the system like the back of his hand, and his reaction to my disposable razors was different from that of my sixteen-year-old cousin to a Bon Jovi tape. "How many shaves is it good for?" he asked.

I shrugged. "One—I don't really know . . ."

He eyed me skeptically.

"Look," I said, somewhat miffed that my answer could be interpreted as an attempt to embellish capitalism (although, way back, I would not have put it past my uncle to embellish Socialism). "If it's the last one in the package, I might use it again." Meaning that sometimes I'm too lazy to run out to the store. "Other than that—at fifteen cents a razor—you understand?"

He nodded heavily. "Seventy years after the Revolution and we still don't have fucking disposable razors."

Seeing my mother was the worst shock. Her work load had eased: she was semiretired, working part-time as a school doctor. But she had aged horribly, even by Russian standards: at sixty-three, a carbon copy of my late grandmother. Her health was failing, her teeth gone, and her disposition, never too kind, even further deteriorated. Every moment I spent at their house she was nagging, reproaching, complaining. I could well believe Mila's descriptions of their screaming matches—I remembered my own experiences. Vladik, Mila, three-year-old Kostya—all were targets for her constantly foul mood.

But not me. I was smothered with love, caring, affection—all at someone else's expense. She tried to get poor Kostya out of my lap because I might be tired; she yelled at Mila to give me the only comfortable chair in the kitchen because I might be uncomfortable; the relentless, breathless assault went on . . . My assurances that at thirty-seven I was perfectly capable of taking care of myself—moreover, that being comfortable at someone else's expense made me uncomfortable—were ignored. I closed my eyes: the one-bedroom apartment that she, Mila, and Kostya occupy was filled with high-pitched invective, just as our Syzran apartment had been. My father was long gone, but my mother had not changed; there was still no peace in the house.

The apartment also badly needed repairs (for which a chunk of the proceeds from the sale of the PC was earmarked): spackling, painting, fixing. Amid the squalor I recognized relics from the past: a half-broken chair, moth-eaten rugs, and my old books, many of them now piled up in the corner due to lack of space—James Fenimore Cooper, Jack London, Jules Verne. I wished I had more time to spend just dusting them and touching their yellowed pages. But I had familial duties; the clan was waiting to see what Olga's grandson had come to.

The retailing generation was in poor shape. Many had died, including Uncle Boris the Main Meat Man; some were bedridden, like his wife, Anya. But the spirit of Beirut was alive: to avoid giving offense, it was paramount not to disclose that a certain relative had been visited first. This was especially true in the case of Uncle Yuri, the richest living uncle.

When we lived in Plekhanovka, there had never been fewer than six of us in two rooms, with no central heating or indoor plumbing. But Uncle Yuri and Aunt Mira seemed to have countless rooms, with dark, polished furniture and sets of crystal on the sideboards. A rare family visit to them was the equivalent of a royal audience. The table was set with caviar and smoked fish; tea was served out of a matching tea service, not tin mugs; and they never ran out of liqueur-filled chocolates.

These memories went through my mind as Mila and I walked to Uncle Yuri's apartment on Danilevsky Street. She had not visited them in years, she said, and it occurred to me that, had I stayed in Kharkov, I would still be "Olga's grandson," to be ignored.

Before leaving the States, I had been counseled by Aunt Zhenya, my mother's cousin, who now lives in Boston: "You must sweep them off their feet! Put on your best suit, necktie— the works. God forbid you'd show up at Uncle Yuri's looking like this." She disapprovingly pointed at my T-shirt and Levi's and delivered an Old World coup de grâce: "It's not for yourself. It's for your late Grandma Olga that you must show them."

I had no intention of following Aunt Zhenya's advice; I don't even own a suit. Yet, hesitantly, I changed from a T-shirt into a button-down—and not one step further.

Now we passed five-storey turn-of-the-century buildings that still looked solid and massive, crossed courtyards that were still quiet and pleasant, but the signs of decay were obvious: cracks in the façades, broken benches, a front door with no handle, dimly lit hallways. Have the mighty fallen, I wondered, or has it always been like this? Was it our own poverty that made these buildings look palatial?

Both Uncle Yuri and Aunt Mira were in their eighties now. Both had recently undergone surgery. Aunt Mira could barely see or hear. She just sat there, leaning on her crutch, an old woman with a hideously expensive golden brooch on her crêpe de chine dress. Uncle Yuri, the ex–Fish King, still carried on and served us homemade preserves.

While we chatted politely, I took in the apartment: the faded wallpaper, the plastic covers on the furniture, the doilies atop the TV. I excused myself to go to the bathroom and peeked into the next room, a small bedroom. There seemed to be another room, but I felt uncomfortable prying further. The bathroom tiles were moldy and yellow with age. To cover up for my spying, I pulled the chain; it was a tough pull. We could be in an average Old World Brooklyn neighborhood, I thought, although to my sister it was still a four-color spread from *Apartment Life*.

Before we left, Uncle Yuri proudly handed me a souvenir: a studio-made black-and-white picture of Aunt Mira and himself. In his white suit with rows of military decorations, with a small, almost shy smile, he looked quite winning. The back of the photo carried Uncle Yuri's full name and address, from a simple rubber stamp that you can order for a few bucks in any

New York copy shop. I mentioned it to my sister. She shrugged: "It's the latest rage here."

"Uncle Yuri is doing all right," said Uncle Vladik the next day as he valiantly fought Kharkov traffic. "He's got enough stashed away. Bought co-ops for both his kids."

By then I had seen the co-ops: modest middle-class apartments on the outskirts—comfortable but hardly deluxe by American standards. I chuckled at Vladik's description of the feud between Uncle Yuri's son and daughter, who had not talked to each other for years. What with the size of Uncle Yuri's fortune, it was *Dallas* scaled down for Kharkov.

I was received warmly at both homes. I smacked my lips politely, but the chicken was no match for Kentucky Fried. *Zakuski*—hors d'oeuvres—were impeccable, from stewed eggplant to caviar. With their co-op apartments and new Lada cars, my hosts were sitting pretty. Yet they asked, "Should we leave?"

I was taken aback. The cream of the clan fleeing to Brooklyn? They would have to charter a flotilla to ship their belongings! They were scared, explained Anatoly, the husband of Uncle Yuri's granddaughter Jana; the country was edging toward chaos, and all their worldly goods could turn to dust overnight. They yearned for stability. They sounded like the Russian aristocracy on the eve of the October Revolution.

Fourteen years before, not only had they been prospering quietly amid misery, but emigrating was a hell of a gamble, too—it took someone like myself, without one hope in the world, to take the leap. Now, under Gorbachev, not only was the country going down the tubes, but emigration had become a comparatively easier procedure, too. It was not just my wealthy relatives; my mother showed me off to her friends on a daily basis, and all echoed the same question: "Should we leave?"

At my first "briefing" I was torn apart. How truthful should I be about the employment prospects of a fifty-year-old teacher of Ukrainian? What did I know about how much welfare one could get in New York? I picked my words carefully, trying neither to sound Pollyannaish nor to shatter their faith in the Promised Land. It is hard being a god—a messiah—an American, I thought. Finally, as I was trying to explain to them that if you live on the Tel Aviv seashore, you barely felt the *intifada*, I stopped short. I realized I sounded like many American Jews, urging Soviet Jews to go to Israel instead of America. Was I sincere in saying that Israel is an easier place for the Soviets to adjust to? Or, like many Americans, was I more concerned with my own breathing space?

Such moments were rare. No paeans to the beauty of Galilee or the magic of Jerusalem could outshine the visions of long, sleek cars and gigantic department stores: in America "they have everything". Yet it would have been hypocritical of me, a brief visitor from the Land of Plenty, to accuse my listeners of greed. For an average person, life in Russia is just too plain hard to think any differently.

In 1975, when I left, I thought that the lot of the Soviet consumer could not get any worse. I was wrong. Then, in cities like Moscow or Kharkov, basics like bread, eggs, milk, and yogurt were available freely; the lines were for fancy stuff like ham. In 1989 the dairy section of a large food store on Kharkov's main street did not have a single dairy product. In the next section the entire display case featured one lonely stick of bologna-like sausage, too green to be eaten safely. Most of the space was occupied by some canned fish I had never heard of. I brought back to New York some ration cards for sugar and soap and pinned them over my desk—as a reminder.

The barter economy, where everyone has something to trade (the way my mother's patients had supplied us with food in Syzran), has not disappeared, but the supply of food has shrunk dramatically, and the time spent foraging for it has gone up. One day Mila and I were walking miles away from her place when she suddenly made a beeline for a bakery. "Do you want to carry the bread all the way home?" I asked. (Fat chance of getting a shopping bag in a Soviet food store, too.)

"There's no line here," she said. It looked like a line to me— but, to her, a dozen people was not a line.

It was the Customs Inspector's reaction to my bars of soap that had first made me feel like a Rip Van Winkle awakening from a fourteen-year sleep. But it was *brekhalovka*, a free-form gathering outside Kharkov's Shevchenko Park, that really brought it home to me. I remembered that people used to congregate there in my time, too, but that was to discuss the misfortunes of the local soccer team. Now the soccer fans were on the fringes, and the rest of the crowd, broken up into small groups, discussed . . . well, everything: How could Stalin have happened? Where is Gorbachev taking us? And, most important, where has all the food gone?

It was a heated discussion, no holds barred, no looking over your shoulder: a verbal free-for-all. The kind that in my time would have landed all of them behind bars. Some of the opinions (especially regarding the West) sounded naïve, some of the speakers were tipsy, few listened to others' arguments, but I was awash with exhilaration: the muzzle was off, and it would take a cataclysm, it seemed, a Tiananmen Square–like massacre to put it back on.

By now Russians are used to such miniature Hyde Parks, and the next day my rapturous descriptions were met with sour smiles. It is not that my relatives are an atypically cynical lot. The accepted term itself, *"brekhalovka,"* is pejorative: *"brekhun"* means "liar" or "windbag." Time and again, both in Kharkov and Moscow, my American-bred positive attitude slammed into a wall of pessimism and despair: Why would the Party mandarins give up their privileges? What will the 18 million bureaucrats do for a living? The ethnics—just watch them carve each other up. And what will happen when they go after the Jews? Each of them had a story of anti-Semitic threats to tell. The writing was on the wall, they agreed.

Russians and Americans treat rumors differently. In New York a rumor materializes in embryonic form in the pages of tabloids before it develops into a full-fledged one. If it can't clear the tabloids—well . . . The stories of nationalists who would not let Jews on the subway, of swastikas painted on Jewish apartments, I took with a grain of salt. I could not ignore the anti-Semitic outbursts of "patriotic" groups like Pamyat, either; later, in Moscow, I would see Pamyat activists in person, I would hear their arguments firsthand—and, yes, they do mean business. They may be a hopeless minority as I write this, yet they create a most pernicious effect by fanning the rumors; and in Russia, despite the newly vigorous media, rumor remains a quasi-legitimate news source. When enough people believe gossip, it can turn into reality.

Yet so much was my mind affected by the American media's adulation of glasnost—Gorbachev waving on Times Square, Sakharov elected to Parliament, samizdat being published officially—that I persisted in my optimistic arguments. "Don't you think that *you* could do something?" (i.e., instead of leaving). But I stopped there. I recognized the question. It was not unlike the one that Americans had asked me so often: "If the regime's so bad, why can't the people do something about it?"

After all my "on-the-one-hand"s and "on-the-other-hand"s, the question lingered: "*What should we do?*" "If you have to ask," I said, "maybe you shouldn't go. Every émigré I know had a hard time in the beginning, and everybody is doing well now. But first you must have a fire in your belly; you must feel there is no other way."

If in New York the hyphen in my "Russian-American" appellation seemed like a vaguely drawn, sometimes barely visible line, now in Russia it became a solid metal bar that weighed on me more and more. As an American, I rooted for Gorbachev and glasnost; as a Russian, I understood those wanting to leave.

Kharkov's airport, serving a city of 1.6 million, must have been designed as a train station. You pass through its small, stocky building in a minute and find yourself amid the crowd on the steps outside, listening to the announcements. Some of them are puzzling at first: "Three tickets for Minsk!" "Two tickets for Kiev!" Then you realize that these are the leftovers. Especially in summer a ticket—for anywhere—cannot be obtained in a normal way; you must have connections. Part of the crowd is mobbing the lonely ticket window, also outside. In American terms, most people are flying standby. I need to use the john, but the only one available is on the other side of the building. It is also outside, and flooded after the rain. I decide to pass. The wait is unbearable.

Finally the flight is announced. The tickets are checked at

one of three gates. Another mob scene: everyone seems to have at least three pieces of luggage. I hug Vladik and Mila and promise to send everybody invitations to visit America—by now, more a matter of red tape than anything else. Although I am relieved to be going, there is a sudden lump in my throat as I push through the check-in and squeeze myself into the covered waiting area. Like cattle, we are run through veering, fenced passages to the bus that takes us to the plane. After bumpy taxiing, we take off for Moscow.

Two

There were a lot of things to attend to in my three weeks in Moscow. Natasha and I had to cut through rolls of red tape to regain custody of Ilya. I wanted to see my father, who would be coming to Moscow. I wanted to see my old friends. I had to get a ticket to Prague—no mean feat in Moscow—to see friends there. I had to help Mila sell the PC. Finally, I had to gather material for the *Boston Globe* piece. This program was anything but realistic. After a week I collapsed: I just could not get up in the morning.

In a way, I had only myself to blame. Granted, there was the emotional roller coaster, the compressed excitement, the wonderment of seeing everything with different eyes. But, from the practical viewpoint, I had lost the knack, the myriad tactics that ensure a Soviet citizen's daily survival. On my first day, in sweltering July heat, I lucked into a lineless (well, half a dozen people) store to buy mineral water. The salesgirl set three bottles in front of me. I stared at her: *How am I supposed to carry these?* She stared back: *What's wrong?* I realized there were no plastic bags—no bags at all. (I could have anticipated that from my shopping sorties with Mila, but in Kharkov I had been an honored visitor, unconcerned with such trivia as *bags*; left to fend for myself, I fell on my face.) Later my friends chuckled, "You Americans."

The next day I joined a friend for lunch at Peking Restaurant. We were second in line, with a group of three young girls, modestly dressed, ahead of us. After half an hour's wait it became clear that the smug, meaty-faced doorman had his own door policy, which had nothing to do with the line. "Give him [a bribe]," my friend whispered. I looked at the doorman, then at the girls. "I can't do it," I whispered to the friend. "It isn't right."

I didn't mind the bribe, I explained; my wallet swelled with cash. I could not bring myself to cut in front of the girls. For me, who had changed dollars at the "informal" rate, the bribe was only thirty-three cents; but to these girls it was *five rubles*—possibly, what one of them made in a day. We went to another restaurant, then another, until, reeling from hunger, we found one where we were seated. For ten rubles.

I gave in to the cabdriver-doorman mafia. I wrapped a ten-ruble note around my finger to show the doormen I was a serious customer. The alternative was going hungry (fast food is nonexistent in Russia; the new McDonald's, besides being the largest in the world, will surely be the slowest-serving). I stopped balking at paying triple cab fares; the alternative was taking the subway and getting only a fraction of everything done.

It was ironic. In my student days restaurants had been easy to get into, and cabs plentiful, but I had no money. Now that I had wads of money, and felt like an Arab oil prince, no one wanted it. An especially obnoxious doorman sneered in my face when I offered him rubles: "What do I want with your *fantiki* [candy wrappers]? Give me some real money—green!" Cab drivers outside major hotels routinely demanded a pack of Marlboros to turn on the meter.

I did try to stand my ground—perhaps too hard. On arrival, I put away my dark-blue passport and credit cards; I did not want the privileges they bestowed. It took me forty-eight hours to reconsider. En route to a party, I stopped by a liquor store.

The sight of a long, weaving line horrified me. I grabbed a cab and sped toward Beryozka, a hard-currency store, for a bottle of Scotch.

After days of trying to buy a ticket to Prague for rubles, I turned to American Express, cursing myself for even having tried to live like a local. Communism had succeeded, I concluded, in breeding the toughest species in the world—the Soviet citizen. I dare any of my fellow New Yorkers to see how long it would take them to pull out their Visa cards.

Late at night, drained and beaten, I felt a serious need for a drink. Should I try to bribe another obnoxious doorman? Restaurants close at twelve . . . Enough of this farce! I headed for the Intourist Hotel's hard-currency bar, open till four.

The bar is a sleazy, faceless, overpriced joint where tourists sing-along after a day of sightseeing, hookers prey on German and Japanese businessmen, and their pimps wait outside. I felt no exhilaration at buying drinks myself, rather than, as in the old days, being treated by my tourists (as a Soviet citizen, I had not been permitted to own dollars). This was a place to get smashed, not to relax. I could not even invite any Moscow girls without a hassle at the door; they were automatically presumed to be hookers. The savvier among them refused to come in, anyway: "If racketeers [pimps] spot me here," Olga explained, "they'll think I'm a hooker and come after me later, demanding protection money."

From the safety of my New York apartment I can laugh at my naïveté. Had I reached for my dollars and credit cards right away—like a true American—I would have spared myself much misery. In trying to be a Soviet, I was, in fact, playing Dostoyevsky's Prince Myshkin, a type that disappeared from Soviet society long ago. It was only when I began to deploy all my resources, moral considerations aside, that I acted in a true Soviet spirit.

My acting the part of a deprived Muscovite I confined to myself. On our first day Natasha and I resolutely headed for Beryozka, to complement with Coke and chewing gum our gifts of jeans, tapes, and Walkman. Like any Soviet teenager, Ilya was fascinated with all things Western.

I had no illusions about the immensity of the task of building a father-son relationship practically from scratch. At the airport, waiting for Natasha's flight, I met Ilya: a tall, gawky fifteen-year-old. I sensed his reticence, his fear of the unknown. Until a few months ago, when we called from New York, he had had no parents. If I were him, I thought, I'd crack up. But he held together. I sensed he was used to keeping to himself. Living with his grandmother, this was perhaps the best survival tactic.

Natasha's mother had gained weight and now sported a bushy mustache, but she had not grown mellower or saner. To her, this was a soap opera in which she had to hog the spotlight (she had done some acting in her youth). She would not leave us alone: dousing Ilya with obsessive affection, pulling him away from potential draughts, bragging about his grades, complaining about his smoking and about those nympho sluts who tried to seduce him wherever he went—all in the same breath. He was boiling but in control. I liked that. Considering the psychological similarities between his grandmother and my mother, he certainly had more patience than I'd had at his age.

He, Natasha, and I spent hours together taking walks, going to lunch, play-acting a family. The strain between Natasha and me—in two weeks we were seeing more of each other than in a year in New York—was beginning to show. I, too, was piqued by the minute indignities of Soviet life, but she was seething, about the greasy food, the rude people. She had become much more American than I: she exercises religiously, counts calories, and verges on a stroke if a cigarette is lit within fifty feet of her. She went into a feminist fit when an elderly waiter (who would not serve us till we guaranteed a huge tip) ignored her, expecting *me*—the man—to order for everybody. "I'm leaving this fucking country *now*!"

Ilya looked as if he were about to cry. I did not know what to say. Not only might he have thought that her anger had something to do with him, but, after fifteen years in Russia, it was humanly impossible for him not to have acquired *some* sense of patriotism. "Your mother has a point," I said, and explained to him the difference between Western and Soviet attitudes.

"You've got to get a hold on yourself," I told her later. "The kid's already been through a lot, with our abandonment and his grandmother's round-the-clock badgering."

"I know," she said. "But I hate this place so much."

Her nerves were as frazzled as mine. Round and round we went, from lawyer to family court to notary public. On top of it, her mother flip-flopped daily on the decision to give up Ilya. One day she would promise to sign, the next day she would take it back. One day she would give Ilya only to me, because Natasha was "a nut" and I was "level-headed"; the next day I was "the kike who would make the child a Zionist." Natasha passed her frustration on to Ilya: "The child must know the truth about his monster of a grandmother." Never mind that he might have a different opinion of a woman who had practically brought him up.

We stopped play-acting. I took Ilya to the gym, looking for

ways to get close to him. I was hardly counting on a hugs-and-tears catharsis—not in three weeks. He had developed better defenses than NATO. But I was not discouraged. It would not be easy for us to become a father and a son, but time was on our side. He would be coming to America. I had all the time in the world.

As a foreigner, I had to register at the OVIR, or visa section—the same office where once upon a time I had sweated, waiting for my exit visa. On a warm, sunny morning the tiny building in Kolpachny Lane looked peaceful, even rustic. I passed the long—but orderly—lines for exiting Soviets, on to the foreigners' section. Now the madding crowds were at the American embassy: it was easier to leave Russia than to enter the US. The OVIR official was sweetness itself. The procedure took minutes. I left the place whistling.

My old dorm was five minutes away, but it was shut down for summer repairs. I could not even get past the watchdog of a granny downstairs. My clumsy lie about visiting someone fooled no one. We used to smuggle countless visitors inside—but I had lost that knack, too.

Without an ID, I could not stroll around my alma mater. Yet there was a back entrance for applicants: the admission exams were about to begin. I crossed the courtyard, where mothers were trading gossip about the exams and their offspring were smoking nervously. I went through the lobby—and the hatch of the time machine slid open.

My steps echoed, dream-like, in the dark, abandoned hallways. I shivered. I was a graduate, true, but I had no formal right to be here. The criminal is always drawn to the scene of his crime, whatever it is. The classroom door creaked ominously; I walked in to take a picture, feeling like a spy. The place looked clean but shabby. Judging by the walls, the propaganda had been scaled down: only a few patriotic slogans awakened my memories. The exam schedule was posted outside: not one familiar teacher's name. Two young girls in summer dresses came by to ask me if I had seen such-and-such. I shook my head.

"I used to be a student here," I said.

They seemed unimpressed. "You work as a translator now?"

"Sometimes," I said vaguely. I knew times had changed, but I still wondered whether they should be seen talking to an émigré—wouldn't it hurt their chances of getting to Kuala Lumpur? I said good-bye and left. In the land of glasnost I was still living in 1975 . . .

After I emigrated, writing to my friends back home would not have been prudent: they had their careers to build, and letters from abroad would have caused them problems. Under Gorbachev, one distant acquaintance showed up in New York on a business trip, then another . . . I remained apprehensive. With or without glasnost, calling people out of the blue—who knows what kind of jobs they held?

It turned out to be more than pure paranoia. A few people I met professed joy at seeing me and were never heard from again. Were they indeed afraid for their careers? Perhaps it was the local equivalent of "Let's have lunch *real* soon"—not a uniquely Soviet phenomenon.

Fortunately, it was different with my best friends. They are well established now: Aleksei* has his own patent law firm;

----

* I changed the names: you never know . . .

Oleg is a functionary at the Journalists' Union; Igor has just defended his Ph.D. on the British university novel. I was taken to exclusive clubs at the Writers' Union and the Journalists' Union (the places where I used to beg passes to screenings), where people whose names I could not remember came up to hug me: "Gurevich you sonuvabitch after fourteen years you've got to have a drink with me." Celebrations went endlessly . . .

After my Prague ticket–mineral water misadventures, I was a bit worried: had fourteen years, spent on different planets, torn us hopelessly apart? My Russian had deteriorated, I knew: sometimes I inadvertently translated English expressions literally, and even had trouble finding the right word.

The language picked up fast. "It's like you never left," they kept saying. Yet the appearance was deceptive. Just as my fluent English had led Americans to believe that I needed no explanations of how to go about doing things, now my old friends were making the same mistake, treating me as one of their own, rather than as the foreigner I was. I kept interrupting their stories with questions that proved I was ill-informed: "Why didn't you do this or that? Hasn't glasnost changed all that?"

"Are you being facetious?" they asked. "Have you forgotten what it's like here?"

Fourteen years ago, peeking into a crystal ball, they would have been delighted with their career accomplishments. Seeing their well-run lives, I had mixed feelings: had I stayed, I might have done well, too; the old-boy network is as strong in Russia as elsewhere. Yet I kept hearing the same question time and again: "*Should we leave?*"

In their late thirties, they looked ten years older than Americans their age. They talked a lot about doctors and hospitals. Like all Soviet women, their wives spent their days foraging for food. Even their trips abroad seemed to bring more frustration than joy, so depressing was the comparison with their lives in Russia. Like my Kharkov relatives, my friends described a sense of impotence: the country was going to hell, and their hard-earned status could vanish any day.

I had not known Naum Puhrer well: he was neither a hallway analyst nor a rock & roll buff. There always seemed something pure and naïve about him. Now I was not one bit surprised to learn that he was leaving for Israel—not for Naum the entre-preneurial hustle of Brooklyn.

His farewell party was like the good old days: a tiny apart-ment jammed with guests and packed suitcases and devoid of furniture; a familiar mix of joy—*Finally! Off we go!*—and sad-ness—*The city will be a little emptier now*—in the air . . .

Many of the guests were from Naum's Hebrew class, in-cluding their *mora*, the teacher. The latter, a short man our age, with a thin, sparse beard (Naum's, by contrast, was rich and bushy: a poster Zionist, no less), seemed piqued at seeing his acolytes form a circle around me to hear tales of America; he made some caustic barbs about Brooklyn go-getters. I smiled affably and changed the subject to Israel, where I had spent six months on a kibbutz in the Upper Galilee.

On our long ride home we were pleasantly warm after many glasses of vodka amid fervent toasts of *"Ha-shana ha-ba'a b'-Yerushalayim"* ("Next year in Jerusalem"). Aleksei remarked that he was amazed to see me bow out of verbal sparring with the *mora*. "You've mellowed. Way back, you'd go straight for the jugular."

Naum asked me to meet him a few days later, to talk about Israel. We had many brandies in a Kalinin Avenue bar (would I have thought, years ago, that nice Jewish boys like Aleksei and Naum would be matching me glass for glass?), and, as we hugged and vowed to see each other again—in Jerusalem or New York—Naum suddenly said, "You've really changed, you know. You're more like a normal person now. America must be good for you."

"Nah," I said. What was he doing, paying me compliments? "It's just age. We're not getting younger, heh-heh." But I wondered what had contributed more to my "mellowness": getting along in years or prolonged exposure to freedom?

Aleksei's and Naum's remarks made me think: it was not just my alleged loss of verbal aggressiveness (many of my American friends would disagree), it was linked to my loss of the Soviet knack for survival. The latter seems to inevitably involve a lack of civility, and, perhaps, plain rudeness.

Many out-of-towners think of New Yorkers as being rude. I disagree: I think we're merely practical. We don't waste time over a casual brush on the sidewalk—the way Londoners sometimes do—when a brief " 'Scuse me" is enough. In Russia I was made to feel like an out-of-towner in New York.

In Kharkov, when Mila and I walked down Sumskaya, the main drag, I was shoved seven times within ten minutes (after that I stopped counting) in traffic that was not half as hectic as Wall Street at noon. In Moscow it was the same: no orderly lines for buses, say (unlike at a store, where a saleswoman could threaten to stop the sale); every man for himself, elbows turned outward—naked Darwinian survival of the fittest. All right, I thought, so Russians are no different from Israelis (who do not accept the label of rudeness, and call it informality). But Russian rudeness seems to go further; it feels like pure hostility.

Everyone I talked to blamed the harsh economic situation:

too many people spending too much time fighting one another for too few things. Glasnost made it worse: the animosity that may have been kept in check under Brezhnev was now out in the open. In subway trains, restaurants, stores, I witnessed people erupting in fits of anger. Words fly: it is "you damn Armenians/Latvians/Jews/Bolshevik parasites" who are to blame for everything; it seemed as though a mere "Hey, watch where you're going!" could lead to fisticuffs.

Linking lack of common civility directly to the Party's ruinous policies seems too facile, though, like blaming the Party for my divorce or the rift between me and my father. Things are seldom so clear-cut. But whatever the roots of the Soviets' uncivility, its fruits were sometimes horrifying.

At a bar at the Rossiya Hotel, an old man, already quite tipsy, kept badgering the bartender to pour him "another two hundred" (grams of brandy) ahead of the line. He was puny and disheveled, and the knot in his tie was edging toward his armpit—a pathetic sight. Finally, the bartender, a big, ruddy-faced dyed blonde, lost her patience. "I'm sick and tired of you damn veterans! When will you ever die out, all of you?" I realized that the man had been pointing at his World War II decorations, using them to cut in front of the line.

The men in the line laughed encouragingly. "That's right, Mama! *Vo dayot*—she really told him!"

A part of me laughed with the rest. The scene undeniably had a comic side: the puny drunk and the Rubenesque bartender. But what made me cringe was less her outburst than the other customers' laughter: after all, my father had been in the war, too.

A friend whom I told about this merely shrugged: "Veterans are unpopular these days. They shop at special veteran stores and then go and use their ration cards at the regular ones."

So—back to economics. Perhaps I should stop resisting and accept the Party as the root of all evil. But I cannot recall such an air of hostility fourteen years before. If it did exist then, I don't remember being particularly aghast about it; I must have been like everybody else. We both have changed, Russia and I; and we went different ways . . .

To speak with my father in Syzran, I had to place a call with the operator. It came within an hour. His voice sounded odd and unfamiliar, coming in bursts through crackling static. He wanted to come to Moscow, he said eagerly, but had to wait for the delivery of spark plugs for his car. It was hard to analyze emotions when both of us had to yell and half the words were drowned out. I tried to see his point of view: perhaps in Russia spare parts came once a year. But he was coming by train, not by car. In fact, I was pissed off.

He reached me at my cousin Leonid's a few days before my departure, when I was ready to give up on him. He was calling from Moscow, he said; he really would like to see me. He realized I was busy, so whatever time I could spare . . . He and Aunt Natasha were staying at her daughter's on the outskirts of Moscow, an hour's travel from my place on the Arbat, so we had to fix the time in advance. Was tomorrow around eleven good for me?

Fourteen years of silence, three weeks of getting spark plugs—drop everything, roll out the carpet, strike up the band? I was angry. I felt pressured. Eleven is fine, I said.

There seemed something operatic about the full, wet kiss he gave me on the lips—but perhaps it was the norm here. Right off he told me about the tomatoes, onions, and radishes they grew on their small plot outside Syzran. They had even brought along a large plastic bag of gooseberries—about five pounds—and a small one of tomatoes. His hands were rough, with broken, black-rimmed fingernails.

Aunt Natasha hurried to the kitchen to rinse the berries, and I got a good look at him. He seemed to have shrunk, but he showed a bit of a potbelly. His receded hairline held its ground where I remembered it. He had a healthy tan. All in all, he was in good shape for his sixty-six years; he could even pass for a Florida retiree. By American standards, his gray suit, with an ink spot over the breast pocket, belonged in a Salvation Army bin. I smiled because I knew that he didn't really care. In the Air Force he had worn a uniform and didn't have to worry about choosing his clothes.

I made tea, over their polite protests. We talked about New York, writing, gardening; we seemed to be groping in the dark along the edges of the Big Unspoken that lay between us. Aunt Natasha's obsequiousness was getting in the way: she bowed and attempted to kiss my hand, trying to show gratitude for my visit. We took a walk on the Arbat, an old city quarter turned into a pedestrian mall, and had some *khachapury*—baked bread and cheese—at a Georgian cafeteria. He tried to pay; I softly took his hand away. He made a mess trying to pour a glass of mint drink out of the container. Such a klutz, I thought. But he was not clumsy, just nervous.

Before he left, I gave him a copy of my novel. The dust jacket note mentioned him and his service in the Air Force (the editor had naïvely picked this as a selling point). He held the bright, glossy book as if it had come from outer space, and glanced at my picture as if disbelieving that I had actually written it. He ran his hand along the jacket with obvious respect. "Well," he said, "that's really something." He was one of the few people, I thought, who never queried me about the sales figures.

A day later he and Aunt Natasha met Ilya, Natasha, and me at the Izmailovo subway station. In the same operatic manner Father opened his arms and gave all three of us wet kisses on the lips. I was not used to so much body contact; he made me feel WASPish. Out of the corner of my eye I observed Ilya. He was polite, yet from my own Kharkov childhood I recognized a little boredom with the family ritual—seeds of the future "attitude," I thought. At the same time, he seemed genuinely curious about his newly discovered grandfather: it might be a relief from hothouse life with his grandmother.

We had to take a bus to go to their house. It was raining brutally. Out of habit, I stepped off the sidewalk, to flag a cab. Father stopped me—"No need." I groaned: *Oh God now he is parading his we-simple-folks-don't-need-fancy-cabs attitude, to save me the money I didn't know what to do with anyway.* And he refused my offer of an umbrella—getting drenched in the cold rain, risking pneumonia. Acting macho at sixty-six, I thought irritatedly as I sneezed from my wanderings in the rain the night before.

Fortunately, the bus came within minutes. Father and I got off before the rest, to stop at a liquor store. A line about two hundred strong weaved outside. By now I had learned my lesson. I quickly spotted an enterprising wino who, for a mere ruble, got us two bottles of vodka. The line looked the other way; not a whimper of protest.

"Must be your ribbons," I said jocularly. Soviet officers wear their medals on festive occasions but pin simple plastic-coated ribbons—each corresponds to a medal—on their coats for everyday wear. Father wore his even in retirement.

He waved. "It's like a Party card nowadays . . . No one cares." Suddenly he told me that a few years back he had almost been "elected" Secretary of the local Party cell. "Until someone remembered that you were in the States . . ."

I laughed. And I had thought that once he retired, my emigration could not hurt him. "Take it easy," I said. "One less sin to atone for."

I regretted my patronizing tone the moment I said it. He waved again: "It doesn't matter now." But from his tone it seemed that it *had* mattered then.

We passed the identical gray shoeboxes of the project. We might as well be in Syzran, I thought.

He gave a short laugh. "Maybe it was your American sneakers, not my ribbons, that shut them up in the line."

Later, at the apartment, he asked if he could try on my Reeboks. The fit was excellent, he declared; then he pointed at his brown, Soviet-made sneakers. "Want to trade?"

"That's okay," I said. "I'll leave you mine."

By that time my cold had gotten worse. I could barely participate in the prodigal-son feast (fried chicken, fried greenish sausage, stewed eggplant, and, mercifully, a lot of vodka). It seemed to go well—a simple act of reacquaintance, of reforging links. Through the aspirins-and-vodka fog I heard Aunt Natasha's nonstop ranting about the chaos that Gorbachev had thrown Russia into and the good old days when people had worked hard and needed none of that freedom. Father retorted weakly that life had never been so Edenic, but mostly he talked to Ilya about fishing on the Volga. If nothing else, I've gotten those two together, I thought—not a total loss.

As we were leaving, he whispered in the doorway, "Son, I know you have dollars in New York, but here—let me give you something . . . a hundred rubles . . ."

A hundred rubles amounted to slightly less than his monthly pension. What should I do? Laugh? cry? try to explain that, no, I didn't have much in the way of dollars in New York? that, at the rate I had exchanged, he was in effect offering me *ten* dollars? Or, viewed differently, the tape recorder or the typewriter, twenty years too late.

"I'll manage," I said. "Thanks anyway."

We met for the last time the day before I left. I had to buy going-away presents—cigarettes for Igor, Scotch for Aleksei—and suggested that we meet outside Beryozka in the Rossiya Hotel. He came alone (Aunt Natasha was not feeling well) and would not enter the store: "I can wait outside." He seemed intimidated by the doorman, who had rows of ribbons to match his own.

"Nonsense." I pulled him along.

We passed the jewelry and the furs, heading straight for the food section. He seemed stunned. How could I convey to him that any Korean grocery in New York was stocked better? I realized I didn't know how to talk to him; I was afraid to hurt his feelings. "Is there something you want?" I squeezed out.

"No, no," he shook his head. "We don't need anything."

Right, I thought, recalling my friend Irene's description (she had visited her mother in Syzran): to buy anything, she khad to be at the store at seven in the morning; by ten the place was swept clean. "C'mon, help yourself. It's not that expensive."

"I don't want you to spend money on me," he said firmly.

Oh, God. "Well, if you change your mind, let me know." I did my shopping in a minute—a Cutty, a carton of Marlboros—

and browsed, to give him a chance to overcome . . . his modesty? his patriotism?

Finally, I got tired of studying medals on Uzbek wine labels. There is an end to every comedy. On the way to the register he shyly picked up a tiny pack of Georgian tea. "Can I . . . ?"

Impatiently I grabbed a dozen—they cost about sixty-five cents apiece—and dropped them into the shopping basket. "Anything else?"

"I really don't want to put you out . . ."

"Please."

He picked out a package of cookies for Aunt Natasha and a can of Tuborg for her grandson. "Do you have enough . . . ?"

What kind of life is this?, I wondered, whipping out my Visa card—nine people out of ten here can't get enough out of you, and the tenth one you have to beg to accept ten bucks' worth of food. I gestured around us: "Anything else you want here?"

He shook his head again. "Maybe . . . do you think they might have some fishing hooks? They're really hard to get . . ."

No fishing hooks, as I expected. Beryozka was set up to milk rich foreigners, not the rod-and-reel crowd. We stepped outside. "How about some American ice cream?" I said, remembering he loved ice cream.

Baskin-Robbins had opened a parlor nearby, a small, clean place with Muzak barely covering the vigorous hum of the air conditioner. Needless to say, only hard currency is honored.

We were the only customers. Father was lost in front of the display case. So was I—how do you translate "Rocky Road"? The saleswoman, made up like a model and wearing a logo'd uniform, offered to help. "What kind of Soviet ice cream do you like?"

"*Plombir*," he said eagerly—vanilla. He got that and a scoop of banana.

There was so much concentration in his face as he brought the spoon to his mouth that I dared not breathe. "You like it?" I asked after he got his first taste.

He nodded slowly, sadly. "That's real ice cream."

Had I arrived in a Rolls-Royce, he would not have been as impressed.

After he had licked the container clean, he rose and held up the cup. "Don't you get a deposit back?"

"We throw them away."

He frowned at the waste. "Will they mind if I keep it?"

"Here." I opened the bag in which I had brought my Reeboks.

Before putting the cup in the bag, he looked around warily; he could not believe he could keep it, he must have thought I was trying to spend money on him again. Then he paused and silently held up the plastic spoon.

I nodded. "Go ahead." I remembered Comma, my high-school teacher, and his packet of dried-up Air France mustard. The best souvenirs in life are free.

As we were leaving, I thanked the saleswoman. She crooned back, "Thank you, please come again."

Outside, Father looked embarrassed. "I did not thank her."

"That's okay," I said, doubting she expected him to.

We returned to my place on the Arbat. I made tea, poured whiskey. He took a sip and made a face: "This is just moonshine!" I shrugged: no accounting for taste. "I thought you'd ask me about how I live," he said.

"I figured you'd tell me yourself."

Following retirement, he had taught physics and drafting at a high school, but after a while he grew frustrated. "They don't want to learn," he said. "No matter how hard you try."

I pictured him pacing in front of the class, explaining the

combustion engine to a roomful of Vankas and Petkas whose sole desire was to break out and wreak havoc.

Then, he went on, he began writing papers for students who took college courses by correspondence. At fifty rubles a shot—

"That's better than school," I said.

"Exactly."

I could not help being amused by the pride in his voice. My father making money on the side—perhaps for the first time in his life. Illegally, too. "Aren't they supposed to write the papers themselves?" I asked.

He gave a weary shrug. "No one gives a damn."

I told him I had brought a whole pack of family pictures from Kharkov. He lit up: "Let's see!"

What a happy family we were, from the looks of these tattered, yellowing pictures. There we are, with Mother's parents, with Father's parents, with friends, in Kharkov, Syzran, Lipetsk—smiling, hugging, kissing, mugging at parties; no hint of screaming, hysterics, tears, curses. My face was the only link between these two worlds. At least, I did not smile in *every* picture, whether due to my less-than-sunny disposition or to my inability to put on a mask. I must have driven the photographers insane.

Father's reaction was purely technical: "I remember taking this one—not enough speed . . . This one came out pretty good, don't you think? . . . Uh-oh, not mine—no way. Let's see, who could have taken it?"

Who cares?, I thought. I knew he was a photography buff, developing and printing his own (no Fotomats in Russia). But now he seemed to be hiding behind his obsession. I was especially irked by the way he wordlessly turned face down every picture with Mother in it. He must have exiled every memory of her to the Siberia of his mind. But I did not confront him.

My childhood memories had made me a pacifist where domestic warfare was concerned. Besides, from having seen my mother on this trip, I was depressed enough already and feeling guilty about resenting her. Finally, I was afraid that, if I stirred up some memories now, chances were he would start, once again, to justify his leaving; to make his case, he would come up with some horrifying episode that had happened behind closed doors. Without knowing what it could be, I knew I could not stomach it.

He asked about other Kharkov relatives, though. I showed him Uncle Yuri's studio photo and sneeringly asked him about the decorations. Somehow I presumed that Uncle Yuri had been a crook all his life. Father shook his head.

"I think he was in the tank troops."

"Really? Then . . ."

"That's what it was like after the war," he said. "You stole or you starved."

We were silent for a while. It was getting late. My eyelids were closing; I had been drinking, and not getting enough sleep. If I had had any thoughts about bringing up the day in May, fourteen years before, when I learned of his cable, by now I was hoping it would not come up. "Father, there's something I need from you. Just one thing. Mila mentioned to you she wants to leave." He nodded. "Well—sign the paper. Don't stand in her way."

He nodded again. I could not decipher the grimace on his face: either he was about to cry, or he was thinking hard about something.

"I just want her to avoid some of my problems," I said. And, before he perceived this as a direct reference to his cable, I added, "You could have saved me a lot of trouble if you had been more honest with me—about politics, about the Party, about everything. It's not easy figuring things out by yourself, you know; I could have taken a straighter road. I did a lot of unnecessary stumbling."

He looked disappointed. From the way he sounded, his tail was already between his legs—did he have a masochistic streak that made him yearn for a more direct accusation? He made a "peh" sound that had a somewhat dismissive tone to it. "What could I have taught you? I was deceived along with everyone else. We all believed . . . until a couple of years ago, when everybody began writing about the camps and everything."

I knew *that*, I thought; perhaps I had misstated my point.

"Besides," he said, "would you have listened? Did you ever listen to anybody? Well . . ." He paused. "Maybe it's all for the better. I'm sure it's been hard for you at times—probably still is, in many ways—"

He picked words with as much care as I had done at the store—did he really think that he could hurt me? He understood as little about my life now as he had when I lived in Moscow.

"—but it looks like it has turned out well for you—"

Despite you?, I thought. Certainly not thanks to you, is it?

"—no matter what . . ." He let it hang in the air.

"If it has turned out well," I said, measuring my words just as carefully, "I'll take full credit for it. If I fuck up, I'll take the rap for it, too. That's the way we live over there, Dad. That's the way I have always wanted to live. Do you understand *why* I couldn't live here?"

The moment the last phrase left my lips, I felt it was unnecessary. He was already upset, which was not my intention.

"*Nu, dai-to bog*," he muttered, "God willing . . . All's well that ends well. But, you know," he added in a normal voice, "we never felt unfree here, either. It all depends how you look at it."

"You mean you are satisfied—you do what you want, you have what you want—?"

"Well . . . like I told you, I could use some fishhooks."

That's not what I meant, I was about to say, when it occurred to me that actually it was a very complete answer.

His eyes were wet when we parted on the street. For once, I did not mind the operatic kisses.

"I'll come to Syzran," I said. "Next time. I'll send you some fishhooks."

"The hell with the fishhooks." He sniffled.

"Whatever." The gap was there, dark and vast, still to be bridged; but at least we had made a step.

My departure from Moscow was dramatic enough—last-minute packing, catching the cab in the drenching rain, chaotic mobs at the airport—but nowhere near as dramatic as the one fourteen years earlier. Then I had been leaving; now I was going back. You cannot measure the relief.

Out of the corner of my eye I see a younger me sitting at a table in the cafeteria, forlornly watching the older me depart. I give him a wink, inspired by my American-bred optimism: *Cheer up, kid.*

The walls are falling, the curtains are being ripped off their hooks; my family and friends can visit with increasing ease, and so can I. This is yet another face of freedom. And if freedom sometimes seems like a burden, it's one worth carrying; as a destination, it's also worth all the stumbling on your way to it.